Code in Context

Primary Socialization, Language and Education
Edited by Basil Bernstein
University of London Institute of Education
Sociological Research Unit

Code in Context

Diana S. Adlam

with the assistance of
Geoffrey Turner and
Lesley Lineker

University of London Institute of Education

ROUTLEDGE & KEGAN PAUL

London, Henley and Boston

First published in 1977
by Routledge & Kegan Paul Ltd
39 Store Street,
London WC1E 7DD,
Broadway House,
Newtown Road,
Henley-on-Thames,
Oxon RG9 1EN and
9 Park Street,
Boston, Mass. 02108, USA
Set in Monotype Times, 10 on 11 point by
Kelly, Selwyn and Co., Melksham, Wiltshire
and printed in Great Britain by
Unwin Bros Ltd

ISBN 0 7100 8481 1

Contents

Foreword

Basil Bernstein

In this volume, Adlam and her colleagues present two inter-related studies. The first contrasts aspects of the speech of lower-working-class and middle-class children elicited by a number of situations in a formally structured interview. The second study examines the extent to which there is an underlying consistency in the children's speech across the various eliciting situations. We collected speech from the children in the sample when they were five years of age, and again when they were seven years of age. This volume is wholly concerned with the speech of the seven-year-old children. We repeated, in the second interview, three of the situations we had presented to the children when they were five, and we added two more. The situations we repeated were as follows:

1 the Trotin pictures (described in the text);
2 the Picture Story series (here the child was asked to tell a story based upon a series of pictures);
3 the explanation of the rules of a game.

We also added two other situations, regulative and imaginative.

Regulative situation

Before the children went to school, at a first interview, we asked the mothers a series of questions about how they would control their child. When the children were seven, at the second interview, we presented to the children the same questions and situations and they were asked to reply as if they were the mother. Dr Cook-Gumperz, in the Sociological Research Unit monograph, *Social Control and Socialization*, compared the mothers' and children's strategies of control. In general she found that there were social class differences in the strategies and language of control between the mothers, a modest relation between the mothers' and the children's strategies, but apart from differences in the use of imperatives no class differences

vii

between the children. We believed that the relative absence of class differences could be attributed to the coding grid. This grid was first designed for the mothers' responses and then applied to the children. As a consequence, certain sub-systems of the grid were too gross (the positional appeal sub-system) whereas the personal appeal sub-system was far too delicate to be applied to children of seven years of age. Geoffrey Turner transformed Dr Cook-Gumperz's semantic grid into a set of linguistic networks derived from Halliday's theory, in which the original positional sub-system was made far more delicate. (These matters are explained in the body of the text.) Geoffrey Turner's complete analysis will be published in a future SRU monograph.

Imaginative situation

The children at the second interview were also asked to tell a spontaneous story elicited by figures of a sailor, a little boy and a little girl, a dog and a small bear.

We thus had five situations, three of which had been presented to the children when they were five years of age. The major plan, in line with the requirements of the theory, was to enquire into whether there was an underlying code regulating the children's texts *across* the situations. Our situations correspond to:

1 an instructional context (explaining the rules of a game);
2 a regulative context (the children's strategies of control);
3 an imaginative context (the spontaneous story).

The fourth, the inter-personal, context required by the theory for its experimental investigation, was missing. However, we did have, three of the four. We selected for analysis the Trotin context and the children's explanations of the game as examples of instructional and descriptive contexts; the children's responses to the control questions we considered as an example of the regulative context. We selected the children's 'spontaneous' story as an example of an imaginative context rather than the stories the children told about the series of pictures. Unfortunately, Dr R. Hasan was unable to complete her analysis in time for this study.

We have always been aware that the experimental context is not a context in which the everyday, inter-actional, informal speech of the child can be examined. As I have written elsewhere, we regard the experimental context, *itself*, as an experimental variable. Our interest is in the *ground rule*, or the *performance rule*, the child selects to regulate the text he/she produces in a context which abstracts the child from his/her local social relationships, practices and meanings and where the context provides no guidance as to what counts as an appropriate response.

I consider (and this is not necessarily shared by the authors of this book) that there are crucial implications of the performance rule selected both for existing pedagogic practices, and for our understanding of forms of familial transmission, which we believe orient the child to specific performance rules regulating the texts the child creates in specific contexts.

In the first part of this book, D. Adlam gives an exposition of how she saw the relationships between codes and context. Without wishing to anticipate her discussion or necessarily to qualify it, I regard *code* as referring to a socially constituted regulative principle, tacitly acquired, which integrates:

1 the relevant meanings;
2 the form of their realisation;
3 their evoking contexts.

What we observe are the *productions* of texts. What we infer is the performance or ground rule which regulates the *production* of specific texts. What we infer at a structural level is the regulation on the relationships *between* performance rules and specific contexts. It is this level which refers to codes. Codes are no more directly observable than are grammatical rules. This does not mean that they are any more heuristic devices than the rules of grammar. As codes change, so do what count as relevant meanings, what count as appropriate realisations and what count as evoking contexts. Codes are constituted by social relationships which regulate the selection and structure of meanings and the mode of their *contextual* realisations. The educational system transmits class-regulated elaborated codes (*Class, Codes and Control*, vol. 3). This regulation may not be revealed by classroom studies which limit themselves to the collection of teachers' speech in primary schools. What is crucial is less the speech of the teacher, but more the principle or code used to *edit* the speech, for it is this principle or code which is to be transmitted and which underlies the surface features of momentary and discontinuous classroom activities and practices. Indeed, classroom inter-actional studies, whilst of relevance, deal only with framing, rarely classification.

The empirical studies which follow the Introduction show consistent class differences between the children which are stronger than those found at five years of age. It is important to point out that these class differences are found when the children are matched for 'verbal intelligence scores'. It is equally important to point out that these differences were not expected to be, and in fact never are, absolute. The variation in the lower working class I consider relates to differences in familial transmissions and to their antecedents. We have some evidence that this may well be the case. Adlam found that within, and almost wholly confined to, the lower-working-class children, there was a pronounced move to narrative speech in the Trotin context, and that this feature was more strongly marked in girls. We then examined the relationship between this move to narrative on the part of the girls, and their mothers' scores on schedules, which referred to reported communication and control procedures. Adlam found that there was a relatively strong correlation between mothers who reported that they favoured positional control and less 'educationally' focused communication and the girls who moved to narrative. This finding is of interest because it reveals a relation between a maternal questionnaire *and* the children's speech behaviour. It is, of course, possible that this relationship is to be found, not because there is a *direct* causal relationship between the mothers' reported favoured modes of communication and control and their children's speech, but because the former is associated with *other features* of the mother–child relationship. For example, the more positional mothers in the lower working class may be those who are more prone to narrative speech as a means of reflecting upon or reporting everyday experience than the more person-focused mothers. Reflecting upon everyday experience can take different forms. The girls may be more likely to model themselves on their mothers than the boys, whose major reference is possibly to the peer group. We should also bear in mind that all the interviewers were women.

Lineker's study, which completes the first part of the book, shows class differences in the mode of instruction offered by the children when they explained the game 'Hide and seek' to a child who did not know how to play. The reader should bear in mind that the children were asked this question as the last section of the instructional situation. Initially, the children were given small figures and were asked to show and comment upon how to play the game. Then the researcher took the figures and the child instructed the researcher how to move them appropriately. If the child missed a step in the explanation, this was made explicit. Finally, the child was asked to explain the game to a child who did not know how to play. Thus this context does contain *possible* elements of learning. The differences we find do not relate to differences in the *efficiency* of the instruction, but to differences in the *mode* of instruction. Indeed, it is likely that the context-independent mode, more typical of the middle-class children, is a less efficient mode of instruction, despite its greater consistency of reference sets and explicit sequencing, than the more context dependent mode of the lower-working-class children.

It might be appropriate to comment on the effect of the eliciting context on the speech of children from the different social classes (middle class and lower working class). In general (and particularly when the children were seven years of age) the middle-class and working-class children respond to the interview situation very differently. As we have pointed out many times, there is no difference between the children in the *amount* of speech, indeed, in some situations, the lower-working-class children talk more than the middle-class children. Many people have argued that the class differences between the children when they were talking about the Trotin pictures can be explained in terms of the fact that researcher and child were *both* looking at the pictures. However, this does not explain why the middle-class children's speech at five is relatively more explicit or why at seven the class differences between the children are stronger. Further, in other situations in the interview, this shared perspective was *not present*, yet class differences in the children's orientations were found.

If we take the Trotin situation, or the Picture Story series, the children were given no guide as to how to talk about the pictures. Second, in the situation where the child was asked to explain the rules of a game to a child who did not know how to play, no guide was given to direct the child towards any one form of explanation.

Third, in an experiment to be published later, middle-class and lower-working-class children were asked to group photographs of food (bread, cheese, meat, milk, vegetables, etc.). *Initially*, middle-class children gave rationales for their grouping in terms of a context-independent principle, whereas the working-class children gave rationales in terms of food in the cultural context of use. The children constructed meals of various kinds. Again, the initial instruction to the children was open. The children could sort the photographs in any way they wished.

What accounts for differences between the children in these various situations? These very different situations have one feature in common. The eliciting instruction does not specify the form the response should take. Yet the middle-class children translate this open request into a request for a particular type of response. We know that this translation is independent of the 'measured intelligence' of the children, and that the translation is made in very different situations within a structured context. The translation of an open eliciting question which implicitly or explicitly says 'do it any way you want' into a very specialised response, where the meanings and realisations are less related to the child's everyday experience, makes the response of the child highly context specific. In some way, the child believes that what is required is that his/her response is not to be based upon the meanings and realisations of everyday informal interactions. The interview context (adult–task–child–response–adult evaluation) appears to be seen by the middle-class child as calling for a specialised response irrespective of a question which appears to offer the child a variety of ways of responding. Indeed, the child translates or rather re-codes an open question into a closed question. The child re-codes a weak classification and weak framing request: implicitly 'do it any way you want, and talk about it how you wish' into a strongly classified and strongly framed request: 'do it one way and talk about it one particular way.' How does a child come to understand that this is what is required, this is what is to be assessed? How does the child come to hold this expectation of an adult? Further, how does the child acquire the performance rule whereby he/she constructs the appropriate text? Thus there are inter-related questions; possessing the rule which constructs a specific text *and* recognising that the rule is appropriate to a given context, and using it.

Neither middle-class nor working-class parents are constantly talking to their children in specialised ways nor requiring that their children talk to them in equally specialised ways. Parents ask open-ended questions which are no more than that. However, it may well be that certain contexts imbedded in the flow of parent–child communication are especially marked by the social relationships, their content and their realisations. And in these contexts, questions and answers, explanations and descriptions, expansions, qualifications, may take a very context-specific form. Their format, their inter-actional structure, is different from that associated with everyday local affairs. A different pressure is exerted on the child to produce and receive a different structure of meanings and their appropriate realisations. In these contexts, the meanings and realisations are less imbedded in —although they may arise out of—local social relationships, local practices, local activities. To this extent, the meanings are less directly tied to a *specific* material basis. We would argue that here the meanings, the principles which generate them, become specialised objects in their own right, and the social relationships through which they are realised become specially marked. Indeed, an open question in this context may be used by the parent to test whether the child can produce 'spontaneously' the appropriate reply. The child learns to distinguish between open questions, according to their context; the child learns which open questions are in fact *testing* rather than eliciting questions; the child learns the nature of the response expected; the child learns how to select and structure his/her meanings;

the child learns the appropriate form of their realisation; the child learns the confidence to manage a social relationship where the presuppositions of everyday relationships are temporarily suspended. The analogy with future educational contents is not too difficult to draw. From this point of view, we should distinguish between recognising when a specific text is situationally relevant, possessing the rules to create the text, and using it. Because of the correspondence between features of middle-class familial transmissions and formal educational transmissions, middle-class children have the means to appropriate such transmissions, and their experience is legitimated by the school, which in turn enables the child to *legitimate the school*, irrespective of the immediate relevance of what is to be acquired or the level of the child's performance. What happens when this correspondence is not present? The mutual legitimising of the child of the school and the school of the child is less likely. It is not a mutually validating experience. In this situation, the school is likely to discount the experience of the child, to be followed eventually by the child discounting the experience of the school.

To return to the Trotin task. There is no particular significance about elaborated or less elaborated nominal groups elicited by this task. We believe that it would not be difficult to create a situation where the lower-working-class child would produce a text similar in orientation to that produced by the middle-class child. However, it might be more difficult for such a child to produce spontaneously strategies of control more typical of middle-class modalities. Further, it might be more difficult for such a child to adopt an instructional mode more typical of the middle-class children. From this point of view, there is no special significance about elaborated nominal groups elicited by the Trotin task. The Trotin task is significant only in relation to what the child does in other contexts, and what the child does in other contexts is, according to the theory, a matter of the underlying code. It is the underlying code which regulates the relationships between performance rules, the creation of specific texts and contexts.

If we now consider class-regulated educational codes, we can see that these codes are dependent upon production and they are also relatively autonomous of production (*Class, Codes and Control*, vol. 3, revised edition, 1977 ch. 8). Formal educational codes are the means whereby the workforce *and* its class basis are reproduced. In this sense, educational codes are dependent upon production, upon the mode of work. From this point of view, the dependency of education upon work represents its *general* material base. However, educational codes, although still subject to class regulation, are *also* relatively independent or relatively autonomous of work in that their principles, possibilities and conditions are not *directly* related to the principles, possibilities and conditions of work. If we look at educational codes from this point of view, then there is an *indirect* relation between the codes and work; an indirect relation to a specific material base. Middle-class forms of transmission transmit both messages.

1   The dependency relation translates into the motivation of the child with respect to the school, irrespective of its immediate relevance or interest to the child/pupil.

2   The relative autonomous relation translates into an orientation towards the school's context-independent meanings, and to specific performance rules and texts these create.

At a fundamental level, educational and familial codes correspond. This is what I consider the experimental contexts reveal.

In the second part of this volume, Turner and Adlam inquire into the relationships between the texts the children produce in the instructional, descriptive and regulative contexts. It should be pointed out that the unit for the analysis of codes is not an utterance, a group of clauses, a piece of familial or peer-group talk, but a text, and the social relationships which regulate it and which it realises. An attempt is made to ask whether there is an underlying, regulating code, such that if a child produces context-dependent texts in one situation, does the child produce a similar text in the other two situations? Such an analysis is fraught with difficulties. What is a text? What features of the child's speech in one context can be considered as text-producing features? What is the variation, in each social class group of children, of these text-producing features? For if there is little variation in these features within a social class group, then the correlation between texts in different situations will be low, or negligible.

From a common-sense point of view, there is no reason why there should be any underlying relationship between how a child talks about a set of pictures, a child's strategies in a control context, or how a child explains the rules of a game. Why should the expressions of uncertainty in the Trotin situation bear any relation to the texts produced in other situations? One might consider that any relation, however small, would be a little unusual. Remember that we have already shown on a number of occasions in these monographs that the orientation of the child's speech has little or no connection with 'measured verbal intelligence'.

In the carrying out of this complex and difficult study, we would like to remind the reader that two indices of texts were created. One was based upon the total sample, the other was based upon the specific samples of middle-class and lower-working-class children. That is, working-class children are compared with *each other*, not with middle-class children. We are considering variations *within* the working-class, and variations *within* the middle-class, children. Such an approach, although technically warranted, creates further difficulties. We know that for the middle-class group the modal text is an elaborated variant, whereas with the lower-working-class group the modal text is more likely to be a restricted variant. Thus, within the middle class there is less variation and so by making our index class specific we have probably produced degrees of variation of elaborated variants. Indeed, one of the interesting findings is the degree of homogeneity of the middle-class children, whereas the reader will discover that the lower-working-class children show far less homogeneity. I shall not anticipate the findings of the second study in part II. The intention here is only to alert the reader to some of the problems it posed.

I should emphasise that these analyses were carried out two years ago, which in research is a long time, and it should be appreciated that the authors now might not necessarily subscribe to all the assumptions underlying the theoretical perspective.

Finally, as I have stated elsewhere, the sequencing rules of educational transmissions, the pacing of the transmission (the rate of expected acquisition), its future relevance and its immediate irrelevance are, to say the least, based upon performance rules which the middle-class child embryonically possesses. Class regulates the elaborated codes of education and in the family. However, if we start from the view that all children possess common competences, are eager to find out about their world and control it, we might come to understand the social basis of differences in children's *performances*, how performances are socially constituted, how and why some are legitimised and others not, which might then create conditions for change, at least in education.

Acknowledgments

The research reported in this volume was made possible by grants from the Grant Foundation and the Social Science Research Council. The authors are grateful to Professor Basil Bernstein for continued advice and discussion throughout the preparation of the book. Our thanks go also to Pat Dyehouse and Barbara Cook of the Sociology Department of the University of London Institute of Education for their patience in the typing and re-typing of the manuscript.

Chapter 1 Introduction

Diana Adlam

A volume which takes for its title the relationship between two concepts, both of which are currently more ambiguous than clear, is under some obligation to vindicate their use. To begin by stating a concern with two distinct kinds of context may not seem a very promising prelude to clarity but it is necessary if the studies collected here are to be placed in the wider framework which generated them and therefore is necessary to their full interpretation. This is particularly important in the case of the present volume, since although each paper stands as a self-contained piece of work, taken collectively they explore a significant sociolinguistic topic in some detail. We begin with an outline of the two senses in which context may be considered with respect to the present work.

Bernstein (1973b) suggests that a child's orientation to language is first acquired in the family and is initially determined by the relationships existing therein. The communication patterns to which a child is exposed both reflect the social in the family and give a social basis to his construction of the world; and this in the sense that the child's orientation to language use will extend to his coding of objects as well as his experience of persons. Code is seen as a principle integrating semantic relevance with the form of its contextual realisation. Bernstein has suggested four generalised socialising contexts which are critical in the socialisation of the child. These are the regulative, the instructional, the interpersonal and the imaginative contexts. Bernstein considers that communication elicited by these four familial contexts is governed by elaborated or restricted codes of varying strengths depending upon the extent to which familial communication to the child focuses upon relatively context-dependent or -independent meanings. He argues that different explorations of the grammar and lexes are related to such coding orientations. This first sense of context attempts to describe those ongoing and constantly recurring situations in which code both regulates the form of the transmission and is itself transmitted to the child.

1

The term context is also used throughout this volume to describe those local situations in which speech is elicited or recorded from speakers. The eliciting context has received a great deal of attention in recent sociolinguistic work as investigators have become sensitised to the general problem of situational constraints on language use and have applied their ideas and findings to specifically educational contexts. Since Bernstein's concept of sociolinguistic code cannot be directly observed but must be inferred from speech in context, and since the concept of the child's coding orientation includes his own understanding or construction of this context then it follows, at least from the present theoretical perspective, that neither code nor context can be fully apprehended without a consideration of the relations between them. A child's communicative competence is only made active in context and so cannot be understood without analysis of what is immediately critical for the form this activation takes. At the same time, the meaning of a context for a speaker and therefore his realisation of it is shaped by just this competence or code.

Having underlined the importance of the interaction, we must stress also that analytically the two are separable and that theoretically they are distinct. A child's coding orientation is not identical with his interpretation and realisation of contexts but may be defined independently as a general orientation to the selection and realisation of meaning on the part of an active speaker/hearer. Thus code is further proposed to have a number of non-linguistic implications. And contexts are not conceived as wholly phenomenal, since then we have a very shifting basis for comparison between groups of speakers and for anchoring descriptions of contextualised speech to a more sociological explanation of the ways in which different groups of speakers use language.

These two kinds of context, which we may call contexts of transmission and eliciting contexts, apparently operate at rather different levels of abstraction. Bernstein's four socialising contexts are closely related to the neo-Firthian concept of generalised language functions while it is clear that contexts of elicitation refer to specific situations or situation-types. The two are linked in the present framework by the hypothesis that the code acquired by the child through experience in the contexts of transmission will be realised in a predictable manner in any one context of elicitation. Where contexts of transmission are governed by different codes then children are expected to differ in their orientation to language use and these different coding orientations will be realised in the semantic and linguistic choices made by the child in a range of eliciting situations.

I Codes and contexts of transmission

In Bernstein's thesis class is seen as regulating the distribution of what counts as dominant or privileged meanings and the acceptable form of their realisation. According to this particular thesis class affects the form of transmission and the institutionalisation of elaborated codes in education as well as their distribution between families. Middle-class families are oriented to the meanings and communication patterns of the elaborated code because the class structure points such families towards a structure of social relationships which gives rise to an elaborated code. The structure of social relationships typical of many lower-working-class families gives rise to the semantic orientation and communication patterns of the restricted code again through the action of the wider class structure. In this introduction these more macro-elements of the thesis will concern us only indirectly. This is partly because of limitations of space but also because of the focus of the empirical work reported here. The theoretical consideration of most concern here may be formulated as *the nature of the relationship between sociolinguistic codes and some specific sociolinguistic codings.* This question cannot, however, be divorced from the general framework, and more sociological aspects of the thesis will frequently be invoked. Bernstein has outlined the most relevant sociological concepts in his introduction and a detailed account may be found in Cook-Gumperz (1973).

II Codes and codings: the theoretical formulation

Bernstein defines code as a general orientation to the selection and organisation of meaning and to the form of its realisation in speech. Briefly, elaborated code users are orientated to more universalistic or context-independent[1] meanings which are explicitly realised in speech. Restricted code users are orientated towards more particularistic or context-dependent meanings which are implicitly realised in speech. Code, then, is seen as a tacit rule system regulating the semantic and linguistic choices which a speaker makes in a wide range of situations. Code is not identical with these choices but is realised through them. This relationship of codes to actual speech is formulated as the relationship of codes to *context-specific codings* (or speech variants or texts) and is diagrammed in Figure 1.

In this first section we shall focus on how parental orientation to code will influence the density and nature of communication in the four generalised transmission contexts. It is of some importance to point out that the unit for analysis is the communicative structure of the family in which is embedded the specific communication of a parent or parents to children. However, parents talk to each other, and the form and content of their speech provides for the children a crucial structure of meanings.

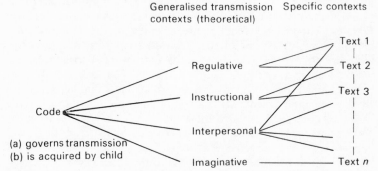

Figure 1   The relationship of code to a variety of context-specific codings

Where the code is elaborated, the four contexts of transmission will be explored and realised in a way that differs systematically from their exploration and realisation through a restricted code. Inevitably the discussion will contain many concrete examples and the specific 'contexts of situation' shown in the diagram here refer to encounters between parent and child. In the next section when we come to consider the interview context the same diagram is relevant, but the contexts of situation under discussion are encounters between children and interviewers and the emphasis is more squarely on attributes of the interview situation. In both cases, however, the relationship of codes to context-specific codings is being explored.

It is suggested that in general elaborated codes are realised through elaborated codings, restricted codes give rise to restricted codings. Such a formulation raises the question of how the surface indices of restricted and elaborated codings are to be identified. What, in any one context, counts as restricted coding and what counts as elaborated coding? This question is fundamental and may be put more specifically.

1   The codes are defined in terms of quite high level concepts such as context-independence/context-dependence; explicit/implicit; universalistic/particularistic.

2   What we are faced with empirically is the talk of a child or parent or teacher in a concrete situation, about a specific topic and often with a well-defined aim.

The problem is how to relate the observable speech to the general concept of code. To say that elaborated coding will be relatively more context-independent than restricted coding does not tell us what are the actual lexical and grammatical indices of one or another variant in a given context. Methodologically the problem is 'solved' in the writing of a coding frame.

The network type of coding frame developed by Bernstein and drawing on the work of linguist Michael Halliday starts with the more general theoretical distinctions and works through to specify the linguistic markers of these distinctions in the particular context under consideration. All the empirical papers in this volume attempt such a derivation. One facet of the theoretical problem can therefore be viewed as the nature of the activity involved in writing context-specific coding frames. By 'context-specific' here we mean that at the linguistic level the coding frame has very little generality beyond this one particular situation. Thus a second aspect of the problem consists in ensuring that varying examples of context-specific speech are coded at comparable levels. For instance, the markers of restricted coding in a control context may differ considerably from the markers of restricted coding in an instructional context (see below for an expansion of this point). In order to tie theory to data and to clarify the framework through which this is done, we must be able both to derive from theory the linguistic markers of restricted coding in the two contexts and to make sure that the two sets of markers are comparable one with the other. These twin aims are really two sides of the same coin. Only if the two sets of markers are realisations of the same more basic distinctions will the coding be comparable across contexts.

At first sight the above may appear obscure. This is partially because the discussion anticipates our presentation of some concrete illustrations of context-specific restricted and elaborated codings. It will be easier, once some such illustrations have been discussed, to examine the question of how the theoretical distinctions between the two codes may be realised and recognised in the distinctions made by speakers in their coding of contexts. It is important, however, that the theoretical problems are to the fore throughout the reading of the following examples and, at the risk of confusing the reader, some further points may be alluded to before the examples are given. All of these will be given fuller consideration presently.

Relating varying context-specific codings

It was noted above that 'the markers of restricted coding in a control context may differ considerably from the markers of restricted coding in an instructional context'. In terms of Figure 1 the critical features of texts 1 through n may vary greatly while still being tied to the more general concept of code. Now in order to infer whether a child is primarily oriented to a restricted code or to an elaborated code it is clearly better to look at a range of his context-specific codings than to restrict the analysis to one single text. This, in fact, is the task of Chapter 4 written by Adlam and Turner. It will become evident that such an analysis is far from simple. It involves the correlating of what, at a surface level, are very different kinds of texts. The texts are of course related at a theoretical level because the same conceptual framework generated each individual coding frame. Keeping the different analyses comparable is a major methodological problem. Examining the consistency of speakers across contexts becomes a test of the thesis itself.

Context-specific coding considered as text

We have said that a central problem in Bernstein's theory (or in 'operationalising' this theory) is that of relating the more abstract or more sociological definitions of code to actual speech in context (codings). In the practical task of analysing such speech the converse problem presents itself. Having derived from theoretical distinctions the corresponding distinctions at the level of lexes and grammar there is a danger of concentrating so exclusively on linguistic features that the object of concern (i.e. semantic orientation) is almost lost sight of completely. For example it may be decided that exophoric pronouns are one index of restricted coding in a descriptive task while expanded nominal groups are an index of elaborated coding in the same situation. The significant thing about a child's response then becomes whether his use of these categories is above or below average. Certainly this is important, but other features contribute to the nature of the text which he offers. Linguistic indices are more important in the pattern formed by them than in the use of any one individually. This notion of a text is crucial in sociolinguistic work and is discussed in detail on p. 16. For the moment let it be noted that from the perspective of the present volume it is a text rather than a phrase, clause or sentence that is taken as the unit of analysis in the investigation of speech. The notion of text is closer to concepts such as context-independent/dependent than are more purely linguistic measures and so provides a link between the two. The patterning of linguistic indices tells us the nature of the text that is offered.

Structured v. naturalistic data

Throughout this book we will tend to take a particular situation (e.g. mother controlling her child, children explaining the rules of a game to an interviewer) and compare and contrast the texts offered by restricted and elaborated code users in this situation. Such an approach may obscure the basic fact that speakers (especially those with power, e.g. parents and teachers) *have a considerable degree of control over the contexts which they choose to code.*[2] Thus while we shall here illustrate how different speakers vary in their exploration and realisation of the same contexts it is also the case that the density of communication over the range of situation types encountered by members of a culture will vary according to code. Thus elaborated code transmitters may use language for the exploration and articulation of feelings and intent to a greater extent than do restricted code transmitters. The latter may centre more of their communications around control than is the case for elaborated code users. Both these examples may be derived from Bernstein's thesis and receive support from Wootton's (1974) study of mother/child interaction. Although our discussion will inevitably centre on comparison and contrast in pre-given situations we shall, wherever possible, allude to corresponding theoretical predictions and empirical findings from less structured situations.

Code realisation in the four general contexts of transmission

In order to clarify the structure of relationships between codes and context-specific codings, Bernstein has delineated four critical socialising contexts. Further, this framework points to the theoretically most relevant situations which the child encounters. It should be stressed that this notion of context does not correspond to the term as it is used in some current sociolinguistic work but is more akin to a generalised function of language as conceived by the neo-Firthian school of linguistics (see especially Halliday, 1973). Thus any one speech encounter might include two or more socialising contexts. Situations in which the child is being controlled would obviously be characterised as regulative contexts but might also be instructional and/or interpersonal. There is a fairly wide range of empirical speech events (at least in the life of the child) which may be characterised according to Bernstein's four contexts of transmission. Bernstein (1971, ch. 9) describes these contexts as follows:

1. The regulative context – these are authority relationships where the child is made aware of the rules of the moral order and their various backings.

2. The instructional context – where the child learns about the objective nature of objects and persons and acquires skills of various kinds.

3. The imaginative context (or innovating) – where the child is encouraged to experiment and re-create his world on his own terms and in his own way.

4. The interpersonal context – where the child is made aware of affective states – his own and others.

What, then, do the theoretical distinctions imply for specific interactions? Halliday (1973) discusses at some length the possible semantic options open to a mother in a situation where her child has returned home after playing in a forbidden place and with a 'trophy' of dubious origin and nature. How is the mother to convey her annoyance at the episode and prevent its recurrence? Halliday gives a whole series of options – she can tell him unequivocally that this is not allowed, she can point out that he has ruined his clothes, she can express disapproval of his playmates, she can threaten to tell his father, she can explain that the place is physically dangerous, etc., etc. The implication of Halliday's network of choices is that where communication is governed by a restricted code then the characteristic pattern of choices will differ from that where the communication is governed by an elaborated code. We must point out, however, that Halliday is here concerned with the construction of a network of choices within the regulative context. It is not possible to infer whether the speech variant is restricted or elaborated from the consideration of any *one* choice in the network. The following sets of statements would be drawn from different systems of the network describing choices in the regulative context. The first set would enter choices in the imperative system whereas the second set would enter choices in the appeal system. The latter makes available to the child information about the intentions and consequences of the child's acts as they relate to him (child-oriented appeals) or as they relate to the controller (parent-oriented appeals). (For a complete account of this system of classification see Cook-Gumperz, 1973.)

Don't do that again.

You'll get smacked.

I told you before about going there and if you do it again you'll lose a week's pocket money.

I'm going to tell your dad this time.

Just look at the state of your clothes, don't you think I've got enough to do without you adding to it?

You mustn't play on rubbish dumps – they're often full of broken glass and old tins and you might get cut.

The first set of statements convey to the child information about explicit hierarchical relationships. He is given no basis for the ruling and so the verbal statement does not transcend the given context. The child can, of course, question 'Why can't I?', but the probability of 'Because I say so' as an answer is quite high.

The child confronted with statements of the second kind also learns that he is supposed to give up this particular play patch. But he learns something besides this. The meaning structure to which he is exposed goes beyond this single incident and he receives both an explicit basis for not repeating this action and an indication of other acts that might meet with nasty consequences – either for himself or for others. The meanings offered to this child transcend the given context while giving an explicit basis for the action within it. This is not to say that, faced with persistent disobedience, this mother might not eventually explode with 'Because I say so now be quiet', but the hypothesis is that the verbally explicit information is likely to be evoked, at least as a first strategy, in a wide range of regulative situations.

We should like to emphasise that abstracted, isolated statements such as those given above are in themselves no firm empirical basis for determining the underlying coding orientation. It is necessary to examine the total pattern of choices to make such an inference. This point will be expanded in our discussion of texts as a unit of analysis.

Consider now an instructional or explanatory context. There is considerable evidence that children differ in the sheer amount of adult instructional speech to which they are exposed outside school. Wootton (1974), in a naturalistic study of parent-child interaction in the home, found that pre-school working-class (WC) children spent much less time in verbal exchanges with their parents than did their middle-class (MC) contemporaries. Beyond this difference in amount of talk, WC mothers were less prepared than MC mothers to answer the children's requests for information or to offer such information spontaneously. Further, the utterances of the MC mother were apparently such as to encourage more 'advanced' questions – in content terms – from their children. A final, intriguing finding was that while WC mothers were often quite prepared to participate actively in their children's fantasy play, MC mothers frequently used such imaginings as an opportunity for the transmission of information. The WC mothers never did this.

Henderson (in Brandis and Henderson, 1970), using a much larger sample of questionnaire-based data, reports results congruent with Wootton's findings. WC mothers were consistently more likely than MC mothers to avoid their children's questions in a number of situations: fantasy questions, requests for information, questions about the meaning of words, etc.

Beyond the finding that MC mothers are more predisposed to make the instructional context a focal part of the child's verbally mediated socialisation, Bernstein suggests that the nature of the communication once such a context has been initiated will differ according to the dominant code. As with the control context it is expected that where the code is elaborated stress will be on the transmission of principles, and that instruction in context will include information relevant outside the particular situation. In such a context, verbal explicitness both realises the mother's intent and sensitises the child to the relevance of the principles that lie behind the immediate operation with which he is involved. Henderson's analysis (1970, *op. cit.*) of maternal communication styles provides considerable support for the notion that MC mothers are concerned to teach general rules whereas WC mothers tend to stress aspects of the particular situation. Henderson also gives evidence to suggest that the MC mothers couple this emphasis on general principles with considerable contextual specificity and that WC mothers tend to discriminate less between, for example, topics in terms of explanatory strategy.

Lineker's (Chapter 3) analysis of children's preferred means of explaining the rules of a game (hide-and-seek) provides interesting data as to how these social class differences in maternal orientation to explanation might be realised in the child's approach to such a context, as elicited in an experimental interview. Lineker finds that while MC children are strongly disposed to giving an overall review of the rules in terms of 'general' players and circumstances (e.g. 'someone's got to hide somewhere') many WC children move towards a description of a specific instance of the game in which they have themselves participated (e.g. 'little girl hides in the kitchen').

The interpersonal context enters quite explicitly into some of the control examples given above – as when the child's attention is drawn to the unhappiness which his behaviour has caused his mother. Bernstein and Henderson found that MC mothers relative to WC mothers judged that the transmission of interpersonal skills would be much more difficult without language than would the transmission of manual skills. Thus MC mothers emphasise the verbal exploration of affect and intent. Wootton, in the study referred to above, also found that MC mothers were far more likely to make explicit reference to feelings and personal states. In fact, Wootton (personal communication) found that WC *mothers* made less explicit reference to the interpersonal area than did MC *children* although in general adults make such references far more extensively than do children. These findings suggest that MC families place some emphasis on drawing the attention of their children to the affective states of others and on encouraging the children to be explicit about their individual meanings in this area. Detailed study of the inter-personal function of language has tended to focus on its role in regulative situations; in the present framework, on how control and interpersonal contexts relate together. An interesting aspect of Wootton's analysis was the finding that for all families, most references to intent were made outside control situations (although in both control and non-control situations the class differential was highly significant).

Both conceptually and empirically, the interpersonal and innova-tive contexts have been studied in less detail than have the regulative and instructional functions of language. This is especially true of the imaginative context, but even the current limited state of our know-ledge would suggest that the most interesting sub-cultural differences in the exploration of this context occur in the extent to which it is made situation-specific for the child, and particularly in the way it is related to the other three language functions. Briefly, both Wootton's analysis and the SRU research suggest that there is far greater ten-sion and interaction between the imaginative and instructional contexts for MC than for WC children. We have already mentioned that MC mothers are much more likely than WC mothers to use their children's fantasy play as an opportunity to transmit informa-tion. In the speech of the children also WC children are much more likely than MC children to use narrative speech when asked ex-plicitly for instruction or for description (which, it is suggested, involves a strong instructional element in the context of adult/child interaction). This is clearly shown in both Lineker's and Adlam's papers in this volume and has been corroborated by others, in-cluding Lancia in Belgium. It has also been shown by Turner that in the interview context, MC children require very explicit requests before they will move into a hypothetical mode whereas WC children do this more freely. And Hasan (personal communication) finds that when asked to make up a bedtime story, MC children are more con-strained and give more tightly and traditionally structured answers than do their WC peers. Taken together, this rather heterogeneous group of findings would suggest that MC children are learning to mark off contexts according to the social relationships and questions asked, whereas some WC children are in similar contexts pre-dominantly oriented to narrative speech. While this may allow them sometimes to make more fluent and free use of the narrative mode, it also implies a different understanding of the parameters of speech contexts and a different classification and patterning of uses of language than that which is acquired by the MC child. It would appear that the tension that exists in MC transmission between report and innovation on the one hand, and instruction and investigation on the other, is a likely determining influence.

We have tried to show how different orientations to code will create different patterns of communication and control in the familial socialisation of the child. Where a restricted code governs transmission, the speech variants will tend towards restriction in all four socialising contexts. Similarly, where an elaborated code governs the transmission, the four general socialising contexts will tend to elicit elaborated variants or codings. This does not mean that where the code is restricted, there will never be any context-specific elaborated codings. Conversely, Bernstein has continually stressed that where the dominant code is elaborated, a whole range of situations will be more appropriately handled through restricted codings. This issue is fully considered below. Here it remains to discuss how the speech itself is to be described, and this will profitably be done in relation to child language in order to provide an introduction to the kinds of analysis which the reader may expect to encounter in the papers which follow. Two aspects of the problem will be singled out for analysis. First, the identification of the critical features of speech variants will be discussed. Since code is defined in terms of semantics, as a general orientation to meaning, then what is significant at the level of lexes and grammar may differ considerably from one situation to another. Second, we will consider the general problem of the appropriate unit of linguistic analysis for sociolinguistic work. It will be argued that any attempt to understand the relationship between social structure and language use should aim for a textual characterisation of speech; that detailed analysis of the mean frequency of certain lexical and grammatical items in the speech of any social group is not in itself an adequate characterisation of the nature of that speech from a social perspective. Both these discussions of course take up points initially raised in our consideration of the relationship between codes and codings at the beginning of this section.

III   Codes and codings: the description of speech

The critical features of speech variants

The linguistic realisations of code have been described here in terms of an orientation to the *selection* and *realisation* of meaning on the part of speakers – to the creation of meaning and the form of its encoding in speech. But the two are not independent. In the examples drawn from the regulative and instructional contexts (pp. 8, 10) it was suggested that speakers could focus either on more local issues – particularistic meanings – or that they could focus on the principles behind the immediate event – universalistic meanings – as well. Thus in these two contexts children are being sensitised to different orders of meaning according to whether the dominant code is elaborated or restricted. Because they are more tied to the immediate situation, particularistic meanings have also been termed more context-dependent than the universalistic type, which are apparently more generally applicable and so more context-independent.

But this distinction of context-independence and context-dependence has also been used to describe the explicitness of the speech. Thus when the children were given Trotin pictures to describe, there was variation in the extent to which they made their meanings explicit and specific. Some of the children gave speech that could be understood by listeners outside the immediate interaction, whereas others gave speech that was much more context-dependent in that the listener had need of the eliciting material in order fully to understand the child's utterance. The first of the following two statements is of this more context-dependent type, whereas the second is relatively less embedded in the eliciting situation:

he's doing that
the guard man's pushing a luggage cart

Now in practice, this distinction between the child's selection of meaning and his orientation to its realisation is quite blurred. If a child understands that he is to be verbally explicit in certain kinds of communication situations then this will affect what he talks about as well as how. Similarly, the choice of, say, an imperative control strategy itself constrains the form of the linguistic realisation. Beyond this, the form of an utterance can itself be of semantic significance, especially in the social meaning which it carries (see next section).

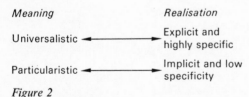

Figure 2

It is apparent that the semantic and lexical/grammatical aspects of language in use cannot be divorced. Semantic options will limit the range of possible formal choices, and formal options (influenced, for example, by the speaker/listener relationship) will affect meaning in a variety of ways. But it is the case that the relationship between universalistic meanings and explicit speech and between particularistic meanings and implicit speech is not of the order shown in Figure 2.

It is important to spell this out because the terms context-independent and context-dependent have been applied to both levels and it would be easy to infer that the relation between the levels was simple. But in Lineker's analysis, many of the children who gave particularistic accounts of hide-and-seek used fairly explicit linguistic constructions. What, for example, is the difference in explicitness between the following?

> someone's got to hide in a good place
> little girl goes and hides in the cupboard

Conversely, the difference in meaning between the following cannot be described in terms of general/particular

> he's doing that
> the guard man's pushing a luggage cart

yet Adlam (Chapter 2) calls the first context-dependent, the second more context-independent.

However, if we consider the implicit variants of the two instructional examples, both transform into

> she's got to hide there

In other words, making the realisation implicit, making an utterance implicit at the level of lexes and grammar, automatically renders the meaning more context-dependent. This would seem to imply that context-independent meaning must be realised explicitly. But the converse does not hold – context-dependent or particularistic meanings can be realised explicitly or implicitly; which is not to say that there is no important difference between

> little girl goes and hides in the cupboard
> she goes and hides there

The specific context will determine the significance of each facet of language for coding orientation.

Our model of the relationship between the semantic and lexico-grammatical levels then looks more like Figure 3.

The hypothesis that sociolinguistic code may be inferred from the nature of the speech variants in the four socialising contexts (or, more precisely, specific situations relevant to these) demands that the level at which these variants are characterised is compatible between contexts. The terms context-independent and context-dependent are useful because whether the distinctive features of elaborated and restricted variants are expected largely at the level of meaning or largely at the level of realisation (e.g. Adlam, Chapter 2), at the social level, the basis of the orientation remains the same. Both particularistic meanings and implicit speech are realisations of a social situation which, for the speaker, involves reduced distance

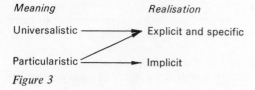

Figure 3

between himself and other aspects of the setting. Both universalistic meanings and explicit speech are part of a speaker/setting relationship of increased distance; both the meaning and the form of its encoding in speech have less need of the eliciting context in order to be decoded by a listener. For this reason Bernstein can say that explicit speech is universalistic in nature in the sense that the meaning is more universally available, is available to more listeners. And implicit speech can be called particularistic in the sense that only particular others – those with whom the speaker has certain shared knowledge either in terms of their common history or in terms of the immediate context – can fully decode the message.

Because both the selection and realisation of meaning are of social origin, it is difficult to make the distinction at all. Indeed the grounds for so doing are more pragmatic than explanatory and our essential concern is to point to the different emphases or foci which investigation of child speech can adopt. Meaning reverberates on speech, syntactic and lexical choices can be viewed as more delicate semantic options, grammatical form is an index of semantic organisation. We tease out the levels in order to understand their interaction and to show that apparently disparate surface features of speech have a common social motivation and therefore may be equally relevant to social theory.

Having stressed the dialectical relationship between the social, semantic and grammatical aspects of speaking we can briefly take an analytic perspective and suggest that the three pairs of terms: universalistic/particularistic; implicit/explicit; context-independent/ context-dependent, might be applied to the levels of, respectively, meaning, lexical/grammatical choice and text. This third level – that of text – includes the other two and, since it derives directly from the more general theory, is an important means of ensuring that the description of speech in one context is comparable with the description in another. The characterising of speech in context as an elaborated or a restricted variant will depend on the extent to which the speech shows a context-independent orientation to meaning and to its realisation. The context itself will determine what specific features of the utterance are to be the focus of attention. Thus the instructional task can focus on the child's overall approach to explanation; the control task can look at the child's tendency to use imperative as opposed to more informative and contingent strategies; the imaginative task is concerned both with linguistic cohesion and with questions of structure.

It should now be clear why Bernstein's concern with assessing the nature of the speech variants across a range of contexts is not a simple one. If the issue were to determine whether the child who used subordinate clauses in describing a picture postcard also used such constructions in his control speech, then we should not be too surprised if this were the case. However, it is not immediately apparent why children who opt for imperative control strategies should also explain hide-and-seek in terms of particular players and places. The 'consistency' predicted by Bernstein's framework refers to consistency in the contextual realisation of the child's general orientation to sociolinguistic code. To put it tritely, the linguistic realisation of code depends on context (as Bernstein has used it) as well as on code.

Our concern with arriving at a theoretically derived textual description of any one speech variant stems partly from just this surface discontinuity in the different contextual realisations of code. The notion that individual linguistic indices should be used only as a guide to the textual characteristics of speech will be considered in some detail. This is a basic tenet of the present perspective as well as having quite general relevance.

Textual descriptions

Many studies to date have been concerned to demonstrate differences between sub-cultural groups in individual linguistic measures, e.g. number of pronouns or frequency of relative clauses. We are here arguing that such an approach gives inadequate information about the child's orientation to language use and that the appropriate unit of analysis for sociolinguistic research is a text. Clearly, word counts and the like will relate to a textual description of the speech. Indeed, such a description will usually be based on more detailed linguistic analyses. The point is that the significance of individual indices is given less by their incidence or frequency in the child's speech and more by how they pattern with other measures. Adlam in discussing the results of the analysis of descriptive speech reported in Chapter 2 writes:

It may have been noted that in no case was a (linguistic) category used exclusively and extensively by one group of children – that, in fact, the differences observed were often superficially slight, representing variations in tendency, in orientation to one or another kind of speech. And this is what we would expect. The children are speaking the same language and they have all been given a standardised set of questions about a standardised task. *Nevertheless it is our conviction that quite small variations in the extent to which certain semantic and linguistic elements are employed, will combine and interact to give crucial differences in the overall patterning of the speech and that these will emerge quite clearly when we look at texts as a whole* (italics original).

Clearly it is of fundamental importance to explicate the linguistic indices which will differentiate texts in a theoretically relevant way. The problem is really one of losing the wood through an overriding concern with the taxonomic properties of trees and, to labour the metaphor, of then being unable to say very much about the conditions which generate different kinds of forest. In the above case, the theoretical dimension with which we were concerned was Bernstein's distinction between context-independent and context-dependent speech. These concepts refer to properties of texts but were operationalised through the identification of critical semantic and grammatical features. As will be seen in Chapter 2, the problem of then using these quantitative measures as a basis for a more global description of each child's speech is not a simple one. Lineker's analysis (Chapter 3) is more satisfactory in this regard since her coding procedure made an initial distinction in terms of the child's overall approach to the task of instruction.

Staying for a moment with the descriptive task, in which children were asked about three detailed picture postcards depicting work by Trotin, we can make more concrete the distinction between textual and linguistic feature analyses. As stated above, the descriptive analysis was concerned with the explicitness and specificity of the child's speech, with the degree to which it could be understood independently of the eliciting context. Some children made their descriptions much more context-dependent than others. Context-dependent speech is characterised as relying on external situational features for its interpretation. Exophoric pronouns (e.g. he, she, this, that, *not* referring back to an item previously specified linguistically) have their referents in the context of situation and have therefore been explored as an index of context-dependence, especially in descriptive and narrative tasks (Hawkins, 1969; Hasan, 1968; Adlam, Chapter 2). It has been shown that exophora differentiates texts intuitively and sub-cultural groups empirically in that working-class children in an interview context tend to make greater use of such pronouns and adverbs than do middle-class children. However, the incidence of exophorics does not in itself define a text as either context-independent or context-dependent. The way in which such constructions pattern with other linguistic features is the essential consideration. Consider the following examples:

> lady sitting there   man walking along
> little girl's got a train   lady's going shopping   shops
> trains   ladies   dogs   those men

This short excerpt contains one exophoric reference in 11 headwords, but it could not be characterised as showing a strong orientation to context-independent speech. A lack of exophoric reference means something quite different in the above text than it does in the following sample of speech:

> people are at the station waiting for their train   maybe they're going on holiday   there's a house at the side with smoke coming out of the chimney   she's got a big suitcase to go in the train

Thus largely because of the second child's inclusion of certain indices such as highly specific reference or general statements, the two children differ considerably in the extent to which they have constructed context-independent texts. In terms of an analysis confined to the incidence of discrete linguistic categories, however, these children score similarly on a critical measure.

A further reason for making a text the linguistic unit of analysis is brought out very clearly when we examine the child's speech across contexts (Chapter 4). For example, we may want to compare the child's orientation to descriptive speech with his speech in the control task. A preference for certain choices within the imperative form of control is suggested as one characteristic of transmission governed by a restricted code (Bernstein, 1971, ch. 9) but, following the argument applied to exophora in description, the child's preference for imperative strategies cannot be taken in isolation. For example, his tendency to explicate the reasons for the command is also of interest. It follows from this that attempts to investigate whether a child's coding orientation is consistent across contexts will gain a misleading picture if correlations are made, for example, between frequency of exophoric constructions and frequency of imperative forms. The appropriate analysis is one which compares the child's orientation to language use, in the two tasks. By aiming for a textual characterisation of speech we allow more meaningful comparisons of very different kinds of texts generated by very different sociolinguistic contexts.

The above discussion throws considerable doubt on the kind of single-phrase illustrations of restricted and elaborated code use sprinkled rather liberally throughout this introduction. We can of course argue limitations of space but would be in fundamental agreement with such a criticism. In the last section of this volume the reader will find reprinted a number of complete interview transcripts, and we would emphasise that it is at this level that we seek to understand the child's use of language. Further, we are not only suggesting that the emphasis on individual structural aspects of speech is misplaced and that the textual patterning of such aspects is primary. The argument applies also to more semantically focused analyses as when the incidence of imperative control strategies was pointed out above to be only one index of restricted forms of control to be considered in the light of the child's tendency also to make more informative options. The categories used in the analysis of control, such as imperatives, reasoning and concessions, are primarily semantic rather than grammatical (given the fluidity of that distinction) but the necessity of centring on their overall patterning still holds.

In conclusion, it can be said that a central concern of this volume is to show how Bernstein's theory of restricted and elaborated codes can generate a useful description of socially based differences in how children use language in a variety of situations. And further, that such descriptions may be meaningfully compared across these situations. Chapter 4 reports a comparison of the orientation of 200 children to language use in control, descriptive and instructional contexts and finds that the children do indeed show some consistency in whether their coding orientations are restricted or elaborated. Now these tasks (the control, descriptive and instructional) were constructed to correspond to Bernstein's initial socialising contexts as outlined above. It should be noted, however, that the collection of speech from the children was in a sense indirect. Their speech was not recorded in actual contexts of transmission, but in tasks expected to realise the coding orientation acquired in such contexts. And these tasks were presented in interview form. The question then arises whether or not the procedure of data collection exerted a critical influence on the data obtained. The answer to this is broadly that it did, but to understand the significance of the context of elicitation in Bernstein's theory we must discuss in more detail the social assumptions underlying the two codes. Such a discussion will profitably include extended reference to other sociolinguistic enquiries into the effect of context on language use.

IV   The context of situation

The notion of the context of situation is not new in linguistic writings, but having been obscured by the appearance of Chomskyan theory it has only recently found a new stage in sociolinguistics. Turner's paper includes an analysis of the Firthian and neo-Firthian tradition in linguistics which has always been concerned with linguistic function and with context, but we will here concentrate on how the notion of context has figured in recent sociolinguistic work, largely in America.

A wide range of empirical research now exists to show how aspects of the situation in which a speaker (or writer) finds himself will constrain what is said and how. Such work ranges from investigations of quite broad problems such as the appropriateness of evaluative statements in situations of varying formality through more linguistically oriented studies of the effects of topic, listener, locale, role relationships and function on a speaker's phonology, grammar, lexes and, amongst multilinguals and dialectals, variety. For example, Labov (1964) has shown that the presence of the post-vocalic /r/ in the speech of New Yorkers is a function both of the social status of the speaker and of the formality of the situation (casual speech through word lists). And it is well established that among bilinguals the code used will vary as a function of recipient, setting, topic etc. or some combination of these (Ervin-Tripp, 1964; Blom and Gumperz, 1972).

Just as context constrains what a speaker says and the form in which he clothes it, so a listener uses context in interpreting the meaning of what is said both directly and in the wider sense of using the speech as a clue to the social attributes or intentions of the speaker. Only references to the context of situation, for example, will decide whether a statement such as 'it's much too hot in here' is to be understood as simple description, a request to turn off the heating or open a window, or a reproach for wasting electricity, etc. If spoken by a guest who is not a close friend in the home of a middle-class English family, such a statement might also be considered inappropriate and its author abrupt or rude. Unless, of course, the speaker was a visitor from an exotic country, and the host 'enlightened' about cultural diversity, in which case the incident might be ignored. And so on. Gumperz and Hernandez-Chavez (1972) show how code-switching amongst bilinguals is used to signal changes in intimacy and distance during conversation. In their study, what seems at first sight to be random switching from Spanish to English is found to realise subtle variations in social meaning.

This is not the place to attempt an overview of the kind of research to which we alluded above. Rather it is important to see how the aims and findings of 'descriptive sociolinguistic' or ethnography-of-speaking approaches to child language may be related to the present series of studies and their theoretical backing. The goal of much micro sociolinguistic work is a description of who says what in what form to whom, where, when and for which purpose. Such a formulation is most readily applicable in situations of multilingualism or dialect variation, since where this is absent or not the central concern it becomes extremely difficult to decide on what counts as variation in form (see, for example, Hasan (1973) on the distinctions code, register and dialect). It is more appropriate to rephrase the problem as it bears on the work of the SRU – where all the children are speaking the same language and dialect variation is not a primary focus of interest – as what constellation of contextual variables will evoke which *kinds of codings* in different groups of children. And this is not a trivial quibble over the formulation of the problem; it involves the basic distinction between code in Bernstein's sense and, for example, dialect or language variety, and also between the nature of the meanings carried by their use. Hasan (1973) makes this distinction between code and dialect as follows:

> Two outstanding differences between the two immediately draw attention to themselves: while the extra-linguistic factor(s) correlating with social dialect are incidental, those correlating with code are said to be causal; if the relationship between the two in the former case is simply that of co-occurrence, the relationship between the two in the case of code is that of logical dependence which presupposed co-occurrence. Secondly, while social dialect is defined by reference to its distinctive formal properties, the code is defined by reference to its semantic properties, thus involving consideration of the formal levels only indirectly. That is to say, it can be argued that the semantic properties of the codes can be predicted from the elements of the social structure which, in fact, give rise to them.

This distinction is, perhaps, best illustrated by considering situations where code use and dialect use overlap. In communities employing more than one language variety there is often concurrence between when a variety is used and what it is used for. Much of the research in this area has, in fact, demonstrated just this – that one variety is used in relaxed situations and that an alternative is used in and marks more formal contexts (Fishman, 1965; Blom and Gumperz, 1972). Whether a speaker uses a restricted or an elaborated code is also dependent on the social situation, on the role relationship between speaker and listener. Restricted coding realises relationships based on shared assumptions and shared meanings where explication in speech would be awkward and redundant; elaborate coding rests on different assumptions (e.g. takes less for granted in the speaker/listener relationship) and is used to explain, to instruct, to probe behind the apparent. However, because a dialect or language is the appropriate means of speech in informal situations and therefore is often used to realise a restricted code, this does not mean that such a variety *is* a restricted code. There is no fundamental reason why variety A, appropriate to informal contexts, could not be used to elaborate meanings of a universalistic kind and, conversely, why variety B, appropriate to formal contexts, could not embody the condensed implicit symbols of solidarity; which is not to say that such usage would come easily to speakers (see, for example, Ervin-Tripp's interview with Japanese women who, though fluent in English through intermarriage, had great difficulty in discussing matters of personal significance in the English tongue).

We can make this argument even more concrete. Imagine a situation where a young girl has been given an unexpected present by her current boyfriend. Imagine further that this particular young lady is Scottish and that speech in her home shows fairly marked dialect features. She works, however, in a rather expensive jewellery shop and her speech to customers shows a strong reduction in these features. In this situation of receiving a gift she might say something along the lines of: 'Fit a bonnie thing. I dinnae ken fit tae say', and accompany this with much non-verbal communication such as smiling, blushing, opening the eyes in surprise and kissing the giver. Now, she is less likely to say: 'It's beautiful. I really don't know what to say', since this would bring a note of formality to the situation. But there is no *logical* reason why she should not, and perhaps if she married an Englishman and went to live in the South then a similar situation twenty years later would evoke just this response, which by then would have lost the connotation of coolness. What she is highly unlikely to do is to respond with the following statement:

'This 24 carat gold bracelet is made by the most skilled craftsman and strikes me as a fine work of art. It must have cost you an entire week's wage and I am quite overwhelmed that your feelings for me should have led you to buy it. I feel quite undeserving of such a gift but on the other hand if you wish to symbolise the importance our relationship has for you then I think it quite an appropriate realisation of your intention',

delivered with minimal non-verbal activity. Such explicit description and explanation is inconceivable in such a setting and if it did occur would have alarming consequences for the nature of the relationship between the participants. Finally, to complete the argument, there is no reason why the final text above should not be rendered in Doric (except that the phonological transcription is quite beyond my grasp), in which form it would be equally disturbing.

Coding orientation, then, follows logically from the nature of the eliciting context itself while dialect, although it can be used in very subtle ways to define and redefine contexts, is only incidentally related to them. We might say that while coding orientation *realises* the social context, dialect or variety is used to *mark* the social context.

This raises a whole number of issues, some of which we will explore in detail. First, the meanings carried and realised by code use are likely to be of a different nature to those carried and realised through dialect use. Second, the form of investigation appropriate to these two aspects of the relation between social structure and language is likely to be different. An ethnographic approach is almost dictated by what we have referred to as descriptive sociolinguistics, while it is unlikely to be very efficient in the adequate exploration of code. Third, the kinds of linguistic analysis needed and therefore the slant of the linguistic theory adopted are likely to be different. In determining the dialect used by a speaker we look for a particular pattern of phonological, lexical and grammatical choices, and although the social context will be fundamental in determining which choices are made, the analysis of the speech can be carried out without reference to this context. We do not need information about locale, the topic of conversation or the person to whom it is directed to decide whether a person is using Welsh or English, although very detailed ethnographic data may be required in order to reveal the full range of meaning carried by that choice. An analysis of code use, however, is basically functional and therefore cannot be undertaken without reference to the eliciting context (see sections on 'Codes and codings').

A fourth problem concerns the nature of context. Is it, in fact, a social or a social/psychological variable? And this raises also the question of the nature of social control. Is a child's linguistic performance subject to the kind of external control that acts upon cheekiness, sullenness and aggression, or does it point also to the social constraints on the realisation of mental structures, on the formation of consciousness?

Finally, we can look to how these two approaches to social aspects of language use might have some very definite convergences. The issue of the influence of such factors as topic or listener on whether a speaker uses Spanish or American English, Clydebank Glaswegian or BBC Standard is not identical to the problem of the influence of topic or listener on whether a speaker chooses to condense his verbally realised meanings or to articulate and elaborate their nature and origins. Nevertheless there are situational constraints on both these aspects of speech use, and the influences of context on coding orientation can be clarified considerably by the work which examines the more general issue of the social constraints on language use.

One implication of explicating the norms of appropriateness which obtain for a speaker or group of speakers across the spectrum of their uses of language is that we shall more adequately understand communicative interference. Not only will the realisation and interpretation of meaning within a community be made more comprehensible but situations where different patterns of rules for use of language lead to miscommunication will also become clearer.

Studies of the use of terms of address provide neat examples of this kind of confusion (Brown and Gilman, 1960; Kantorovich, 1966; Ervin-Tripp, 1964). As long as we share a system of rules with those around us, it is easy to manipulate terms of address to imply deference or show solidarity, but where a newcomer to a group has a different system of sociolinguistic rules, misinterpretation is likely to result. For example, if the speaker but not the listener has a system in which familiarity, not merely solidarity, is required for use of a first name, he will use 'Mr Smith' instead of 'John' and be regarded as aloof by his listener. Again, he will feel first-name usage by the other in the dyad to be intrusive.

Such situations of mis-match are particularly important in education. Children whose speech patterns are not that of the school may find that they are not understood in the classroom, that the full meaning of their speech fails to reach the teacher and that their responses to her are somehow not appropriate. And as Hymes (1972) has pointed out, 'If one rejects a child's speech, one probably communicates rejection of the child.'

The plight of children whose natural language or dialect is punished or forbidden in the school has been documented by a number of writers and it has also been shown, most clearly by Labov, that even where a child's communicative skills are not actively prohibited, the context of the classroom may be one in which he finds it impossible or irrelevant to make any use of these at all. Hence arose the myth of the non-verbal child. Polgar (1960) describes how Eskimo children interpreted the normal loudness of voice and directness of their American teachers as anger and how she, in turn, took their respectful, fearful silence to be a sign of sullenness and unwillingness to learn.

Again, however, 'interference' can exist at the level of dialect and at the level of code and in both cases there may be variation in its recognition as well as its implications. Differences in orientation to meaning, however, are likely to be more difficult both to recognise and to manage. Interference at the level of code may often assume a more subtle and perhaps more insidious form than that which leads a teacher to try to change a child's accent or grammar. Bernstein (1975) has suggested that in the open classrooms of British primary schools many working-class children understand differently from middle-class children what is required of them and what they must achieve. A number of ways in which what he refers to as the 'invisible pedagogy' may be selectively visible can be suggested. There may, for example, be different tacit understandings as to what counts as a question – from child or adult – and what counts as an acceptable answer – again from child or adult. The question form in the setting of the classroom may provoke, from the child whose socialistion is geared to the modes of instruction which the school prefers, a very different selection and organisation of meanings and speech from that evoked in the child to whom the open classroom appears to have less to do with instruction and more to do with play. In this case the question form might be said to mark the setting as one in which elaborated coding is appropriate.

The understanding that many of the factors which influence a child's language in the classroom are social before they are linguistic, has brought a new set of questions to bear on the problem of the educational testing situation and the relative failure of many WC children on standard attainment measures. Allied to this is the place of the experimental setting in educational research and its limitations in telling us anything at all about any child, but especially about the child who finds such a context culturally confusing or alien. Specifically it must be asked whether the experimental interview is a suitable medium for the investigation of child language.

Labov, for example, has demonstrated how the formality of the interview setting can intimidate a lower-working-class Black child to the point where he says practically nothing. By manipulating physical (sitting on the floor eating crisps), psychological (having present the speaker's best friend) and social (reducing the height and therefore status difference between interviewer and interviewee) aspects of the interaction, such a non-verbal child could be transformed into an enthusiastic and fluent speaker. Less dramatically, Heider, Cazden and Brown (1968) showed how social-class differences in the extent to which meanings were made explicit could be made to disappear by giving WC children twice as many probes as MC children. Cazden (1971) gives a useful summary of how children's speech varies as aspects of the eliciting context – topic, task, listener, instructions – are changed.

We can examine some implications of this work in the light of our concern with the effects of context on a child's coding orientation, bearing in mind that the studies cited above have been interested in various kinds of speech use and noting that conclusions drawn from one perspective – e.g. the effect of the situation on the realisation of grammatical competence – have often been applied, and sometimes inappropriately, to the whole question of language use.

It has, for example, been suggested that the kind of research reported by Labov and others implies that every effort should be made to overcome the effects of context, otherwise we shall never get at what the child really knows. This view would appear either to emphasise grammatical rather than communicative competence or else to confuse the two, but its origins are not hard to trace. The importance of demonstrating linguistic competence in Black children springs firstly from a concern to correct the picture of the verbally destitute child painted by deficit theory; and secondly, from a more academic interest in explicating the relationships, in terms of transformational grammar, between standard English and Black vernacular. In pursuing the second aim and demonstrating that Black children have as complex a grammatical competence as any child, Labov has succeeded also in achieving the first. But as Hymes (1972) points out, the demonstration of grammatical competence does not sign the death warrant of the notion of linguistic disadvantage.

Certainly it is scientifically absurd to describe children as coming to school 'linguistically deprived' so far as the presence of regular grammar and the capacity for creative use of language in social life are concerned.

But there is the rub. Children may indeed be linguistically deprived if the language of their natural competence is not that of the school; if the contexts that elicit or permit use of that competence are absent in the school; if the purposes to which they put language and the ways in which they do so, are absent or prohibited in the school.

What much of the research directed at the deficit hypothesis shows is, in fact, that 'the contexts that elicit or permit use of that (Black children's) competence are absent in the school' and the importance of these findings cannot be sufficiently stressed. However, we are still a long way from understanding *how* speakers use a particular dialect or language in different contexts. To show that when ghetto children speak freed of the social constraints of the schoolroom or interview their speech is fluent and dense, and that an underlying logic informs what they say, is to illustrate the completeness of their grammatical competence and to tell us something about which contexts will evoke full use of this competence and which contexts will suppress it almost completely. But an analysis of this kind cannot tell us very much about how the child uses that competence as a coding device. The purposes to which he puts language in different contexts and the extent to which his coding orientation clashes or fits with the orientation expected in the classroom are problems raised only obliquely.

We have said that the selection and realisation of meanings governed by code has its basis in the ongoing social relationship. It is thus apparent that the contexts used to elicit speech that will reflect differences in the code used (either by the same speaker across situations or between speakers in objectively similar situations) must be amenable to differences in coding. We can expand this notion.

A restricted code realises social relationships which are predicated on shared knowledge, where the meanings are implicitly realised and communicated because their verbal explication would be redundant, inappropriate and tedious. Such are the situations which obtain between friends in relaxed atmospheres although to be sure some topics may make the assumption of shared knowledge less certain and their introduction may change the context to one which demands more elaborated coding. In general, however, an encounter between people whose social histories have much in common in a setting which has had many counterparts in the course of their shared histories, and where the content of the talk is neither new nor especially problematic, is a paradigmatic setting for the use of restricted coding.

Now if all speakers will be strongly oriented to restricted coding in this kind of situation, what is the nature of contexts realised through elaborated coding – how are we to characterise such contexts and what are the implications of this for research? Elaborated coding realises contexts where the role relationship that obtains between speaker and listener is such that meanings, principles and processes must be made explicit, where reference to a 'common grid' is either difficult or to be suspended (e.g. as when children learn that although a relevant adult knows very well the answer to the question he has just asked, still the child must answer as if the information was novel). It therefore follows that in order to investigate the presence and extent of orientation to an elaborated code, speech should be elicited in situations which will activate such an orientation. The relationship between speaker and listener, which may be partly given by aspects of the physical situation, is critical if the child who is oriented to elaborated code use in appropriate situations is to understand this situation as appropriate. It is further clear that since sociolinguistic code use *is* the social realised in the linguistic, it is on the social context as the child constructs it that we must focus. Situations to which some children respond with elaborated code use are understood differently *at the social level* by these children than by children who realise the same objective context through restricted codings.

It can now be seen that the kinds of situation used by Labov in order to elicit 'natural' speech from Black children are much more likely to be realised through restricted codings than through elaborated codings. Since the speech was analysed grammatically rather than functionally, it is impossible to test this hypothesis without access to the data – it would be a valuable undertaking. Interesting, however, is the finding in the studies reported here that those children who interpreted the interview context as one in which the relationships between speaker and listener and between speaker and topic were ones of reduced distance and who we, therefore, infer were oriented to a restricted code in this context, were frequently the children who gave the longest and most fluent texts. Often it was the most explicit children or those offering context-independent responses who spoke least. This suggests that their understanding of the context as one in which very little could be taken for granted in the speaker/hearer relationship included a concern with 'accuracy'. The analogy with aspects of the classroom needs no emphasising and it is reasonable to assume that the nature of the speech elicited by an interviewer will shed some light on the way children talk to teachers. Bernstein highlights the role of the interview as follows.

The setting, tasks, social relationships and meanings are independent of the child's normal settings, tasks, relationships and meanings. In this sense, the experimental setting is a *context-independent* setting for the child. Now some children in this setting produce speech or responses which differ markedly from the speech or meanings of other children. Why do the children differ in their interpretation of the context? It certainly has nothing to do with the children's tacit understanding of grammar, and little to do with differences in the children's vocabulary. I suggest that what we are witnessing are differences in the *ground rules* the children are using to generate their meanings and so their speech. One group of children are applying rules for the creation of context-independent speech whereas another group of children are doing this to a lesser extent.

And Adlam (in Chapter 2) adds:

In terms of the given context, there is nothing inefficient about context-dependent speech or relatively implicit meaning. Again, it is not to be supposed that children whose tacit understanding leads to the production of a restricted variant in the interview situation are incapable of any degree of elaboration. But the assumption is that such children would require very explicit instructions in order to produce an elaborated variant under these conditions. What is important is that different groups of children spontaneously and consistently offer different orders of meaning and different linguistic realisations, and that these differences are indicative of different orientations to the setting as a whole.

The child's orientation to meaning – his relationship to listener and to task – is constrained in this as in any other situation but it is in just such formally framed interactions that we expect differences in the nature of his socialisation to be made manifest in his speech.

The interview is an eliciting context which might be expected to realise differences in the nature of the transmission contexts which the child has experienced. Those children for whom communication in the home is regulated by an elaborated code will tend towards elaborated coding in such a context; those children for whom cultural transmission is governed by a restricted code will tend towards restricted coding in the same situation. And this is because the children differently construct the context itself.

This formulation, in the light of much of the work in the general sociolinguistic field, leads to two kinds of question. The first may be put quite bluntly. It says 'What if you are wrong?' This issue, raised in a more considered way, is treated in some detail in Chapter 4 and includes the possibility that, in fact, the empirical research has not measured differences in the child's general orientation to meaning but only (although it is quite a big 'only') differences in willingness to make particular linguistic choices in this one context. It is conceivable, in other words, that those children who made restricted codings in the interview context would without difficulty switch to elaborated code use in another situation. This is the problem posed by Labov and others, and although we have argued above that such studies have demonstrated the effect of context on use of grammatical knowledge rather than on coding orientation, the issue remains that contextual constraints on coding orientation may not be completely confined to the kinds of 'perceived role relationships' which we have discussed. If the children were intimidated by the situation then they would say very little and be disinclined to use language for purposes of exploration and explicitness – their 're- stricted codings' would be a mark of anxiety or rejection rather than a realisation of shared assumptions and reduced personal distance. Empirically, this appears quite unlikely. In the research of the SRU it is the middle-class more often than the working-class children who show the greatest constraint. The most 'verbal' (in terms of quantity and rapidity of speech) children are almost without exception work- ing class and, interestingly, it is often just these children who are most readily characterised as giving restricted variants. While it is clearly the case that the verbal reticence of the children in Labov's research was due to their anxiety in or disdain for the interview con- text, this does not appear to have been a factor in the British work. To say that children are using language in an implicit, context- dependent way is not to say that they are not using language at all. On the other hand, if the context is such that the child will not make use of this natural language then clearly nothing at all can be said about his orientation to its use as a coding device. Quite simply, we have to try to understand the different levels at which the context of situation can influence language use and then to try to understand which of these is critical in any one empirical situation.

Before leaving this question additional empirical evidence may be mentioned (see Chapter 4 for extended discussion) which argues against the suggestion that social class differences in coding orienta- tion are a function of the interview situation pure and simple. The consistency of responses across tasks – where consistency is measured in terms of orientation to meaning and speech use and only indirectly concerns grammatical and lexical features – and the tendency for a child's speech to correlate with his mother's attitude to language use both suggest that the concept of a general coding propensity is necessary for an adequate understanding of the social aspects of language in use.

The second range of issues highlighted by our concern with situational constraints on coding orientation in fact follows from the above discussion and centres on how we are to delineate and charac- terise the specific features of the context which are important for the elicitation of elaborated coding. Bernstein has said that what is critical is the child's perception of his own social role – not only vis-à-vis his listener but also vis-à-vis the topic in itself and as it is to be communicated to his listener. Presumably, however, this understanding of the social relationship is itself influenced by features such as setting, the form and content of discourse, etc. We have emphasised that the child's speech in context cannot be understood without reference to the child's social history as evinced in his orientation to code. Neither can it be understood without reference to the eliciting context, and it is possible that there exist some very specific features of situations which mark them, for some children, as situations in which the role relationship is one of distance and the appropriate coding is elaborated. But clearly such features could only be so interpreted by a child who had experience of and could handle the necessary role. Other children would understand them differently. We are thinking here of highly specific features – perhaps single phrases like 'Tell me about . . .'.

Perhaps the primary value of the focus on social relationships is to stress that it is the context as constructed by the child that is important. Paradoxically, this argues for collecting speech in quite standardised situations, for only then can we argue that systematic variation in speech is a reflection of different interpretations of and orientation to meaning in the same situation. It also suggests that we look at the same child's speech over a range of situations in order to see what for him are the critical differentiating features. The SRU has made a start in this direction and the intention is to make a more comprehensive exploration over the next three years.

In summary, an elaborated coding orientation is identified with a general propensity to take on a social role of distance – at the intrapersonal as well as the interpersonal level. In one sense, it is just because he has this context-independent orientation that the individual is led to interpret a wide range of contexts as situations where things must be objectified and made explicit. Context-independent meanings and speech are the realisation of a social perception rooted in the individual's history and beyond. Context-dependent meanings and implicit speech are the realisation of a different order of social relationships, also rooted in the individual's history. At the same time, there will be certain age-, sex- or class-specific contextual features which will intensify or mark the appropriateness of one or other of these orientations once established. Such features may be said to act upon code use in a similar way to that in which they act upon other aspects of language use, but it should be stressed that they do so by underlining what is relevant in the social relationship. And it is the linguistic realisation of the role relation that is seen as necessary for coding orientation but not for other sociolinguistic dimensions. Bernstein's basic proposition is that the typical form and therefore interpretation of the social will differ quite consistently between sub-cultural groups, and that this is reflected in the selection of relevant meanings and the form of their realisation in a wide and significant range of situations.

V   Code in context

Two related forms of contextual constraint on language use have been explored in the discussion so far. Clearly these constraints are not peculiar to Bernstein's theoretical framework but their influence on speech is given a specific, and we believe useful, focus when seen in terms of subcultural differences in the structure of transmission. First, it was suggested that within a transmission system whatever the dominant code, the content and purpose of any one interaction will exert a fundamental influence on the discourse. The features of language which command attention will vary according to which socialising context or language function is to hand. Beyond this, whether the dominant code is restricted or elaborated will affect both the semantic areas which are given emphasis within each context, and the extent to which each of the four socialising contexts is initiated and explored by the mother with her child. It is further suggested that such variation in contents and contexts will influence the form of the communication.

If the first kind of contextual influence on speech may be broadly identified with 'function' or 'topic', the second discussion considered aspects of the context of situation, taking the speaker/listener relationship as fundamental. It was seen that the nature of this relationship exerts a strong influence on many aspects of language use, including the degree to which meanings are made explicit and specific in speech. Further it was suggested that since the code governing transmission in the home is rooted in the social structure which includes the material basis of the family, the child's acquisition of sociolinguistic competence must include acquisition of knowledge about social roles and relationships. Thus his interpretation of what is appropriate in the context of any one interaction will depend, at least initially, on his experience of social relationships in the family. A specific hypothesis is that the child's tendency to assume that language must carry the burden of communication between himself and another is significantly determined by the forms of communication which mediate socialisation.

Together these ideas are central to the questions put by the present series of papers. The underlying theme of the volume will now be considered in relation to these two senses of 'code in context' and we shall go on to sketch a more general framework in which the present argument might be placed.

The aim is to make detailed analyses of a number of specific texts constructed by each child and then to relate these, both singly and as a series, to the code which lies behind them. The children who took part in this investigation were asked to speak about a range of topics in a standard interview setting, the eliciting materials being designed to tap the child's coding orientation in the four contexts identified by Bernstein. Thus while the maternal interview sought information about patterns of mother/child communication in situations relevant to the regulative, instructional, interpersonal and innovating functions of language, the collection of speech from the children attempted to see how such patterns of communication might be reflected in the child's use of language – again in response to situations representing the four generalised contexts. This sense of 'code in context' then refers to the necessity of looking to how a child speaks – the speech variants he adopts – in a range of 'contexts' in order that we may infer his orientation to code. The general framework is diagrammed, in simplified fashion, in Fig. 1 on page 4. The specific texts analysed in the following chapters are examples of instructional, regulative and descriptive speech.

By using a standard interview as our context of elicitation we achieve a dual goal. First, the questions put to each child are designed to point him towards speech that is centred around one of the four socialising contexts. Thus the structured nature of the interview aids the analysis set out above. Second, the role relationship and material setting of the interview constitute a context of elicitation which, so theory predicts, will be differently interpreted and therefore differently realised in speech according to whether the child's general orientation is to a restricted code or an elaborated code.

Perhaps the critical paper in this volume is Adlam's and Turner's analysis of the relationships between the codings or texts offered by almost 200 children in the control, instructional and descriptive tasks. Although clearly the detailed analysis of each of these contexts is a prerequisite to the investigation of their interrelationships, it is this final paper that raises most clearly the key theoretical and methodological issues, at least as far as the linguistic work is concerned. For example, in asking whether children are consistent in their orientation to language use across these three rather different tasks we are led to an empirical test of the hypothesis that some underlying principle or code is structuring the meanings and speech which they offer. Again, the nature of the codes is illuminated by considering, in concert, their various contextually specific realisations. At the level of research methodology, this analysis underscores the importance of the problem of arriving at a textual description of the children's speech and also raises some critical questions regarding the appropriate statistical treatment of sociolinguistic data.

What this study lacks is an explicit linking of the child's speech to the form of transmission in his home. The link is made indirectly by the finding that working-class children show a tendency consistently to give more restricted speech variants while middle-class children are more likely to make elaborated codings in the three situations. And we know already that there is a strong association between social class and forms of transmission (Bernstein and Brandis in Brandis and Henderson, 1970; Bernstein (ed.), 1973a). A report of an investigation into the relationship between family transmission structures and the children's responses to the interview is in preparation. However, since the research reported here has something of a linguistic bias it might be helpful to redress the balance by placing the present questions in a more general context.

Transmission, acquisition and realisation

As a theory of cultural transmission Bernstein's framework addresses itself to three broad issues. First, what are the principles regulating the transmission of cultural meanings; what is made relevant for the child and how is it made relevant? Second, how is the nature and process of acquisition to be described; what does the child learn at the tacit as well as the overt level? And finally, how is this acquisition realised in specific contexts; how can such contextually specific realisations be understood so that our conception of the acquisition matrix becomes clearer?

Such questions obviously have relevance beyond their application to linguistic and communicative skills, which might be considered as one very critical facet of acquisition. But at every level we assume that much of what the child learns he learns in a tacit way, and that even in an explicitly instructional situation the child learns much more than the adults intended teaching. Specific ways of speaking, individual practical tasks, particular means of solving problems – such skills are not learned discretely, in isolation, but are also the basis on which the child builds a set of rules that orient him to selected aspects of new situations and thereby relate different experiences in a coherent way. Constrained by the transmission system, his actions are nevertheless born of his own construction of the reality which that system makes available to him.

There is thus a tension set up between principles of transmission and the process of acquisition. The socialiser has certain notions about what the child should learn and also how best to teach him. These generate specific practices to which the child is exposed but which cannot be divorced from the ideas which lie behind them nor from the tacit cultural knowledge which will affect both the conscious ideology and the actual teaching practices.

The child towards whom this transmission is directed will learn something of its specific contents but will infer also a way of organising and acting upon experience that accords not only with the explicit and tacit cultural knowledge of the socialiser but also with the prevailing stock of rules and strategies he has himself built up. There may be a considerable gap between what is transmitted and what is acquired. A great deal of what is taught may be transformed, ignored or simply not seen. A great deal is certainly acquired that is never intentionally transmitted. Occasions on which there is direct match between the adult's conscious transmission and what is learned by the child are surely rare. The distinction between transmission and acquisition is of crucial importance. Nevertheless, it is a distinction that it is dangerous to overplay. The way in which transmission constrains acquisition is our central concern. To frame the basic question in this way is not to see the child as passive nor to imply that the main function of socialisation is to limit, inhibit and conventionalise. Only by recognising and understanding the nature and modality of control is it feasible to raise questions about the possibilities available and the potential for exploration open to an active child in a social world.

The present model sees transmission agencies as concerned, both explicitly and at a covert level, to make aspects of the environment selectively relevant for the socialised such that he comes to attend to some features more readily than others; such that he has certain expectations about what may or may not occur; such that he has a tacit understanding of what is an appropriate response from him. The process may be thought of as analogous to or an extension of the process of perception. What is perceived, its spatial and temporal relations to other perceptions, what appears ambiguous as well as modes of resolving that ambiguity – all are shaped by the structure of transmission. And similarly with the cultural transmission of ways of thinking, acting and believing as well as the contexts and contents typically articulated thereby. On the basis of such selectively focused experiences, the child acquires an understanding which enables him to make sense of new situations and act within them accordingly. Clearly this has implications for what happens when a child of one culture meets situations controlled by the principles and members of another.

There are perhaps two complementary methods of trying to understand the social basis of the acquisition matrix and its nature. First, we may attempt to uncover what lies behind transmission and regulates its form. What are the principles governing activity and speech, social relationships and material setting in the child's interaction with the cultural world? Such an approach centres on what is made relevant for the child and how it is made relevant. Second, it is possible to consider the problem of what is acquired by looking more directly at the child; at the situationally specific realisations of the acquisition matrix. We would expect on the basis of the above argument that, for example, his speech and his activities will be consistent across situations in accordance with the ground rules he has acquired. The problem then becomes one of the basis and various manifestations of that consistency. In particular, a social perspective is interested to show how a variety of situationally specific behaviour can be seen as realisations of an acquisition matrix that is rooted in the social context of transmission.

The above outline is framed in the most general terms. It would encompass, at the level of empirical enquiry, the entire range and patterning of symbolic systems characterising a social group as well as the entire range and patterning of behaviour shown by the child. The research endeavours reported here are not so ambitious. The symbolic system under study is language, we are centrally concerned with the child, with the nature of what is learned – and we have examined a fairly limited range of speech situations. The studies do, however, concern children for whom familial transmission is known to differ considerably, and social class is shown to be the chief discriminator both in terms of communication and control patterns and in terms of the children's orientation to language use. Further, the speech situations studied are sufficiently dissimilar for the finding of consistency in orientation not to be a truism. The findings suggest that the concept of code has considerable power in the analysis of the child's acquisition of knowledge.

Detailed exploration of the link between acquisition and the structure of transmission is the central concern of the final SRU report. The presence of integrated theory coupled with the powerful associations found between social class and language use does, however, permit considerable discussion of the transmission/acquisition relationship in the present papers. The focus of this volume is nevertheless on the second of the two perspectives outlined on the previous page. The analyses look at different linguistic realisations of the sociolinguistic code which the child is thought initially to acquire in the home. If this code is seen as one aspect of what is acquired in familial transmission then we are considering, separately (Chapters 2 and 3) and in concert (Chapter 4) some contextually specific realisations of this facet of the general acquisition matrix. Such analyses promise to shed considerable light on what different children are learning about communication and language use as well as allowing extensive discussion about the antecedents and possible implications of their knowledge. Bernstein (1975) states: 'It is a matter of considerable sociological and sociolinguistic interest how it is that certain rules generate distinctive texts. It then becomes important to understand the different forms of socialisation into distinctive underlying rules' (p. 11). The first sentence encapsulates the theme of this volume, the second expresses the question that is constantly to the fore.

Structure of the book

Each chapter in this volume constitutes a complete empirical study. Each was originally written as a self-contained report. Inevitably, therefore, there is some overlap particularly in the theoretical sections of each chapter. We have tried to keep this to a minimum in order to avoid redundancy. In some cases, however, points made and concepts drawn out have been retained even where there is repetition or revision in another chapter. We feel this is necessary in order to maintain the cohesion of the individual studies.

Notes

1 In an important sense there are no context-independent meanings. Meanings arise in contexts and are constrained by them. Formal education can be considered as an agency which regulates the selection, form and focusing of meanings, practices, social relationships and contexts which give access to elaborated codes. Thus context-independent meanings are always regulated by the recontextualising procedures of education.

2 This is oversimplification. The material and economic structure will constrain quite strongly the contexts that, for example, a mother or teacher may explore with a child. A small room with six boisterous children severely limits the time which a mother may devote to anything other than control. The focus on instruction, 'play and learn' and discovery characteristic of the middle classes demands the provision of books and special toys, plenty of space and an adult with time to guide and to answer questions.

Chapter 2   The descriptive context

Diana Adlam

Introduction

Bernstein's theory of sociolinguistic codes involves conceptual levels which vary both in content and in degree of abstraction. At the most general level, we are concerned with social relationships and their influence on the symbolic orders made available and transmitted through the culture. Still on a predominantly theoretical plane, we would wish to examine the explanatory and conceptual power of notions such as positional and personal family types, or universalistic and particularistic orders of meaning. In his theoretical writings, Bernstein has made very explicit the nature of these concepts, and their hypothesised interrelationships.

At the empirical level, an attempt is made to operationalise these higher-order concepts (see Brandis for an elucidation of the substantive nature of the different family structures) and, further, they are used in order to shape our hypotheses about, for example, the semantic and linguistic characteristics of the speech which the children will offer. The recent theoretical focus on contextual constraints at all levels would suggest that this speech will be influenced not only by characteristics of the children – the degree to which alternative modes of interpretation and expression have been made available to them in the process of socialisation – but also by specific attributes of the particular eliciting context.

The present study is concerned with the speech of.seven-year-old children in response to a request to describe three highly detailed and colourful picture postcards (hereafter referred to as the 'Trotin' cards, after the artist, Hector Trotin). This was one of a series of linguistic tasks given to the children in the form of an interview. Bernstein (1973b) has pointed out that the most crucial aspect of the interview situation as a whole would appear to be that different groups of children interpret the tasks in very different ways:

The setting, tasks, social relationships and meanings are independent of the child's normal settings, tasks, relationships and meanings. In this sense, the experimental setting is a context-independent setting for the child. Now some children in this setting produce speech or responses which differ markedly from the speech or meanings of other children. Why do the children differ in their interpretation of the context? It certainly has nothing to do with differences in the children's tacit understanding of grammar, and little to do with differences in the children's vocabulary. I suggest that what we are witnessing are differences in the ground rules the children are using to generate their meanings and so their speech. One group of children are applying rules for the creation of context-independent speech, whereas another group of children are doing this to a lesser extent.

In terms of the given context, there is nothing inefficient about context-dependent speech or relatively implicit meaning. Again, it is not to be supposed that children whose tacit understanding leads to the production of a restricted variant in the interview situation are incapable of any degree of elaboration. But the assumption is that such children would require very explicit instructions in order to produce an elaborated variant under these conditions. What is important is that different groups of children spontaneously and consistently offer different orders of meaning and different linguistic realisations, and that these differences are indicative of different orientations to the setting as a whole.

At the most general level, these different orientations may be identified with the concept of code. The main hypothesis then becomes that middle-class children have acquired the ground rules which allow them to cope adequately (in terms of the educational system) with context-independent settings, and that the interview situation satisfies the conditions for such a setting.[1]

If the notions of elaborated and restricted codes may now be identified with a basic orientation or rule-system, what is the relationship with speech? Bernstein (1971) makes the distinction between code and speech variant and suggests that only under certain conditions can, say, a restricted speech variant be taken as indicative that the speaker is operating with a restricted code. It is necessary, for example, to obtain samples of speech over a range of critical contexts before we can make inferences about code.

The meanings generated by the interpretive rules which are code, are realised linguistically in the speech variants which we may observe. Thus Bernstein has come more and more to emphasise the semantic aspect of language (important here is the influence of linguists such as Halliday). The effect of the social structure on the meanings made available and relevant in the process of socialisation – particularly moral and cognitive socialisation – has come to be seen as fundamental.

Access to an elaborated code means access to a world and language of universalistic meanings. The notion of universality is both more general in what it subsumes and more specific in its implications than the concept of context-independence, which it might be said to include. Universalistic meanings are realised in such a way that they are available to all. They are context-independent and highly explicit. But more than this, such an orientation gives access to the rationality and organisation behind principles of knowledge and of control which are made verbally explicit and thereby both comprehensible and an integral part of the child's experience – symbolic and real – of the world. Similarly, with the notion that the world of the restricted code is a world of particularistic meanings – meanings available only to those who share with the speaker certain crucial assumptions and perspectives. Particularistic meanings are realised implicitly, and this tends to preclude both the need and the possibility of the explication principles. Those that are acknowledged are announced; many are outside the relevant scheme of things.

The sociological, psychological and linguistic implications of this framework have been developed in detail by Bernstein.

The present investigation is concerned with the descriptive context, and it is necessary to examine the particular tasks before we can make assumptions about the specific linguistic nature of either code as it is elicited by stimuli such as the Trotin cards. In other words, although the elaborated and restricted codes are now given context-independent definitions in terms of semantics, any one analysis depends on the application of the general model to the task at hand. The specific features of the speech variants will differ between contexts, and analyses of speech in a range of contexts will inevitably tell us more about different aspects of the rules which the child is using to generate and realise his meanings. As long as hypotheses about context-specific characteristics of the codes are always derivable from the more general definitions, and given that we are clear about the level of the differences between contexts, then we are at least half way to operationalising the theoretical constructs. Thus both Bernstein and Cook (1965) and Turner (1973a) have provided empirical valid-ation for the concepts of universalistic and particularistic orders of meaning, by demonstrating their realisations in the regulative context.

The hypotheses in the present analysis, then, concern the nature of context-independent and of context-dependent descriptive speech.

But the empirical investigations also have an exploratory function and we therefore expect the analysis to give us some information about the nature of such speech as well as to test hypotheses derived from theory and from previous empirical research.

Peter Hawkins had already analysed the children's responses to the Trotin cards at age five. His analysis took the form of a very detailed study of the nominal group, and the present coding frame evolved from a preliminary analysis very similar to this. Hawkins found, as anticipated, that working-class children used more pronouns than middle-class children, and that these tended to be exophoric, i.e. to depend on the eliciting context for their interpretation. This tendency has two important consequences. First, the child who uses exophoric reference is generating a context-dependent description – his meanings are implicit. Second, a preference for pronominal usage largely precludes the use of modification and qualification which, at least in terms of the Trotin cards, serve a differentiating function and further free the speech from the surrounding context. By way of illustration, consider the following two statements, describing the same event and taken from the second speech sample:

he's pushing that into there
there's a man with a cap pushing a luggage thing
into the side of the train

The pilot study indicated that again at age seven, the middle-class children were being more explicit and more specific. It seemed, however, that by confining the analysis to the nominal group structure, we would be ignoring some of the more significant explicit realisations – those involving complex qualification and predication. It appeared that the way in which children qualified nouns and pronouns was more important than the niceties of modification (although this may be a function of the particular task) and that this part of Hawkins's frame, although useful, was not sufficiently delicate. Further, it was felt that a more detailed study of qualification and predication might tap something of the semantic basis of the child's speech and thus be more consonant with recent theoretical developments.

There were two constraints on the latter aspiration. The first, and most important, stems from the nature of the stimuli themselves. The Trotin cards will evoke a concrete descriptive mode from most children because the characters and events in the cards are so immediately relevant. The material is readily definable at the perceptual level and it was therefore expected that in this context the main differences would occur in the way in which the children *realised* their meanings. The coding frame was therefore predicated on the hypothesis that the children would differ in the degree to which their overt speech was context-independent – such speech involving greater explicitness and a higher degree of specificity. The basic divisions, however, were semantic, and it became clear in the course of the analysis that even with material as constrained as picture postcards, the children's differing basic orientations will lead to wide variation in the meanings which are generated.

The second constraint is linked with the first. It follows from our discussion of the characteristics of the eliciting context that semantic differences will be at a relatively high level of delicacy and that explication of their exact nature will require a very fine analysis indeed. Dorothy Henderson is currently working on such an analysis and the present study may be regarded as a crude attempt to define areas of importance, and to provide some specification of the linguistic variables involved. It may be the case that in an effort to give some basic picture of the nature of the speech variants in the descriptive context, we have missed some crucial differences at the level of code. It is beyond doubt that Henderson's study will give far greater insight into the children's tacit understanding of the communicative situation.

Individual hypotheses concerning the patterning of linguistic variables are best included with a description and explanation of the coding frame. Let it just be reiterated that, given that the children will differ in the degree to which they interpret the interview setting as context-independent, our aim is to explore and to test hypotheses concerning the nature of the differences between context-dependent and context-independent descriptive speech.

The sample

The Sociological Research Unit obtained speech samples from 439 children at age five and similar speech samples from 298 of these children at age seven. The children came from two geographically distinct areas of London, one of which was predominantly WC and the other mainly MC (the correlation between area and social class is 0·74).

At age 7 a factorial sample of 128 children, one with a two-way division on class, verbal ability and sex, had been drawn up by other members of the SRU for the purpose of analysis of the speech. The same sample was used in this study.

Social class was measured in terms of the occupation and education of each parent, according to a procedure worked out by Brandis (in Brandis and Henderson, 1970). On the resultant ten-point scale, the MC children had a mean score of 2·31 (a low score indicating higher social class) and the WC children had an average score of 7·15.

Half the sample scored at the 90th percentile or higher on the Crichton vocabulary scale, with a mean score of 90·83, and half had scores between the 50th and 75th percentiles, with a mean score of 63·84. Thus we have children of high measured ability (HIQ) and of average measured ability (MIQ).

The factorial sample may be diagrammed as follows:

	MC		WC	
	HIQ	MIQ	HIQ	MIQ
B	16	16	16	16
G	16	16	16	16

Tasks

The children were given a variety of tasks and we will here consider their responses to a request to describe three highly detailed picture postcard reproductions of paintings by the Belgian artist Hector Trotin.

The cards were presented one at a time and the children asked to describe what was going on in the picture, what the people were doing and what the picture was all about. Other questions specific to each card were also asked, but the responses to these were not included in the analysis and in any case involve very little of the speech.

The coding frame

As has been explained in the introduction, the present coding frame represents a re-orientation of Hawkins's nominal group analysis. The nominal group covers structures such as the following:

M	H	Q
the pretty young	lady	at the gate

The 'head' is obligatory whereas qualification and modification are optional and of varying degrees of complexity. Many of Hawkins's 'headword' categories have been included or introduced elsewhere, and modification *per se* is not analysed but serves as an indication of specificity within the qualifier.

Hawkins's analysis of qualification included the following:

(1) one-word qualifiers, e.g. they *all*;
(2) rank-shifted adjuncts, e.g. the boys *in the water*;
(3) rank-shifted clauses, e.g. the man *who belongs to the station*;
(4) rank-shifted nominants, e.g. the *lady's* dress.

Constructions (1) and (4) were not included in the analysis and (2) and (3) were re-grouped according to function. Thus (2) above becomes an explicit reference to location. Beyond rank-shifted adjuncts and clauses as qualifiers, the frame also examined predication. In one sense we merely included action as another form of qualification. Semantically information about 'action' qualifies the headword as much as information about location, relation etc. But structurally the analysis is no longer confined to the nominal group. However, the dividing line is to some extent arbitrary, and it could have been argued that Hawkins's use of the concept of rank-shift was rather too free for an essentially structural analysis. The two studies are, therefore, to some extent comparable.

Only what has previously been defined as 'task speech' was coded in this analysis. Thus anecdotal accounts of the child's own experience, questions to the interviewer and comments about the nature and purpose of the task and apparatus were omitted. Responses to card-specific probes were also excluded as were indicators of hesitation (e.g. 'I think', 'it could be') although the speech pertaining to the particular referent was examined. Hesitation phenomena have already been subject to detailed analysis by Turner and Henderson.

Classification of headwords

With the exceptions mentioned above, all nouns and pronouns uttered by the child were coded as headwords. Adverbs, epithets and relative pronouns were never coded as headwords, and this represents a reduction of Hawkins's frame. However, such constructions are covered by some of the categories below, where they appear to occur more naturally within the context of the present study (e.g. A1 below corresponds fairly closely to Hawkins's adverb at head and certainly includes all instances which would be coded therein). Nouns and pronouns, then, were subdivided according to the following criteria.

(1) *Nouns*
All common and proper nouns were coded here (but see (5) below). Context-independent speech uses nouns rather than pronouns in

order to make explicit its referents. The Trotin cards depict detailed scenes with many different figures and objects, and it was therefore expected that all children would use a high proportion of common nouns but that middle-class children would use relatively more than working-class.

(2) *Anaphoric pronouns*
This category includes pronouns whose referent had already been linguistically specified either by the child or by the interviewer:

that man's just coming out of his little house
that little dog's going to run after him.

A pronoun which takes the same referent as a previously uttered exophoric pronoun is also coded anaphoric:

they're running to get on the train
they're going to miss it.

By the age of seven, some children use determiners and ordinators in an anaphoric fashion and such usage is also listed here:

there are two cats, a brown *one* and a white *one*.

In response to the probe 'what are the people doing?' an utterance beginning 'they're' was given anaphoric coding as was, for example, a construction involving three consectuive occurrences of phrases beginning 'some of them'.

Finally, some children responded to this probe with a verb alone or a verb phrase, e.g.

'What are the people doing, Johnny?'
'Walking going to get the train.'

It was considered that here the pronoun is implied and so the speech is coded as including one anaphoric pronoun. This controls for the possibility of some children having an undue number of qualifiers in proportion to the number of heads.

It was not expected that there would be any sociologically relevant differences in this category. Pronominal usage precludes the possibility of much differentiation but lack of anaphora usually means redundancy in the form of repetition of nouns and noun phrases. The category is of crucial importance, however, in that the remaining pronouns of the same form class constitute, to a large extent, the realisation of implicit meaning.

(3) *Third-person exophoric pronouns*
All third-person pronouns whose referent is not linguistically

specified, but present in the context of the task, are coded here. The use of exophora is important in the realisation of context-dependent speech, and such pronouns are used as an index of implicit meaning in the analysis of qualification (see below). When the subject of an utterance is an exophoric pronoun, the child's meanings are not available to listeners outside the speech context. Not having used videotape, it is impossible to say whether the meanings were made available for even the interviewer (e.g. through pointing) but in any case, a succession of utterances whose subjects are not made explicit leaves the meanings embedded, to a very considerable extent, in the eliciting context.

It was expected that Hawkins's finding of much greater exophoric reference in the working class would be repeated.

(4) P *determiners and ordinators* (exophoric)
This category is again confined to exophoric referents but only when the words are used at the head not when they serve to modify, e.g.

> '*that*'s a house',
> '*one*'s getting on the train'
> '*some* are running'

Again, a high incidence of such exophoric usage characterises context-dependent speech.

Hawkins did not find a significantly greater use of such words by any sub-group of children on this task, but this may have been due to the infrequency of the category among younger children. It was therefore expected, in accordance with the theory, that WC children would take up the option more often than MC children.

(5) *Indefinites*
This category includes all the indefinite pronouns (somebody, everyone) as well as occurrences of 'people' and 'things'. Although not strictly pronouns, such words were considered, functionally, to belong to the indefinite category.

Studies of the regulative (Turner) and instructional (Lineker) contexts had shown that 'universal' meanings were often linguistically realised by the use of such pronouns. As has been already pointed out, the descriptive context limits the extent to which the child can elaborate principles and explanations. It was felt, however, that where context-independent speech does not give a very detailed and specific description it may operate at a high level of generality, perhaps supplemented by a greater specificity. For example,

'all the people are going somewhere',
'some are going to Southend',
'some are going on holiday maybe'.

Hawkins reported a higher usage of indefinite pronouns among the middle class (but note that the present category is broader) and it was expected that this finding would be replicated.

It must be admitted that at the start of the analysis it was not altogether clear what such a finding would signify or imply. Only later did the place of such words in the patterning of descriptive speech become apparent.

Unstructured words
These took no qualifier but could be modified and/or preceded by 'there', e.g.

there's a house
little girl   little boy
there's green grass   flowers   some trees

Hawkins found that the use of unstructured nouns or 'listing' was more characteristic of the working-class children. By age seven, however, working-class girls were tending to introduce a lot of cohesive, narrative speech into their description. It was hypothesised that there would be a significant interaction between class and sex with much greater variance within the working class. Middle-class children, on the whole, were expected to put their observations within some sort of verbally realised context and therefore to have relatively few unstructured words.

Nouns and pronouns were also divided according to whether they occurred at the head of the unit or within the qualifier. For example, in 'a man playing a guitar', 'man' and 'guitar' are both coded 'noun' but the former is at the head of the unit, the latter within the qualifier.

In complex utterances a word can occur both within one qualifier and at the head of another unit, e.g. 'a man pushing a barrow with apples in it'. Here 'barrow' and perhaps 'apples' function both in qualification and as subjects. For ease of coding it was decided to count all such occurrences as within qualification. The decision is to some extent arbitrary but would seem to give rise to no spurious theoretically important results as long as the coding is consistent.

An exception is made for complex relative clauses such as: 'the pavement at the side where people are walking and buying things'. Here 'people' is rated at head. This construction is easily recognised since the qualifier as a whole is marked D3 (see below).

It is when a child gives extra information about a person, object or event that the differences between context-dependent and context-independent speech become most obvious and most important:

a man *over there*; a man *by the side of the street*
a boy *pulling it*; a boy *pulling a toy train*
he's *watching her*; the man is *watching the lady with the basket*
a man *wearing one of those*; a *man dressed in a guard's suit*.

It was expected that middle-class children would have a greater proportion of nouns within the qualifier than would working-class children. The use of nouns and modified nouns as object and as complement are the chief linguistic realisations of explicitness.

Conversely it was anticipated that working-class children would use more exophoric reference (categories 3 and 4) at these points. It was tentatively hypothesised that such constructions would be very rare indeed for middle-class children (partly because exophoric reference to location is not covered in the 'headwords' classification and this is the most preferred type among all children).

No differences were expected in the relative distribution of anaphoric pronouns and no hypotheses were put forward as to the structuring of indefinite pronouns.

The analysis of qualification
The frame for the analysis of qualification was semantically based, i.e. a unit was coded as referring to

location: *the man on the seat*
relation: *the man with the blue hat*
action: *the people eating their tea*
or elaboration: *the lady who helps in the kitchen*.

These categories are not mutually exclusive in that an elaboration may, as in the last example, subsume information pertaining to other categories. These divisions are coarse, but seemed sufficient, first in view of our focus on linguistic realisations, second because any sociologically or cognitively crucial semantic differences were likely to be picked up in the 'elaboration' category, and third because a more delicate semantic network would be redundant in view of Henderson's forthcoming study.

Each of the first three categories (location, relation, action) was subdivided according to whether the referent was implicit (i.e. context-dependent) or explicit (context-independent). Explicit utterances were then coded for their degree of specificity, which could be high or low. This relatively simple two-way division does impose a ceiling on the data such that some highly detailed utterances receive the same coding as those reaching the criteria for explicitness and high specificity.

The criteria for coding specificity and explicitness are structurally based. Thus any qualifier including an exophoric referent is coded implicit. This means that an exophoric pronoun coded within the qualifier (see above) also serves as the criterion for coding that qualifier as implicit. But in this part of the frame we have the additional information that the use of exophora realises either an 'action' or a 'relation' qualification. ('Location' is realised by the exophoric adverbs 'here' and 'there'.) Future work may omit the counts of exophora in qualification if this proves to be a workable criterion for the realisation of implicit meaning. It is expected that working-class children will show a greater frequency of such constructions in all three categories than will middle-class children.

Explicit, low specificity in location or relation is given by the inclusion of a noun or anaphoric pronoun within the qualifier, and a high-specificity coding requires that this noun be modified (see examples below).

Utterances realising action sequences will be of low specificity if the verb takes no object and of high specificity when the object is present. Intransitive verbs were initially coded as being of low specificity but this obviously clouds the picture.[2] Such verbs often occur together with an explicit reference to location or relation in the form of an adjunct or adverbial phrase. Compare, for example,

'the man playing the guitar';
'the man walking along the road'.

In analysis the two types of construction were treated as equivalent 'high specificity action' forms.

Explicit speech frees the child's meanings and utterances from the confines of the eliciting context. The greater the degree to which he verbally explicates his meanings, the greater the extent of the availability of his meanings, and this in two senses. First, more hypothetical listeners will understand him, and second those same listeners will have access to more of what he means. Of course, either or both of these effects may be seen to have very little relevance, in which case it is only sensible to keep one's language embedded in the context which generated it. We expect middle-class children to show a preference for explicit realisation and especially for high specificity, although this only in a relative sense since such constructions will be infrequent. Only the most pedantic child would religiously pepper his speech with adjectives and modifiers ad infinitum.

Working-class children, on the other hand, will have a greater incidence of implicit constructions, although the stimulus will tend to evoke a high proportion of concrete speech from all children.

The elaboration category refers to information about a person, object or event which is not covered by the above categories. It is a rather more heterogeneous class and is best explained by means of examples. No provision was made for implicit constructions although these are possible and there were one or two instances in the sample (e.g. 'it's one of those'). We have, so to speak, three degrees of specificity. The first includes two main types of construction.

(1) the window is open
    the people are busy (cf. Hawkins's 'epithet at head')
(2) that's a train
    he's a policeman   ⌈ Such constructions usually have an
                       │ exophoric subject. The reader can note
(3) it's a market   ⟨ in passing that the third example is
                       ⌊ rather different from the first two.

The next degree of elaboration includes the following types:

the man *who is playing* has a black jacket
they are bringing food *to eat*
the lady's cross *because of the cats*

And finally

the man *who is playing the guitar* (*by the side of the road*)
the lady is upstairs *because she wasn't invited to the party*
he's watching *to see if the cats will jump down*
there's a fire in that house *because smoke's coming out of the
    chimney.*

As well as encompassing 'reasons' and 'purpose', then, D2 and D3 cover Hawkins's 'rank-shifted clause as qualifier', although by age seven the children are offering far more complex constructions. The degree of specificity is determined by the grammatical criterion outlined above for coding the first three semantic divisions. Usually, in fact, D2 will include A2, B2 or C2 and similarly with D3.

Hypotheses about this group of constructions were not clear, but beyond the broad assumption that middle-class children would offer more of this type of information and in a more explicit fashion, reasoning was expected to be a feature of context-independent speech, particularly where children justify their own inferences about the card (see last example above).

Specific hypotheses about speech coded in these categories, however, were very much shaped by the data and results examined through the rest of the coding frame, and these will be presented in detail later. This approach is felt to be defensible in so far as the empirical investigation is seen to have an exploratory aspect and not to follow a rigorous 'hypothetic deductive' approach.

For each category, then, we expect working-class children more often to realise their meanings through an implicit construction. All children are expected to give a great deal of explicit speech at a low order of specificity, and this is mainly a function of the stimulus cards. Middle-class children may show a tendency to give more of this kind of speech, but we hypothesise particularly that they will more often include constructions of a high order of specificity.

Any differences in the types of meanings generated were expected to be manifest within the 'elaboration' group of categories. Hypotheses were tentative but it was suggested that middle-class children would show a preference for reasoning and especially elaborated reasoning and also for the types of differentiating constructions realised chiefly by relative clauses. Again, more detailed hypotheses were formulated once the analysis had been partially completed.

The frame may be schematised as follows:

A. *Location* $\lceil$*implicit* (1)

B. *Relation* $\{$ *explicit* $\lceil$*low specificity* (2)

C. *Action* $\lfloor$ $\lfloor$*high specificity* (3)

D. *Elaboration* $\{$
$\lceil$*low specificity* (1)
medium specificity (2)
$\lfloor$*high specificity* (3)

their luggage *is going in there*	C2 A1
they're *all going to market*	C2 A2
aeroplane *in the sky*	A2
some flowers *on top of the wall*	A3
that lady's *got one of those*	B1
a man *wheeling a barrow with apples*	C3 B2
a lady *in a red spotted dress is picking flowers*	B3 C3
there's *a man with an umbrella and a walking stick*	B2 B3
this man *is pushing that into there*	C1 A1
he's *kicking it*	C1
they're all *sitting writing*	C2 C2
water's *running down the kerb*	C2 A2
a man *playing his guitar*	C3
people *buying all sorts of things*	C3 (NB, ceiling effect)

the men *are busy with their wires*	D1 B2
there's *a bunch of carrots in the shop*	D1 A2
they're *sitting at the table waiting to eat*	C2 A2 C2 D2
the shopkeepers they *got signs for somebody* *come in*	B2 D2 C2
two cats *on the roof, a brown one and a white*	A2 D2
the man *who sings is standing in the road*	D2 C2 C2 A2
there's another train *coming so some people* *waited for that train*	C2 D3 C3
they're *catching a bus 'cos they just come off* *that train*	C3 D3 C2 A2
a flood *somewhere because there's water* *running round the gutters*	A2 D3 C2 A2
a train *that often come into that station*	D3 C2 A2

The role of verbal ability

The present sample was selected in order that we might assess the role of verbal ability in the speech which the children produce. We are only very indirectly concerned, however, with the effect of cognition on language. Rather a sociolinguistic thesis focuses on how a child's measured ability acts, *through his socialisation*, to affect his speech.[3]

It is Bernstein's contention that socialisation of the child is more homogeneous within the MC than the WC – both at home and at school. We therefore predict that observable, role-relevant aspects of the child (e.g. his age, sex, intelligence, race) will have more influence on the behaviours he learns if he is WC or part of a 'positional' social system.

It is therefore expected that high measured ability will correlate with a context-independent response but that this relationship will be much more pronounced in the WC. Similarly, we expect any sex differences to be accentuated in, or even confined to, the WC sample.

Treatment of results

A major difficulty in deciding on the most appropriate methods of statistical analysis of the data was posed by the immense variation in the amounts of speech offered by the children. For example, the number of headwords produced varied from 20 to 357 and the qualifying constructions ranged in number from 17 to 293.

Of greater importance than the absolute size of the variance is the fact that there were highly significant differences in output between the factorial sub-groups. This problem had already been faced by Henderson and Turner in their analysis of uncertainty sequences in the same sample of children. Henderson looked in detail at these differences and found that both class and sex were important variables. Verbal ability did not significantly affect production.

The total verbal output of each group of children is shown in Table 2.1.

Table 2.1   Total number of words for each group of children

		MC	WC
HIQ	B	8,190	7,448
HIQ	G	6,176	10,595
MIQ	B	6,176	9,361
MIQ	G	7,531	9,600

Analysis of variance showed highly significant differences between the classes and between the sexes ($p < 0.001$ in both cases). Table 2.2 emphasises that while the MC as a whole gave less speech it is WC girls who are the atypical group.

Table 2.2   Total number of words for each class and sex group of children

	MC	WC
Boys	14,568	16,809
Girls	13,707	20,215

Obviously such clear-cut differences in quantity of speech make a statistical analysis based on raw scores totally misleading. The most appropriate solution, and that used by Henderson and Turner, is to convert the raw scores to proportions. For each child, the number of words in each class of headwords is expressed as a proportion of his total number of headwords and similarly with qualification, the denominator in this case being his total instances of qualification.

Such a technique is not without difficulties. The chief problem with the present sample inhered in the tendency for children with a very high output to use a wide range of categories and for children with a very low output to make use of a relatively restricted range.

The reason for this is not clear, but it seems intuitively plausible that a child who gives an output of around 500 words will make at least one highly specific reference to the location of an object. Similarly the child who says very little, perhaps fifty words in all, may be explicit and concise yet fail to use more than one of the high-specificity categories which in any case were used infrequently by all children.

Now many of the qualification categories are used by less than 75 per cent of the sample and are therefore not amenable to parametric methods of analysis. A chi-squared analysis based on the number of children in each group who use, regardless of frequency, or do not use a particular category is all that may be attempted. It follows that if any one group of children is giving a significantly greater overall output then that group may have a spuriously high incidence of 'presence' of any given category. Conversely, a group of children with an especially low output may have more 'absence' counts than if they had merely said rather more.

It is of course the case that the children at the two ends of the distribution of verbal output are not randomly drawn from the factorial sub-groups. Working-class girls account for most of the very high output children whereas the majority of the children with a very low output are middle-class girls.

If we hypothesise that a particular category will be more characteristic of middle-class speech and go on to test this using a chi-squared analysis of presence or absence then the 'true' size of the difference may be obscured by this fact of differences in output between the groups. Conversely, if we expect greater use by the working class then the size of this difference may be exaggerated when the test of significance is based on the number of children in any one group who use the category at all.

The variation in output itself may be of some theoretical significance – a direct consequence of differing orientations to the task situation. This possibility will be briefly discussed below. For the present, we can merely note the difficulties involved and their implications, but having no logical grounds for assuming that greater quantity of speech will lead to more variation in kind of speech, we have no sound justification for altering our significance levels. The crucial categories are most often those of which we expect a preference by middle-class children, and consequently verbal production differences most often work against our hypotheses.

Where most of the children gave exemplars of a category (e.g. with most headwords and most explicit, low-specificity constructions) the converted scores were subject to three-way analysis of variance.

Where a category was infrequently used, a chi-squared[4] analysis of presence or absence was performed. Such an analysis allows the combination of categories when the incidence of use is very low, and such combinations were carried out when theoretically defensible.

The results will be presented in an order similar to the explanation of the categories of the coding frame. There will be an extended examination of the 'elaboration' group of categories in order to allow presentation of hypotheses and ideas which developed in the course of the analysis.

Results

Nouns

The groups did not differ significantly in their overall tendency to give common and proper nouns. Table 2.3 gives the mean percentage of nouns for each factorial group.

Table 2.3   Noun use as a percentage of total heads

		MC	WC
HIQ	B	67	70
HIQ	G	62	67
MIQ	B	64	67
MIQ	G	64	62

In general, then, the children take up the option of using a noun rather than a pronoun. This is not surprising in view of the detailed nature of the Trotin cards, which tends to elicit a high frequency of concrete speech.

The structural position of nouns, however, differed between the classes. Table 2.4 shows the proportion of total nouns which were uttered as the subject of a unit.

Table 2.4   Percentage of total nouns used as subject

		MC	WC
HIQ	B	36	43
HIQ	G	35	39
MIQ	B	33	40
MIQ	G	38	39

Analysis of variance showed the middle class to be more likely to bias noun use towards the qualifier ($F = 5\cdot7664$, $p < 0\cdot025$). This indicates that, as anticipated, MC children will show a preference for explicit qualification.

Table 2.5   Anaphoric pronoun use as a percentage of total heads

		MC	WC
HIQ	B	13	11
HIQ	G	13	12
MIQ	B	11	12
MIQ	G	13	14

Anaphoric pronouns

Hawkins's finding of no differences in frequency of anaphoric pronouns was repeated in this study. Table 2.5 shows the average percentage use of anaphoric pronouns for each group. Again, there were no differences in the structural distribution of such words.

Third-person exophoric pronouns

While the above two categories were used by all children, eight of the subjects used no third-person exophoric pronouns at all and in general the frequency of use is rather low. Table 2.6 shows the average proportional use of this category.

Table 2.6   Third-person exophoric pronouns as a percentage of total heads

		MC	WC
HIQ	B	5·2	7·1
HIQ	G	3·2	6·3
MIQ	B	6·9	7·6
MIQ	G	5·9	9·1

Analysis of variance showed a significant preference by WC children ($F = 5\cdot8148$, $p < 0\cdot02$) and by children of average verbal ability ($F = 4\cdot4444$, $p < 0\cdot05$). Thus social class is a stronger influence than ability.

Only 38 out of the 128 children used this category as part of any qualifier. Of these, 27 were WC and 11 MC. A chi-squared analysis was carried out on these numbers ($\chi^2 = 8\cdot42$, $p < 0\cdot01$). There were no IQ or sex differences.

Thus WC children show a greater tendency to realise their meanings implicitly, and this is particularly apparent when they come to provide some linguistic context for any given subject. Children of average measured ability are also more likely to take up the implicit option, but this tendency is not as strong as the class preference and does not extend to qualifying constructions.

Exophoric pronouns – determiners and ordinators

Of the total sample just over two-thirds (38 children) use this category at all. Fifty-five WC and 33 MC took up the option at least once and a chi-squared analysis of use shows this difference to be highly significant ($\chi^2 = 16\cdot04$, $p < 0\cdot001$). The verbal ability and sex distributions are at the chance level. Clearly, WC children are more likely to use this type of exophoric realisation.

Table 2.7 shows the number of children who, opting for this class, will also use the exophorics in qualifying a subject.

Table 2.7   Children using category at all and (in brackets) those giving exophoric determiners and ordinators in the qualifier

	MC	WC	Total
HIQ	16 (1)	27 (11)	43 (12)
MIQ	17 (7)	28 (18)	45 (25)
Total	33 (8)	55 (29)	88 (37)

A chi-squared analysis showed that more WC than MC children ($\chi^2 = 5\cdot76$, $p < 0\cdot02$) and that more MIQ than HIQ children ($\chi^2 = 5\cdot81$, $p < 0\cdot02$) do not confine their use of this category to the realisation of subject elements.

Given that WC children are far more likely to use this category, they are also more likely to include such exophoric pronouns in their qualifying constructions. Children of average verbal ability, although no more likely than their high ability counterparts to realise their meanings through exophoric determiners, do show a greater tendency to make use of such implicit realisation in qualification. It is of interest that only one MC child with a high measured ability made use of this construction.

Indefinite words

All children used this category at least once and the average frequency for each group is given in Table 2.8.

Table 2.8   Indefinite words as a percentage of total heads

	MC	WC
HIQ B	13	10
HIQ G	21	11
MIQ B	15	11
MIQ G	15	11

An analysis of variance was made and it was shown that MC children take up the option far more frequently than WC children ($F = 18\cdot2558$, $p < 0\cdot001$). Girls show a tendency to use indefinites more frequently ($F = 4\cdot5814$, $p < 0\cdot05$) and this is apparently due to the exceptionally high use by MC HIQ girls.

The sample as a whole used about three-quarters of their indefinite words to realise the subject of a unit. There were no significant deviations from this tendency.

The emergent pattern of word use indicates that whereas all children are giving a relatively high proportion of nouns, social class strongly affects the child's other speech preferences. Thus exophoric pronouns account for a much higher proportion of the remaining headwords in the speech of WC children while indefinite words are the chief preferred option of MC children. Measured ability has a somewhat weaker effect on the choice of exophora but is totally unrelated to the use of indefinite words.

Table 2.9 shows the average proportional use of the headword categories for each social class (i.e. if an MC child gives 100 headwords then, on average, 64 will be nouns, 12 anaphoric pronouns, etc.).

Table 2.9   Percentage breakdown of headword use by social class

	MC	WC
Nouns	64·3	66·3
Anaphora	12·5	12·1
Exophora (3rd person)	5·3	7·5
Exophora (det. + ord.)	1·7	3·0
Indefinites	16·0	11·1

Among WC children, exophoric reference is used as frequently as the indefinite type, but the latter occurs more than twice as often as exophora in the speech of MC children.

Table 2.10 gives a similar breakdown by ability and here it is apparent that although high verbal ability acts to reduce the preference for exophoric options, measured intelligence exerts a minor influence on the patterning of speech when compared to social class.

Table 2.10   Percentage breakdown of headword use by ability

	HIQ	MIQ
Nouns	66·6	64·1
Anaphora	12·2	12·4
Exophora (3rd person)	5·4	7·4
Exophora (det. + ord.)	2·0	2·8
Indefinite	13·6	13·4

The results concerning the structural positions of the various classes of headwords suggest that MC children are more likely to include nouns in their qualifying constructions where the WC child includes a relatively higher proportion of exophoric pronouns. It should be emphasised that these results concern relative distribution irrespective of overall frequency of use of a category. Thus MC children not only use less exophora than WC children, they also show a greater tendency to confine such use to the realisation of subject elements. Again, although there are no class differences in the relative distribution of indefinite pronouns, MC children, having a higher absolute use, will realise a greater proportion of subjects *and* qualifiers through such speech elements.

Unstructured words

There was a great deal of variation among the children in the extent to which they 'listed' objects and characters in the cards. Such words (the vast majority were nouns) were therefore expressed as a proportion of the remainder of the child's output as counted above. These figures are summarised in Table 2.11.

An analysis of variance was made and it was seen that girls gave fewer unstructured words than did boys ($F = 9·1071, p < 0·005$). The sex difference is stronger in the WC and would appear to be due largely to the tendency of WC girls to introduce a great deal of narrative into their descriptions (see below, p. 74).

Table 2.11   Unstructured words as a percentage of total heads

		MC	WC
HIQ	B	7	18
HIQ	G	6	11
MIQ	B	15	15
MIQ	G	11	7

There was also a significant interaction between class and ability ($F = 7.6667, p < 0.01$) seen on closer inspection to be due to the small proportion of unstructured words offered by MC HIQ children. This group avoids the narrative style but the children do provide some semantic and linguistic context for their observations.

Our chief interest in these results lies with the information they give about the children's differing interpretations of what was required of them in the interview in general and in this task in particular.

Analysis of qualification

The location categories

Implicit location

The criterion for coding a unit as an implicit reference to location was for that unit to include the exophoric adverbs 'here' or 'there', whether or not these were preceded by a preposition. Hawkins confirmed his hypothesis that the category 'adverb at head' would be a feature of WC speech although prepositional use was obligatory in his frame.

Three-quarters of the children used such constructions but the frequency of use was generally rather low and it was decided to limit the analysis to non-parametric methods. Of 97 children who used the category, 57 were WC and 40 were MC. This difference is highly significant ($\chi^2 = 10.9, p < 0.001$) but distribution by ability and sex is within chance limits.

The prediction that implicit realisations will be more characteristic of WC speech is therefore confirmed. Analysis of the remaining location categories will show whether this is contrasted by a preference for explicit realisations by MC children.

Explicit location

Before considering variations in specificity we will examine the relative tendencies of the children to use any explicit reference to location in their descriptions. All children took up this option and Table 2.12 shows the mean proportions of total qualifiers thus coded for each group.

Table 2.12   Explicit location as a percentage of total qualifiers

		MC	WC
HIQ	B	27·3	25·5
HIQ	G	24·7	23·6
MIQ	B	24·8	22·4
MIQ	G	23·8	17·8

An analysis of variance was made and the F-ratios for the main variables are shown in Table 2.13.

Table 2.13   Analysis of variance of explicit location

Source	V	F	p
Class	2·44	4·88	0·05
Ability	3·03	6·06	0·025
Sex	2·02	4·04	0·05

Thus MC children, those of high measured ability and boys all tended more frequently to specify the location of an object. Verbal ability would appear to have the greatest influence but the data show that both ability and sex differences are almost totally confined to the WC. This is chiefly, although not completely, due to the low incidence amongst average-ability girls in this group.

Table 2.14   Explicit, low-specificity location as a percentage of total qualifiers

		MC	WC
HIQ	B	24·3	24·2
HIQ	G	23	21·4
MIQ	B	23	21·3
MIQ	G	23·3	16·7

We must now consider relative preferences for the two levels of specificity. The low-specificity option was taken up at least once by all children and the mean proportional scores are given in Table 2.14.

Analysis of variance yielded the main variable F-ratios and associated probability values shown in Table 2.15. None of the interactions was significant.

Table 2.15   Analysis of variance of explicit low-specificity location

Source	V	F	p
Class	1·67	4·3947	0·05
Ability	1·90	5·000	0·05
Sex	1·85	4·8684	0·05

Thus the same tendencies are apparent in the low-specificity option as were operative for the explicit utterances as a group. This will obviously be the case, since the vast majority of explicit utterances come into this category. The effects of class and ability are weaker, however, and this suggests that these variables are important for the use of high specificity. That is, when we exclude the high-specificity constructions, the effects of class and ability are attenuated. The effect of sex, on the other hand, appears to be accentuated with the exclusion of the high-specificity option.

Apparently the child's social background, his measured verbal ability and his sex all influence the extent to which he will explicitly realise locational information, and the evidence suggests, albeit obliquely, that the first two variables are even stronger determinants of his tendency to make such utterances highly specific in nature.

However, the high-specificity category was infrequent and used by only 71 children, of whom 39 were MC and 32 WC. This difference does not reach an acceptable level of significance ($\chi^2 = 1·14$) although this analysis suffers from the difficulties posed by differential production outlined above. At this level, then, the data do not confirm our hypothesis as to differential access to highly specific constructions.

The relation categories

Implicit relation
This proved to be a very infrequent option for the sample, with only 9 users in all. Of these, 8 were WC and 1 MC.[5] The WC MIQ sample accounts for 7 of the children and 5 of these are boys.

Such small numbers cannot meaningfully be subject to statistical investigation, but it is obvious that these constructions are highly context-dependent (e.g. 'a man with one of those' gives even the listener in context very little information) and that they are used mostly by WC children, especially boys of average measured ability.

Explicit relation

Most of the children (56 MC and 54 WC) made at least one explicit reference of a relational kind. The mean proportional scores for each group are given in Table 2.16.

Table 2.16   Explicit relation as a percentage of total qualifiers

	MC	WC
HIQ B	6·4	5·0
HIQ G	6·3	5·6
MIQ B	6·6	7·5[6]
MIQ G	6·4	4·1

It may be seen that the category is generally low in frequency and an analysis of variance showed no significant differences.

Table 2.17   Explicit, low-specificity relation as a percentage of total qualifiers

	MC	WC
HIQ B	4·8	4·8
HIQ G	3·2	4·8
MIQ B	5·0	5·5
MIQ G	5·0	3·0

Considering only the low-specificity constructions, we have the mean proportions shown in Table 2.17. Again there are no significant differences, but it can be seen that the MC means decrease more than the WC means when the high-specificity constructions are excluded. Thus between one-quarter and one-half of relational information given by the MC is made highly specific whereas only about one-tenth of comparable WC speech is thus explicated.

The inference that MC children are oriented towards greater

specificity is again somewhat oblique. The frequencies are extremely low and we cannot talk about central tendencies, since less than half the children use the category and they do so to widely differing degrees.

As with high specificity in location, it is necessary to look at differential access. Thirty-three MC and 32 WC children realised relational information with highly specific constructions. This difference is not quite significant ($\chi^2 = 3.16$, $p < 0.07$). Ability and sex differences are within chance limits.

High specificity in location and relation

The data so far considered have all suggested that MC children are rather more oriented towards use of high specificity than are WC children. We do not, however, have any firm statistical basis for such a conclusion.

In view of the fact that none of the results contradicts our predictions, and considering also the problem of differential speech production, categories A3 and B3 were combined. That is, we looked at children who had taken up either option or both options. There were 82 such children, of whom 47 were MC and 35 WC. A chi-squared analysis showed that significantly more MC than WC children used highly specific realisations ($\chi^2 = 4.12$, $p < 0.05$). The general patterning of the data therefore confirms our hypothesis that MC children will have greater access to such constructions.

The action categories

Implicit action
Predicators with an exophoric pronoun as object were offered by 42 children. Of these, 33 were WC and 9 MC, the difference in children using the category being highly significant ($\chi^2 = 18.76$, $p < 0.001$). Verbal ability would also appear to affect choice of this category although the value of chi-squared is not quite significant ($\chi^2 = 3.54$, $p < 0.07$). Sixteen high-ability and 26 medium-ability children took up the option and the difference is most pronounced in the middle class, where only one high-ability child used the category.

Social class, then, is the most important influence on the likelihood that a child will use this category.

Explicit action, low specificity
Action clauses realised by a verb and prepositional phrase (e.g. *people walking to the train*) were not included in the investigation of low-specificity action, the analysis being confined to verbs realised without any complement, for example:

they're walking
she's sitting
lady's eating

As indicated above, it is appreciated that verbs differ in the extent to which they can appropriately stand alone, but to analyse the data in terms of such distinctions, with the concomitant problem of differentiation between types of complement, would have required a frame too delicate for present purposes.

All children gave at least one instance of this category and the mean percentage scores are given in Table 2.18.

Table 2.18   Explicit, low-specificity action as a percentage of total qualifiers

		MC	WC
HIQ	B	12	15
HIQ	G	14	15
MIQ	B	15	19
MIQ	G	14	19

An analysis of variance was made and both social class ($F = 7.5833, p < 0.01$) and measured ability ($F = 4.9167, p < 0.05$) were found to be important in the frequency with which children opted for such constructions. Further inspection showed that the atypical group were WC MIQ children who realised action clauses in this way significantly more frequently than any other group.

Explicit action, high specificity
The mean proportional scores for verbs taking an object and for verbs with a prepositional phrase at complement are given in Tables 2.19 and 2.20. All children used both categories.

Table 2.19   Verb and prepositional phrase constructions as a percentage of total qualifiers

		MC	WC
HIQ	B	13	15
HIQ	G	14	15
MIQ	B	16	13
MIQ	G	14	12

Table 2.20   Verb and object constructions as a percentage of total qualifiers

		MC	WC
HIQ	B	20	21
HIQ	G	22	19
MIQ	B	21	17
MIQ	G	22	22

There are no differences between the groups in their preference for these constructions. Neither are there any significant differences in the frequency with which the children realise the action categories as a group. The mean proportional scores for predicators are given in Table 2.21.

Table 2.21   Predicators as a percentage of total qualifiers

		MC	WC
HIQ	B	47·2	51·1
HIQ	G	50·3	51·1
MIQ	B	49·6	50·5
MIQ	G	50·6	56·3

The trend is for WC children to choose these constructions, but it is non-significant and a reflection of their greater use of the low-specificity type.

The elaboration categories

By the time the linguistic analysis was complete, it was apparent that these categories were by no means pure. Further, many of the types of speech offered were infrequent and it was clear that the division into three 'levels of specificity' had represented a premature conception of what the data would involve. Many of the categories subsequently investigated were semantically quite separate, and although levels of elaboration within these categories were easily identifiable, such a division often represented a level of delicacy unwarranted by the frequency of instances.

The original results never underwent statistical investigation, but it seemed that despite the inadequacy of the coding categories there were some important differences in the speech being offered. Clearly, we had to set up additional hypotheses about the nature and extent of the differences. This task was postponed until after the preliminary analysis of the rest of the data in order that we might use these results in the formulation of additional predictions.

Three main areas of possible significance were identified. The first evolved from the finding that middle-class children used more indefinite pronouns than their working-class peers, and was intended to cast further light on this tendency. Second, an analysis of reasoning, purpose and justification was undertaken; and third we looked at the use of relative clauses, particularly their function as a defining device.

In the interests of simplicity, the results of each sub-analysis will be presented along with the rationale for investigation and the technique of coding. Such a presentation is justified by the fact that it mirrors the development of the research.

Indefinites and generality

We have seen that all children give a great deal of concrete description, with the middle class showing a relative tendency towards greater detail. Working-class children use more exophoric pronouns, and these are the chief indices of context-dependence, reflected in the implicit realisations which are relatively absent from MC descriptions.

MC children give a much higher proportion of indefinite words but we have yet to ascertain their particular role and significance. One inference might be that such usage is indicative of a more general orientation which leads the children to make overall non-specific statements about the cards, in addition to the basic descriptive material which they offer. It was noted that not a few children gave the following type of statement:

> it's a tea party
> it's a railway station
> it's a market place.

Now these were coded at D1, because of their structural similarity to the following:

> that's a mouse
> it's a dog
> those are policemen.

(Where additional information was given, for example 'it's the celebration after the wedding', the item was coded at D2, but degree of elaboration was largely ignored in the statistical analysis.)

Semantically, however, the two are quite distinct. The first gives a global or thematic description of the card as a whole, the second gives the briefest elaboration of an exophoric realisation. We tentatively suggest that in so far as differences in orientation to and availability of universalistic and particularistic orders of meaning (see Bernstein, 1971, ch. 9) will be realised in a descriptive context, it is here that they may be found. Our use of these terms perhaps requires some further explanation. It is suggested that the interpretative rules which orient the elaborated code user allow the maintenance of a certain cognitive distance between stimulus and respondent. Thus while the elaboration of principles, as described in the regulative context, is largely precluded by the nature of the stimulus, the child will nevertheless provide some general frame which serves as an anchor or reference point for the more specific descriptive material. By encapsulating the theme to which the description pertains, the speaker increases the universality of his meaning and, concomitantly, the context-independence of his speech.

The interpretative rules characteristic of the restricted code user tie him firmly and closely to the eliciting context so that his observations are realised implicitly or are highly concretised. He focuses on particular aspects of the card and realises his meanings in such a way that they are available only to selected listeners. The structures here labelled particularistic are very like simple listing but with the implication of a more integral relationship with the communication context. Our first additional hypothesis, then, is that the universalistic type will be more characteristic of the middle class and that the particularistic type will be more characteristic of the working class. The categories were not frequent ones (although some children gave a fairly high number of the particularistic type) and non-parametric analyses are appropriate.

Fifty-two children made general statements about the cards and of these 33 were MC and 19 WC. This difference was clearly significant ($\chi^2 = 5.56$, $p < 0.02$). In addition, MC children appeared more likely to elaborate these statements (i.e. 10 MC and 4 WC gave such constructions coded at D2).

The more particularistic realisations were used by 57 children of whom 41 were WC and 16 MC. This difference is again highly significant ($\chi^2 = 18.32$, $p < 0.001$). Table 2.22 shows the pattern of preference of these constructions among the social classes. The IQ and sex differences were not significant.

Clearly, MC children are more oriented to spontaneously offer an overall thematic description of the picture card. Using a very similar linguistic construction, WC children realise a rather different order of meaning – one that is relatively context-dependent.

Table 2.22 Children opting for universalistic and particularistic statements as defined in the text

	MC	WC
Universal type	33	19
Particular type	16	41

A third level of such constructions was identified, more akin to the particularistic than the universalistic type but rather more context-free.

'That man is pushing the truck; he's a guard'
'That house is a hotel'

Eleven WC and 5 MC children offered such realisations, the difference being non-significant.

Relative clauses

Hawkins noted that relative clauses, although structurally fairly uniform, may serve a variety of functions. He suggested a sub-classification based on 'their degree of dependency on the group head which they follow'. Hawkins identified two main functions and the present analysis adds a third, intermediate level.

First, the qualifying clause can give all the essential information about the head; i.e. it defines the head almost completely:

people who push your luggage (i.e. porters)
one of those things that you push with apples in it $\left.\right\}$ Type A
(i.e. a barrow)

At the other extreme, the relative clause structure may be semantic-ally all but superfluous:

there's a man who's walking along the road   Type C

The relative pronoun can be replaced with 'and he' without de-tracting from the meaning of the observation. Hawkins calls such clauses 'additioning' types. (It could be argued that the use of a relative clause automatically realises an increase in specificity, but the difference in function between this and the previous examples is quite apparent.)

In other instances the referent was given essentially by the head, but the relative clause realised further critical attributes:

a train who often came into that station   Type B

Here the relative clause distinguishes this train from other trains, but the information is still secondary to the fact that it is a train which the child has observed. Such types were not always easy to discriminate from the previous, additioning clauses. It was finally decided that the clause should either realise a long-term attribute, as above, or serve an obviously discriminative purpose as in

> the ones *who want to get off* have to get off first
> the ones *who want to get on* have to get on the last

or, rarely, be anaphoric in function, i.e. refer back to a figure or object previously mentioned.

Now it is perhaps far-fetched to suggest that use of types (A) and (B) indicates the realisation of classificatory systems (i.e. the class of 'people who drive railway trains' is a subclass of the class of 'people' in general) although there is no doubt that such constructions would be an efficient way to realise such a system. But in view of the middle-class child's orientation towards general as well as specific description it was suggested that he might bring these tendencies into relation by way of relative clauses with a comparatively dependent relationship to the head. It was therefore hypothesised that more MC children would use types A and B.

The number of children employing type C was expected to be fairly consistent throughout the sample but we were interested to see whether more MC than WC children used similar 'surface' structures to realise more than one kind of semantic or deep type.

All the categories were infrequently used, the total number of children giving *any* relative clause structure being 42 (21 in each of the social classes).

The first, most dependent type was used by 17 children, 12 of whom were MC and 5 WC. The breakdown by sex showed that 12 boys and 5 girls used the category. The value of chi-squared in both cases is 2·69 ($p = 0\cdot1$). Remembering that the WC children offered far more speech than their MC peers, and considering the infrequency of the category, we would suggest that these figures at least suggest a trend towards greater access by the MC. The same conditions apply to the sex difference, since girls gave significantly more speech than boys.

Type (B) was used by 26 children of whom 15 were MC and 11 WC. This difference was not significant ($\chi^2 = 0\cdot8$).

Type (C) was used by 26 children of whom 12 were MC and 14 WC, the difference again being non-significant.

We then looked at the children who used relative clauses to realise more than one of the functions which we have outlined. Ten MC children used at least two types and a further 4 gave instances of all three options; 6 WC children did not confine their use to one type only and 1 of these offered all three. (It should be noted that half the WC children gave only 1 relative clause.) Thus there is a trend for more MC than WC children to give more than one type of relative clause ($\chi^2 = 2\cdot91, p < 0\cdot1$).

It would appear, then, that while access to this particular structure is not class-based, the functions realised by it are influenced both by social class and by sex. MC children and boys are more likely to add definitive information about the head by way of a relative clause, although the hypothesis is not confirmed at the intermediate level where finer discriminations may be required (or a re-classification with utterances of similar semantic base but different structural form – see Henderson). More MC children as predicted varied the kinds of meaning realised by the one form.

Reasoning

When the coding frame was evolved it was intended to look at the extent to which children gave rationales for what they said. Somewhat naively, it was considered that rationale statements could be identified mainly by the inclusion of 'because' and less frequently by conjunctions such as 'so that' and 'in case'.

Consider the following examples of children's rationale statements –

It's a wedding 'cos there's a bride and a groom and a church in the distance.
They're looking at the balloon because it's high in the air and it's a peculiar shape.
The lady's running 'cos the train's going soon.
She's looking sad because the dog bit her.
That man is there because he's there.

The first statement represents a 'meta-level' justification for the observation. The next three statements are all reasons for things going on in the picture but they represent varying degrees of inference. The final statement is not a 'reason' at all but a repetition of what has been said already.

The extent to which children spontaneously offer rationale statements is obviously of some importance. However, it was felt that within the context of this frame it would be very difficult to make objective decisions about the level of the reasoning. Further, Henderson's forthcoming analysis makes a basic distinction between 'assertive' and 'inferential' statements and is also better equipped to cope with the problems which narrative speech poses in this regard.

We did, however, distinguish between the first type of example above and all other kinds. Our hypothesis was that this would be a feature of context-independent speech and therefore used by more MC children. The child who uses evidence from the card to justify his inferences leaves very little embedded in the context of the communication situation.

As well as rationale statements, we were interested to see how many children assigned a function or purpose to objects and actions in the pictures. In this case, distinctions were made according to the level of elaboration of the function. Thus

(a) grass for the children to play on.
(b) lights to keep people safe when it's night.
(c) food to eat.
(d) glasses for wine.

All such statements can be said to realise the purpose of an object but (a) and (b) are more elaborated. Similarly, with the purpose of actions

(a) that man's standing up to let the lady sit down.
(b) that lady's looking to see if it's her train.
(c) the lady's coming to help.
(d) the man is playing his guitar for money.

In the original frame the more elaborated types were coded at D3, the less complex types at D2.

It was expected that, as with reasoning, children using context-independent speech would be more likely to explicate the function of a few objects or events.

The meta-level rationale statements emerged as very infrequent and used by only 9 children, of whom 7 were MC and 2 WC. No WC MIQ child used the category and the group with the greatest number of users were MC HIQ boys (6 children having instances). Further, all the MC HIQ boys, and only this group, gave more than one example. These figures can only be suggestive, the overall infrequency being most likely a function of the task (there was no indication that such statements were required) and of the age of the children.

There were no differences in the numbers of children taking up the other reasoning option. Twenty-eight MC and 27 WC children gave instances of such statements, but as indicated above the coding procedure was inadequate. We await Henderson's analysis with interest. The finding that 10 out of the 27 WC children who used reasoning were MIQ G, the group that showed a preference for the narrative mode, suggests that the role of reasoning in narrative deserves closer scrutiny. Again, however, a slightly older age group might give more illuminating data.

The results concerning function are again unclear. There were absolutely no differences in the numbers of children who made reference to the purpose of an action except that once again, within the WC sample, MIQ girls account for half the children who gave an elaborated realisation of the function of an action. In this case, the utterances do seem encouraged by the use of imaginative narrative.

The fireman will climb in the window to rescue the people.
The dogs hid in the train to escape from the men who were
    after them.

Thirty-two children used such constructions and 16 gave the more restricted variety. It still remains to explicate the nature of such utterances which do not occur within the context of narrative. Some imaginative provision of context on the part of the speaker is almost always involved

The people are catching the train to go on their holidays.
The lady's stopping to buy some apples

although some examples are more indicative of a structural complexity which reduces repetition

they're walking along to catch the train to go somewhere
they're sitting down for their great big feast or dinner

Again distinguishing criteria would be too subjective and the infrequency of the categories makes it unlikely that such a delicate analysis would be justified here.

Seventeen children elaborated the function of an object and 30 gave a more restricted definition. There is a tendency for more MC children to specify function quite precisely (12 MC, 5 WC users gave $\chi^2 = 2\cdot69, p = 0\cdot1$), although the level of significance is not very respectable. A similar trend exists for the more restricted types, 18 MC and 12 WC children offering examples ($\chi^2 = 1\cdot12, p = $ n.s.). Further, 5 MC children gave both levels of specificity whereas only 1 WC child did so.

In descriptive speech, the extra information added by giving rationales or specifying function does a considerable amount to free the speech from the eliciting context. Where this speech, as sometimes occurs in narrative, bears little relation to this context, reason-giving ceases to have such an explicatory purpose and may become more of a conjunctive device, holding together the thread of the child's imagination.

Our findings are far from clear-cut, but it is suggestive that predicted trends were found in the more analytic of the options investigated here. Thus more MC children appear oriented to justify their own inferences and to include the specification of function in their description of an object.

The use of narrative

Finally we must consider the extent to which children moved into the narrative mode. We have seen how such a tendency can affect the child's language, and will go on to suggest that the introduction of imaginative story-telling may tell us something of the ground rules and assumptions which the child brings to the interview setting.

Narrative occurs when the speaker makes extended inferences which go beyond what is given in the picture. Some children responded to the task by telling fully fledged stories which ran to perhaps two pages of transcript. Such story-telling constituted unambiguously a move into narrative and was evidenced at least once by 12 children. Of these, only 1 was MC and only 1 was a boy. Thus 10 WC girls gave imaginative story-telling, 3 being of high measured ability and 7 of average measured ability.

Less complete use of narrative occurs when the child gives in the course of his description a few sentences about a character which are clearly of his own creation. Arbitrarily, a count was made of children giving five or more clauses in the form of narrative and of those giving less than five.

No differences emerged in the numbers of children giving very limited narrative. Such speech can never go far beyond what is obvious in the card and usually lends a certain linguistic cohesion to the speech. It was not considered to be of any sociological importance.

Nineteen WC and 5 MC children, while not giving a complete imaginative text, did give at least one instance of narrative style which exceeded five clauses in length. This difference is statistically significant ($\chi^2 = 5.14, p < 0.05$) and, further, there is an almost significant difference between the ability groups in the WC where 6 HIQ and 13 MIQ children give limited narrative ($\chi^2 = 2.75, p < 0.1$).

There can be no doubt that WC children, in a descriptive task, more often move into the narrative mode. The tendency to give almost the entire corpus of speech under an imaginative framework is confined to WC girls, but less exclusive narrative is used also by boys, and here it is MIQ children who most often feature this type of speech. The adoption of a narrative style is most characteristic of WC MIQ girls.

Finally it should be pointed out that there is a strong correlation between the tendency to use narrative and the total verbal output. Children who give a great deal of speech are very likely to be those who create an imaginative context. By contrast, other children are constrained both in what they talk about and in how much they say. The theoretical significance of this finding will be discussed below.

Summary of results

Before discussing the data, the statistical results will be briefly summarised.

All children had a high instance of noun use, with the MC having a higher proportion of their total nouns in the qualifying constructions ($p < 0.025$). Third-person exophoric pronouns had a higher frequency of use among WC children ($p < 0.02$) and among children of average measured ability. More WC than MC children used such exophorics within qualification ($p < 0.01$). Again, more WC than MC children use the determiner and ordinator class of exophorics ($p < 0.001$) and the propensity to include these in qualification is shown by more WC children and by more children of average verbal ability ($p < 0.02$). Finally, indefinite words are far more characteristic of the MC ($p < 0.001$) and are preferred by girls ($p < 0.05$). An almost significant third-order interaction shows MC HIQ girls to have the highest incidence of this option, and this is also the group least likely to employ exophoric choices.

From our analysis of qualifying constructions the following results emerged.

The implicit option in location was used by more WC children ($p < 0.001$). The explicit options were more frequently chosen by MC children ($p < 0.05$), by HIQ children ($p < 0.025$) and by boys ($p < 0.05$) with the latter tendencies being much more pronounced within the WC. MC children also showed a trend towards greater specificity but this did not reach statistical significance.

The implicit option in relation was very infrequent but used most often by WC children of average measured ability. The general infrequency of the categories may account for the lack of a clear pattern of use in the explicit options. The high-specificity option appeared to be used by more MC children, and when this category was combined with the corresponding option in location the preference reached statistical significance ($p < 0.05$).

In the action categories, the implicit option was again used more often by WC children ($p < 0.001$) with a trend towards greater use by children of average ability. Within the explicit categories the low-specificity option was used more frequently by WC children ($p < 0.01$) and, to a lesser extent, by children of average ability ($p < 0.05$). The ability difference was more pronounced within the WC. There were no differences in the extent to which the children took up the high-specificity options.

The structures we have labelled 'universalistic' were used by more MC children ($p < 0.02$) while the particularistic types were preferred by WC children ($p < 0.001$). There was a tendency for more MC children to use relative clauses in a defining fashion and also to realise a variety of semantics with this one linguistic form.

The analysis of rationale statements failed to give clear results but there was always a tendency for more MC children to take up the analytic options. Particularly in the analysis of the categories called elaboration, it was seen that some apparent inconsistencies arose from the tendency of some children to adopt a narrative mode. Further analysis showed this alternative style to be almost completely confined to WC children and particularly to girls.

Our caution concerning the problems of differential verbal production should be remembered when reading these results. Where tests of significance are based on chi-squared values, these are likely to be inflated when we predict that more WC children will use a category and depressed when we expect more MC children to do so.

Discussion

This investigation has two facets – first, we attempted to elucidate the differences between context-dependent and context-independent descriptive speech and second to show that middle-class children, having been socialised into and through an elaborated code, would be more likely to offer the latter type. Our primary task is to translate the separate linguistic counts into a coherent picture of the children's responses to the task. Statistical differences are important only in the contribution which they make to the overall patterning of the speech.

The first block of analyses consisted in looking at relative tendencies within a logically connected semantic network. There was, as it were, a central core (usually defined by explicit, low-specificity coding) which constituted a large part of the speech of most children, and we were interested in the extent to which children relied on that core and which options they took up when they moved from it. Thus a consideration of references to location showed that all children gave constructions such as

the lady in the train
the people at the gate
the cats on the roof

but that MC children tended to confine their use to such a type with some children increasing the specificity by the addition of modifiers:

the people at the gate of the house
the cats on the edge of the roof.

Fewer WC children gave this degree of specificity and their reliance on the 'standard' type was less heavy. But many more WC children gave the implicit variants

> the lady in there
> the people out there
> the cats there

The WC pattern was most pronounced amongst MIQ children.

The results concerning the relation categories were less clear but followed the same trend, and increased our confidence in the hypothesis that more MC children show a propensity to greater detail.

An examination of the action categories showed that, again, more WC than MC children took up the implicit option. Further, whereas all children gave a fair proportion of the following types of utterance:

> a man sweeping the street .
> he's walking along the road
> she's sitting on a chair
> cats are watching a feast,

working-class children, and especially those of average verbal ability, were relatively more likely also to include the more context-dependent

> a man sweeping
> he's walking
> she's sitting there
> cats are watching it.

The semantic networks used in these analyses ensure that infrequent categories are logical subdivisions of a larger group and that the conceptual interconnections of the options are clear.

The semantic types investigated under the rubric of 'elaboration' were of a different nature. These could not be called characteristic features of descriptive speech, but are perhaps the most relevant of a wide range of peripheral options which children might spontaneously include. There will, necessarily, be many more such options which appeared rarely, or not at all, in our sample but which would be more prominent with a different task or with children of a different age group.

Nevertheless, we found good corroborative evidence for the notion (suggested by the 'head' analysis) that MC children will include general, even universalistic, statements in their descriptions while WC children will use a similar surface structure to realise a particularistic semantic which is concrete without being contextualised.

The different functions of similar surface structures were again made manifest by the finding that an inter-group consistency in the use of relative clauses concealed a tendency for MC children to use these structures in an analytic fashion. The propensity towards analytic statements, which are clearly context-independent in nature, was further indicated by the tendency of more MC children to give detached rationale statements and specification of object-function.

It may have been noted that in no case was a category used exclusively and extensively by one group of children – that, in fact, the differences observed were often superficially slight, representing variations in tendency, in orientation to one or another kind of speech. And this is what we would expect. The children are speaking the same language and they have all been given a standardised set of questions about a standardised task. *None the less, it is our conviction that quite small variations in the extent to which certain semantic and linguistic elements are employed will combine and interact to give crucial differences in the overall patterning of the speech, and that these will emerge quite clearly when we look at texts as a whole.*

Below are given excerpts from two children's responses to the cards.

The street scene

Child A (middle-class)
This is about some people in the road and there's some dogs and one horse. And lots of signs on the wall and names of the shops on the blinds. There's probably people living on top of the shops. There's a man sweeping water down the road, down the kerb.

What are the people doing?
They're walking about mostly and the one with the broom he's sweeping all the water down the gutter into a drain 'cos it's probably just been raining.

Is anything else happening?
Well, there's a man coming down the road and in the wagon he's pushing there's lots of apples or carrots or strawberries. A girl pushing an engine along with a truck on it.

Child B (working-class)
That man's playing a guitar. That lady's expecting rain. All that that's down there is what somebody's done and that man's got to sweep it all away. That dog's running after her.

What are the people doing?
All the people are lining up to get their tea but they can't stop him 'cos he can't stop in the middle of the road. That man's trying to catch that man up and that man's trying to get past there.

Is anything else happening?
He's standing out there because he wants to.

Excerpts from responses to the second card (wedding scene)

Child A (middle-class)
There's a man got a sword, he's a guard I expect. There's two dogs, one's running about and the other's going to the toilet. Three people at the gate. There's a church and three houses in the background and two cats up on the roof of the house. Lots of flowers in the garden. And steps leading down to the ground from the house. There's a tree. There's flowers in a vase on the posts above the gates.

Child B (working-class)
They're all having a party. She doesn't feel well. All the animals haven't got anything to eat. They've had theirs and they think that's not enough for me, let's go and have all that.

That lady up there she thinks that's not fair they've got all that and she hasn't anything. She's not sitting down because of that fat lady and he's not going to sit next to that fat lady. That lady doesn't mind sitting next to that fat lady nor does that one so they all sat and they all sit down to eat their tea.

All the animals are going away from that fat lady 'cos they don't like her one bit.

These examples illustrate our emphasis on the fact that all children will include a good deal of 'standard description' in their speech. But it must also be clear that the inclusion of just one or two linguistic exophorics immediately renders the child's meaning much less accessible. Further, one very specific reference in the midst of a highly context-dependent utterance has little effect on the explication of the semantic which generated that utterance.

'All the people are lining up to get their tea but they can't stop him 'cos he can't stop in the middle of the road.'

This sentence has three explicit clauses and one high-specificity reference, yet the inclusion of an exophoric 'him' not only leaves the referent in context but obscures the relationship between the two parts of the observation. ('He' must be the man referred to by Child A from whom the people wish to buy their food.) The speaker could have been completely implicit and given the following: 'They are lining up to get some but they can't stop him 'cos he can't stop there': such a degree of context-dependence was very rare although this same child does offer one construction which approaches it: 'all that that's down there is what somebody's done', and it is instructive to note the structural sophistication of her sentence. Apparently our theoretical bias towards semantics is well founded.

The second excerpts are perhaps more illustrative of how different children can have totally different orientations to the pictures. Child A gives a fairly straightforward and detailed description of the card. Child B, on the other hand, concentrates on two aspects of the action – first that some people are excluded from the feast, and second that there is a very fat person in the card whom the others avoid. These observations are largely inferential but the child devotes large chunks of speech to them (not all of which is given here).

The second child has moved into the narrative mode and never, in fact, gives a description as we would define it. Her speech revolves around her imagination and the card is relevant only in so far as it provides the protagonists, and a rudimentary basis for the action, of her story. Minimally, she has created her own linguistic context and thus gives us a type of context-dependent speech rather different from that which we anticipated and described. For it is on the context as the *child* constructs it that our interpretation of *her* speech must depend and for some children this construction apparently diverges considerably from that of the researcher.

We shall argue that this is indicative of a particular orientation to the communication context – one which does not differentiate it from a great many other communication situations and thus is at variance with the interpretation demanded in the comparable instructional situations characteristic of the school.

By contrast, it is suggested that the interpretative rules which orient the elaborated code user lead him both to recognise the critical features of the context and to cope with it appropriately. The topic is constrained because the card has been objectified. And the perspective which leads him to maintain a psychological distance from his subject also defines the interaction with his listener. He understands that the burden of communication has been placed firmly on the speaker. A concern with giving the 'correct' response makes the introduction of rich imaginative material unnecessary to him and he has already the notion of irrelevancy.

Of central importance is the fact that these, mostly middle-class children are oriented towards the role relationship required in the basically instructional setting of the school. It would seem probable that this is because they have experience with similar situations at home and that the instructional (in the broad sense) context is well marked for them – physically, socially and linguistically. In the acquisition of communicative competence[7] they learn to differentiate and deal with such contexts and in a way consonant with the demands of the school.

The child who gives narrative speech is effectively offering a conversational speech style. If he does this across a range of contexts, as seems likely, then it suggests that the contexts themselves are not clearly distinguished from each other. If interaction in the home does not recognise certain critical contexts, and so mark them linguistically, then it may be relatively more difficult for the child to acquire the system of social, perceptual and semantic rules which shape appropriate speech in what are socially defined as relevant situations. It is possible that the WC mother emphasises the narrative form at the expense of other forms. If this is so then we should not be surprised that it is the girls in our sample who so show this tendency.

Not all children who avoid context-independent speech adopt the narrative mode. The context-dependent variant with which we have been concerned in this paper tends to avoid an analytic semantic and to rely on implicit linguistic realisations. The speaker does, however, appear to concur with the researcher's definition of the context – he offers a description. But although he has learned that such situations carry their own constraints he has not acquired the full set of rules for dealing appropriately with them. In as much as his linguistic behaviour, at the semantic as well as the lexical/grammatical level, reflects his own orientation to the situation then it is clear that here, too, is a speaker operating with a different set of ground rules.

The rule system which is code is a tacit understanding which spontaneously generates a particular behaviour – in this case a particular speech variant. Access to an elaborated code comes through experience with appropriate social relationships and, even were this desirable, cannot be taught in the conventional sense. Where such experience is missing or alien, the child will continue to operate on the basis of shared assumptions and his speech will approximate the context-dependent variant described by our results.

At this point it might be apposite to summarise the defining attributes of context-dependent and context-independent descriptive speech. This is a precarious undertaking since such potted accounts tend to become reified and to exist apart from the real situation. We cannot hope to capture the full flavour of the speech, and in any case the boundaries are fluid and will vary in accordance with the requirements of the particular descriptive task; for example, a highly detailed picture of one figure or object would be expected to elicit a more cohesive description whose sub-parts bear an explicit relation to the main referent. Enough has been said for the reader to reconstruct for himself the tone and the characteristics of the speech variants, and for this reason a strong classification by the author would be both an imposition and a distortion.

Finally, it should not be supposed that, in the theoretical framework, a context-independent variant with high specificity is identified with the speech of MC children and a context-dependent variant with low specificity with that of their WC peers. Such a conclusion reduces the present argument to a tautology and implies a too rigid conception of the variables involved.

Social class in this and other papers of the SRU has been measured in terms of a weighted scale based upon the occupation and education of the parents of the children. Whilst it is the case that differences between the parents in terms of this scale are associated with differences in the sociolinguistic choices of the children, it is also the case that there is considerable variance in each social class. Our social class scale is a relatively indelicate differentiator of the social and psychological experience of individuals. We have developed a typology of family structures and their hypothesised related forms of communication. We expect that the subjective consequences of objective class position will vary according to family type. We are at present attempting an empirical analysis which we believe will lead to a description of family types. Although we have shown that context-independent speech is more typical of children whose parents satisfy, on paper, the criteria which define them as middle class, a more stringent test of our hypothesis would be to identify those 'middle-class' children who offered a substantial amount of context-dependent speech and to investigate more thoroughly their family structures; and similarly with those 'working-class' children whose speech is relatively free of implicit realisations (but see discussion of ability below).

The role of IQ

Comparisons of the two ability groups yielded less significant and less consistent results than comparisons by social class. There were, however, some six statistically significant results indicating that HIQ children showed greater preference for a context-independent variant. For three linguistic measures, the IQ difference was almost completely confined to the WC. Again, the almost exclusively WC tendency to adopt the narrative mode was found to have ability correlates.

We have seen that the sample can be divided into three broad response groups – those offering a context-independent variant, those offering a context-dependent variant and those moving into narrative. If we then split by social class we have five groups of children (since the incidence of narrative in the MC is negligible), two of which represent the modal variant for each of the two social classes. Figure 4 schematises this, the modal groups being represented by double lines.

Thus there exists a group of WC children who give speech akin to that of the average MC child. The data suggest that ability will affect membership of this group.

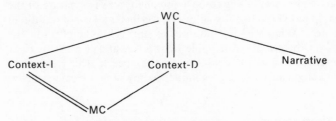

Figure 4   Linguistic response and social class

Two previous findings of the SRU may illuminate the tendency of WC HIQ children to behave, in some ways, like MC children. First, it was shown (Brandis and Henderson, 1970) that a Communication and Control Index correlated highly with the intelligence of the child in the WC. That is, WC mothers who reportedly relied heavily on speech in interaction with their child tended to have children of high measured ability. It would seem logical that children whose mothers emphasise verbal methods of control and instruction should cope more easily with verbal intelligence tests.

Second, Brandis and Bernstein (1974) have shown unequivocally that teachers positively evaluate those children who show high intelligence test scores, independently of their knowledge of those scores. Further, language behaviour was found to correlate both with intelligence and with high evaluation by the teacher. Both these tendencies were more pronounced amongst teachers of the WC.

Remembering that HIQ children in the WC are an atypical group (a fact which a factorial design tends to obscure), it would appear that some of their socialisation experiences are rather different from those of their average-ability peers. In so far as the teacher/pupil relationship is a rewarding one, then these children will find adaptation to the school's demands and orientation not inconsistent with their more general attitudes. But it should be stressed that the effect of IQ in no case overrides the effect of social class.

Just as WC HIQ children are atypical, so are MC children who score around the average mark on IQ tests. However, the speech of such children is not substantially different from that of their high-ability counterparts. The CCI index was found not to correlate with the ability of the child in the MC area and correlations with teachers' ratings, although significant, were consistently weaker (Brandis and Bernstein, 1974). This suggests, as Bernstein has always maintained, that speech socialisation is relatively more homogeneous within the MC.

It is now generally accepted that the correlation between IQ and social class is not something to be 'controlled' for. The nature of the relationship has yet to be satisfactorily described and is not our direct concern here. What we must attempt to unravel is the effect of the variables on the child's observable behaviour, and it must be clear that the effect of measured ability on the speech which the child offers is to a considerable degree influenced by sociological variables.

Concluding remarks

Our attempts to explicate the nature of context-independent and context-dependent descriptive speech and to show their relationship to the social background of the speaker have led to the conclusion that some WC children give responses which are difficult to handle within this framework. Thus these children spontaneously use the interview setting to explore the creative function of language. Their highly imaginative responses suggest an orientation rather different from that of their more constrained peers. An extension of the concept of context-dependence to include explicitly the child's interpretation of the context seems feasible were it not for the strong theoretical and empirical suggestions that the tendency to adopt a narrative form stems from a different aspect of code than do linguistic realisations. (It cannot be stressed enough that 'aspects of code' are theoretical entities and the abstraction of any one can be only for expository purposes. Communicative competencies will tend to be internally consistent because the constituent rules share common social-psychological antecedents.)

Another way of describing the data at the general level, then, might be as follows. We have identified two crucial, but probably not independent, aspects of code or competence and these act to generate the three broad kinds of response which have been described. First, the child's meanings are a function of his interpretation – perceptual, cognitive and social – of the setting. This dimension is roughly comparable to Bernstein's ground rules or the invisible aspect of code.

Second, these meanings are realised through a particular speech variant. This is the visible aspect of code but is clearly an integral part of the overall rule-system or competence which the child has acquired. Inferences from speech to code (i.e. from part to whole) then depend on the identification of crucial features at the micro- (e.g. implicit/explicit) intermediate or semantic (e.g. tendency to give thematic statements, rationales, etc.) and macro- (e.g. degree of adherence to objective referent) levels. Given this, the necessity of examining a range of contexts also becomes apparent.

We should perhaps confine the context independent/dependent terminology to descriptions of the speech and introduce some notion of the tacit knowledge of the classification of settings when referring to the child's interpretation of the communication context. The child's semantic potential – what he can mean and, in any one empirical context, what he does mean – then stands at the interface of these two aspects of his experience and becomes the logical basis of sociolinguistic analysis.

Notes

1 The broad correspondence between the experimental situation and many of the evaluative situations predominating in the current educational system is not hard to see.
2 Our classification of verbs could be taken to a far greater level of delicacy. Halliday gives a detailed discussion of the complications of the English verb system.
3 This is not to deny the importance of cognitive factors in shaping speech—a hypothesis which age comparisons make ridiculous.
4 The formula used included a correction for continuity.
5 It may be of interest to note that this child lived in the WC ILEA.
6 This figure is inflated by one child with a very high score.
7 In Hymes's (1971) sense of the term.

Chapter 3   The instructional context

Lesley Lineker

Introduction

One of the early empirical studies conducted in the SRU by Peter
Robinson involved an analysis of the instructional speech of five-
year-old children in a game situation. The game selected for the
purpose of the study was hide and seek, and the children were asked
to explain to the interviewer how it should be played. The coding
frame used in Robinson's study breaks down into two main sections,
the first dealing with the structure of the game, and the second relating to the way in which the subjects referred to the participants in
the game situation.

However, the two emphases converged in an overall description of
the scripts in terms of a universal–particular distinction. The two
parts of the analysis may also be seen as semantic and linguistic
descriptions, although it is unlikely that these ideas were central to
the coding frame at the time. It is true, nevertheless, that the section
devoted to structure is concerned with the way in which the child
sees the game and its rationale, whereas the second section refers to
the linguistic expression of the terms in which he sees the players.

In the structural section of the coding frame, very few differences
in approach were found either in class or IQ. In the second part,
some differences were found, correlating mainly with IQ, in the
children's ability to make verbally explicit the initial differentiation
between the roles of the players and to maintain that distinction
throughout the explanation. The most important relationship, however, was that between class and markers of particularity. It was
found that the working-class children were more likely to use par-
ticular-type explanations, and although there was no significant
corresponding middle-class relationship with universality, there was
a highly significant correlation between middle-class boys, mainly
from the high IQ group, and the use of nouns as markers of universality.

86

Thus the conclusions that could be drawn from this study indicate that linguistic differences in the realisation of the explanatory role are rare, but the most important finding is that differences can be expected in the way in which the children approach the task. The orientation towards the role of instructor varies according to the social class of the child, resulting in a different kind of speech in the test situation. Since these differences appear to suggest that the middle class are moving towards a universal frame of reference, Robinson infers that they are consistent with the thesis that elaborated code users can achieve greater economy in communication, greater abstraction and precision of expression and greater facility for taking an objective perspective.

This then is the starting point for the present study: an examination of instructional speech in seven-year-old children. Using a game situation in which the children have to give an explanation of the rules of hide and seek imposes a tight control on the semantic and linguistic options available. It is expected, therefore, that any class differences in the realisation of the task would stem from differences in focus or approach. Robinson classified scripts in terms of possession of single markers of universality or particularity:

> to be counted particular, the answer had to mention a particular
> place or time that the game was played in or else be specific
> about the object used in the game or the persons playing it –
> In some cases, abnormal stages were described which seemed
> inessential to the game and these were categorised as particular
> elements. . . . In order to qualify for the universal category, the
> explanation had to contain some linguistic marker of a
> non-limitation of space, time, object or person
> (Robinson, 1973).

Such distinctions involve relatively simple semantic analysis, but their implications can be clearly related to sociolinguistic theory. Within the context of the interview situation, and more specifically the game explanation, there is an obvious link between the concepts of universal/particular and context-dependent/independent. Context dependence is illustrated by the child who invents a situation for his explanation, names the participants in the game – in other words, gives an instruction explicitly embedded in the interviewer's task instruction. A universal instruction, in contrast, attempts to set out the rules of the game as it could be played in any situation, and by definition does not limit it to the circumstances peculiar to the context of the task situation.

One of Bernstein's central ideas had been 'that the form of the social relationship acts selectively upon the meanings to be realised, which in turn activate specific grammatic and lexical choices' (Bernstein, 1971). Robinson's paper related the linguistic options taken up to basic patterns of meaning potential, and from the preference shown by groups of children sociological inferences could be drawn. The aim of the present paper is to examine the instructional speech of children at age seven, two years older than the previous study, and to develop a coding frame along the lines suggested by Robinson's findings while taking into account more recent theoretical developments.

The most important development has been the construction of semantic networks derived from the thesis largely as a result of the empirical studies conducted by members of the SRU (notably Geoffrey Turner) on modes of control. Bernstein acknowledged the importance of this work in providing the 'key' to 'the relationship between the "socio" and the linguistic features' (Bernstein, 1973b). As early as 1962 Bernstein developed a set of concepts making explicit three main types of control: imperative, positional and personal. These concepts were operationalised in the construction of a coding grid to be applied to social control data already collected from mothers and children. Semantic sub-systems were developed in relation to each control situation and each sub-system headed a further range of possible choice systems which were realised and could be described linguistically. Thus, for each linguistic realisation an explicit relationship can be traced with higher-order formulations of the theory.

The application of this principle proves both that it is possible to adopt Professor Halliday's network system of language analysis, and to construct networks related to the theory together with the linguistic choice systems for the realisation of semantic categories. The significance of the adoption of a network system, however, is the possibility of its application to any speech context. In other words, context-specific networks may be set up in order to examine which of the range of linguistic options available within a particular situation are utilised. In this way the characteristics of speech variants may be described.

Empirical studies have identified the characteristics of elaborated and restricted speech variants as these appear in a given situation. The definitions, therefore, are context-specific, and it is important to take into account the significance of the eliciting context in any analysis of children's speech. Because a particular language situation initiates a choice system whose realisations indicate the use of a restricted variant – that is, where the meanings are implicit, context-dependent and particularistic – this does not imply that the speaker is necessarily limited to a restricted code in all speech situations.

The link between speech variants and codes is provided by Halliday's theory of language functions. This involves the identification of a set of distinct language functions which are realised in the grammatical system and the lexis. Halliday believes that in its initial acquisition by the child each language function has its own distinctive grammar. The seven functions identified by Halliday have been condensed by Bernstein to four and conceptualised in terms of 'critical primary socialising contexts'. These are regulative, instructional, interpersonal and imaginative. Since these contexts involve different language functions, their linguistic realisation should also be different. 'The concept code now referred to the regulative principle which controlled the form of the linguistic realisation of the four primary socialising contexts' (Bernstein, 1971).

The nature of the sociolinguistic code which orients a speaker can, therefore, only be inferred from an examination of the speech variant which he offers in any given context. Ideally, we would want to look at his speech across a range of contexts.

The distinction between code and speech variant is a crucial one. A speaker's sociolinguistic code shapes the ground rules which lead him to select a particular pattern of semantic and linguistic options from within the semantic network constructed to describe the given eliciting context. This pattern of options is realised as the speech variant.

Any empirical study, then, must be based on a well-defined context such that analysis of the speech may be logically related to higher-order theoretical concepts. When the context, and thus the language function, have been defined, hypotheses can be advanced about both the semantic and the lexical/grammatical realisation of code.

The present paper is concerned with the instructional function of language, but with a peculiarly limited situation within that range of semantic options. Not only is the context rigidly limited and defined by the interview situation and the wording and administration of the probes, but the meanings available are severely restricted by the imposition of the selected game on each child. In the earlier study of five-year-olds a choice of game was offered to the children and they were also given a great deal more freedom to choose the manner of their explanation, in other words to define their own speech context. (See 'Method' below – Notes on interview situation.)

Such a narrowing of the speech context has been deliberate, since movement within a smaller set of options will necessarily be more limited in its scope and a coding frame may be constructed which will encompass the whole range of meanings available. Selection of a particular game by the interviewer and the presentation to the child of a particular direction for his instruction – asking him to explain the rules to an imaginary third person – means that even the amount of information offered by the child may be measured against reasonably objective criteria. However, this does not mean that the orientation of the child's answer is also constrained. Even acting within the framework given to them the children may perceive the nature of the task differently, and it is the resulting differences in the orientation of their answers that provide the basis of this study. What the rigidly defined context does signify is that orientations will tend to be polarised. This means that a limited number of distinct approaches can be identified and their characteristics defined. Of course, this does not imply that all scripts will fall neatly into predetermined categories, only that within the range of possibilities available, groupings will occur among the scripts. These may be recognised by the possession of certain identifiable linguistic or semantic characteristics. From these groupings theoretical inferences may then be drawn regarding the influences governing the child's attitude to the task, and his method of answering it.

Method

Subjects

At age five speech samples were taken from 439 children and of these further samples were taken from 298 at age seven. Of the latter group, 174 were drawn from schools in a predominantly working-class district of east London, while the remaining 124 came from schools in a largely middle-class area of south-east London. In the present analysis of speech, from the seven-year-olds, material from 128 subjects was used. This population was subdivided according to a factorial design, with a two-way division on sex, social class and verbal intelligence scores, thus giving a sample of sixteen subjects per cell.

The social class of the families to which the children belong was determined by interviewing the mothers, that scale being based on the occupation and education of both parents (Brandis and Henderson, 1970).

It is also the case that eleven children in the working-class groups were from schools which had taken part in an exploratory language-enrichment programme. The programme had been devised by D. M. and G. A. Gahagan in 1964 and had run for three years. Its function had been to encourage children to explore through language different orders of meaning and to give them a greater understanding of the resources of language (see Gahagan and Gahagan, 1970). Children who took part in this project are referred to in the paper as 'E1 children'. The intelligence test score defined 'high' as being at the 90th percentile or higher on the Crichton Vocabulary Scale and 'medium' as at the 50th to 75th. Ten per cent of the total sample (16 children) deviated from this criterion, but satisfactory scores were obtained using the English Picture Vocabulary Test. These tests were administered during the children's third week of their starting school.

Specific aspects of this programme were concerned with the development of instructional speech. A number of other SRU studies have shown that the E1 children's speech in certain contexts differed from the speech of non-E1 working-class children (Robinson and Rackstraw, 1971; Brandis and Henderson, 1970, appendix). In the present study the expectation was that E1 children would be more likely to resemble the middle-class child's orientation to the task.

The second interview took place when the children had been at school for almost six terms. Interviews were individual, lasting for between half and three-quarters of an hour. The children were asked to perform a number of different speech tasks and their responses were tape recorded and later transcribed using traditional orthography, but without any 'editing'. The 'game' task with which we are concerned was in three parts designed to elicit different kinds of instructional speech.

The first stage aimed to make the children play the game of hide and seek by manipulating dolls while giving a commentary on their action. The child was first presented with four small dolls and some boxes to hide behind and then given the following instructions.

'You can pretend these dolls are playing hide and seek, can't you? [Given as expecting the answer 'of course'.] Make them play hide and seek and tell me just what they're doing *all the time*. Tell me what they do *as they do it*. Start now.'

If the child failed to verbalise a stage in the game he was interrupted immediately and given the following probe: 'What have they just done?' If he stopped the action before the total sequence was completed the child could be given a further probe: 'What do they do now?'

The game, hide and seek, was constant through the three parts of the task but the orientation of the instruction was changed. The aim of the second stage was not to elicit any new information but for the child to adopt the role of instructor and command the interviewer to perform the actions of the game. The interviewer took the dolls from the child and gave him the instruction.

'Now *I* want to have a turn. I want to play hide and seek *as well*. Will you tell me what to do with them, as *I go along*? Give me the

dolls. Now tell me what to do with them to make them start playing.'
A further probe, 'Have you forgotten anything?', was to be given to
each child, once only, when he had stopped.

Parts one and two of the task involved a close temporal relationship between the action of the game and the child's instruction – he
could follow the step-by-step exposition of the rule system by
manipulating physical 'props', thus reinforcing the concreteness of
the situation. For the third part the dolls and boxes were removed,
since the aim was the dissociation of the game instruction from a
rehearsal of its actions. The instruction given to the child was,

'Let's pretend that you know a little boy/girl, and he/she can't play
hide and seek. Pretend you're telling him/her how to play the game
so he/she will know *exactly* how to play. Tell him/her about the
whole game at one go. Start now.'

Again a final probe was given when the child had completed his
explanation: 'What else has to be done?'

For the purposes of the present paper only the third part of the
task was analysed. Interviewer inconsistency in the first two parts
meant that the data obtained were unreliable and many of the
children misunderstood the instructions particularly in part two.

Coding

The coding frame used for this analysis has been developed from
several earlier versions and revised after carrying out pilot studies.
Initially, the approach was, like Robinson's, structural rather than
semantic, with the main emphasis on a measure of the child's ability
to communicate the rule system of the game and the details of
linguistic realisation. This represented primarily an assessment of
competence rather than performance. By the age of seven this appeared less important, since it was clear that by this time all children
would have acquired the basic competence for giving instruction in
order to be accepted as members of a peer group. In fact when a
study was made of the objective rule structures given by the children
it was found that nearly all children both understood the sequence
of hide and seek and were able to communicate it. The only real
differences in the success of their instructions resulted from the
restrictions of the speech contexts imposed by the interviewer, which
were not always perfectly understood.

It is therefore an examination of performance in which we are
interested, and this necessitates a much more complex approach.
When looking at methods of approach to the task it is important to
see them as different kinds of performance and to avoid making
value judgments. The efficiency of the transmission of information

within the given speech context may not necessarily correlate with evaluative linguistic measures such as the degree of verbal explicitness in the approach adopted.

The second major disadvantage of a non-semantic approach to the data is the lack of an explicit relationship with the thesis. It is possible to construct a coding frame based on linguistic structures used and to group these in grammatical types, but such a mechanical analysis would be too far removed from higher-order conceptual backing for any useful inferences to be drawn from the results. This is not to deny the value of the groupings of linguistic structures which will become obvious as keys to the methods of realisation of the semantic criteria adopted by different groups of children; this may be regarded as the exploratory part of the coding frame.

In the construction of a coding grid it is important to retain the model suggested by Bernstein in which, diagrammatically, the movement from theory to linguistic realisation of the options available is seen as a steady progression along a line of increasing delicacy through the type of socialisation (i.e. the language function and speech context) to the specification of semantic alternatives and their realisation in terms of grammatical structures. To take a structural basis as the starting point is to begin too far along the scale.

Further, since we are interested in the speech as an index of the child's socio-semantic orientation to the task, specification of the range of possible meanings is a prerequisite of a context-specific coding frame. If a coding frame is based on the range of possible meanings we can then make predictions concerning which groups of options will be taken up by which groups of children, and the relationship of these groups of options with the underlying theory may be explicitly traced.

In the present 'hide and seek' analysis the principal hypothesis concerns the different conceptions of the demands of the task we may expect to be held by the middle- and working-class groups. Although the semantic options and grammatical realisations will be context-specific, it will be possible to make inferences from the results about the nature of instructional language in the two social-class groups. We can predict that those options realised by the middle class will be the universalistic context-independent ones, and their rule giving will be highly specific. Working-class children, however, we should expect to give particularistic, implicit explanations relating their speech to the context and making use much more fully of the information given by the interviewer in the task instruction.

The idea that the child's concept of what is required by the instructions will differ according to his class provides the semantic starting point of the coding frame. If the hypothesis suggests that the middle class will select the more universalistic orders of meaning and the working class the more particularistic, the kinds of semantic options, taking into consideration the limitations of the speech context, can be isolated and described. Such sets of meanings or methods of approach are known in the coding frame as 'mode types'. Obviously such mode types are not absolutes but points on a cline and no complete one-to-one correspondence of mode type and class can be expected. This makes exploration of the linguistic manifestations of the semantic mode types by the groups of children the more significant. It is not only of interest to investigate the semantic options taken up within the range of possibilities but also to see whether children of different groups when adopting the same mode type will realise it in grammatically the same way.

However, the strict control imposed by the task instruction ensures that grammatical realisation within the chosen mode will also be limited in scope. Different 'sets' of grammatical structures may be associated with different modes of instruction, and wide differences between grammatical structures used in different scripts should be an indication that a different mode type has been used. Thus class differences in the types of grammatical structures used should be less apparent when similar modes have been adopted.

Conceptually, development of a method of analysis through division into mode types appears straightforward. Such a division is necessarily semantic since the mode can be regarded as a sub-context, although one which offers a certain choice to the children, within the set speech situation. However, in linguistic description of the scripts, objective identification of the modes is difficult. Even with an expressly semantic basis for coding, classification of scripts obviously has to be according to linguistic structures, since these may be regarded as the visible realisation of semantic intent. Thus certain significant linguistic features of each mode must be identified as indicators of mode type.

The linguistic key to the analysis is provided by reference and cohesion. One of the things which set this speech situation apart from earlier attempts to examine children's responses to the instructional context is its emphasis on the lack of interaction with the interviewer. The children have been asked to adopt the role of instructor and explain the rules of hide and seek 'in one go'. Two things then are being tested: the child's ability to adopt and maintain an unfamiliar role – outside a test situation he would be likely to use demonstration to back up his verbal instruction – and his ability to produce a cohesive body of speech without assistance.

Apart then from those restrictions imposed by the task instruction, the constraints on the child and movement within the semantic networks available result from the manner of his socialisation. In other words, neither the interviewers' speech nor the wording of the probes gives a direction to the child's attitude towards instructional speech. Instructional modes, however, once adopted vary in the complexity both of the grammatical structures that realise them and the reference systems needed to maintain them. In choosing this method of instruction the child is also accepting the responsibility of maintaining that mode, and he may or may not set up his answer in terms that he is able to manipulate. Failure to maintain the mode may be reflected in a move to a less complex one, complete loss of instructional mode probably with a move into narrative or non-task speech, or a high level of mazing. Maintenance of reference without mazing throughout the instruction can also indicate the ease with which the child operates within his chosen conditions.

The linguistic analysis of the scripts is carried out in three sections: initial identification of mode and examination of its maintenance, the degree and kind of mazing in each script, and finally an examination of reference sets. The basis for coding is semantic, but a semantic system is not incompatible with the possibility of developing a much finer grid which would examine in greater detail grammatical realisation. This could be done by extending the existing coding grid 'to the right' – by writing networks for all possible sets of grammatical choice systems within each semantic category.

Three distinct instructional modes have been isolated, although it is possible for one mode to include certain linguistic characteristics of another. (See the Appendix for examples.) The first mode, identified as 'mode A' in the coding frame, is the one which corresponds most clearly to a universalistic approach to the task. The rules of the game are given without dependence on the conditions set out by the interviewer and with no reference to the imaginary third person. This mode is characterised by the use of universal nouns and pronouns, and usually, although not necessarily, complex grammatical structures and a high degree of explicitness.

The second major type, 'mode B', represents the particularistic approach, in which instructional speech is embedded in the speech context. This can be indicated by the child's making explicit his relationship with the context and his adoption of the instructional role by using the second-person pronouns to refer to the second child. He may also include himself in the rule system and assign himself a role in the action. An alternative realisation of this mode involves the relation of a particular instance of the game or relating the game to a particular location, group of players or set of circumstances.

If modes A and B can be viewed as points towards each end of a cline, then the third, mode C, can be seen as holding a place in the centre. It is not strictly accurate to call this a mixed mode although it contains elements of both A and B, since it does represent a possible pure approach to the instructional context. The identification of the mode, usually in the initial definition of the roles, frequently contains characteristics of universal and particular instructional methods, for example in the use of universal nouns in the identification of one role, while the speaker and hypothetical listener are also involved in the activity. The principles of the game are frequently given universally but the instruction will then include some personal application. However, this mode once adopted can be maintained and is distinct from those scripts in which a single mode is adopted initially but not sustained and which result in the breakdown of mode.

Although role speech is more commonly associated with mode B, it is possible for short role-speech sequences to appear in mode A, and for this reason a separate count of role speech is made. In the same way, scene-setting is characteristic of mode B, but it can be used to introduce the wholly universalistic instruction associated with mode A. Separate analysis, outside the main classification for mode types, can also be made for narrative sequences and meta-task speech.

This section of the coding frame includes a study of maintenance or non-maintenance of mode. A subdivision of the former category examines the consistency with which the child refers to the players in his imaginary game (referred to in the coding grid as consistency of subject). This is felt to be important, since while an inconsistency in the number or sex of one group of players or the presence of role switch does not indicate a change in mode, it does point to a weakening in the child's ability to hold the mode.

The next related section of the analysis involves an examination of reference, an important indicator of the child's ability to maintain a cohesive text. The initial role system is suggested by the interviewer's direction, 'pretend that you know a little girl/boy . . .', but this does not constrain the child into adopting any particular system of reference. He may, for example, place himself directly in the instructional context, assigning himself the role of instructor and playing a part in the game. Alternatively, a more generalised approach can be characterised by the use of universal nouns. In either case the child's initial reference system, the way in which he chooses to refer to the participants in his game, reflects his attitude to the task.

For this reason it is important to look at primary role definition, and the coding frame identifies seven relevant categories. The first four may be associated with a universalistic approach. Category (1) covers functional definition, when one or both roles are defined either using a relative clause or a noun such as 'hider'. The next group of categories isolates specific universal nouns or pronouns, (2) 'one'/ 'one of', (3) 'someone'/'somebody', (4) 'person'/'people'.

Categories (5), (6) and (7) are associated with a more particularistic instruction: (5) role definition involving the use of third-person pronouns in which the reference is exophoric; (6) definition in terms of 'you'/'I' or 'we'; and (7) definition using any other particular noun or pronoun, e.g. naming the players.

Role definition is responsible for initiating and clarifying the first reference set. Subsequent pronominal reference to these primary referents is possible, but as soon as a new referent is introduced when one of the roles is redefined, a second reference set is said to have been introduced. The relationship between primary and subsequent reference sets may or may not be consistent: if a child cannot deal with the complexity of the web of reference he has initiated in his role definition, he will either become confused and introduce exophoric reference or role switch or he will modify his system, usually by switching to a more context-dependent mode. Consistency and maintenance of reference sets reflects the child's ability to organise his material into a cohesive body of speech and set up his instructional context in terms that he can manage. (For summary of coding grid and examples, see the Appendix, p. 122.)

The final section of the analysis involves a study of mazing. The amount of mazed speech in each child's text can be seen as a reflection of the fluency with which he manipulates instructional speech. Three basic counts of mazing can be made: (1) presence/absence of mazing for each child; (2) frequency of mazing, i.e. number of words mazed in relation to the total number of words in each script; (3) number of instances of mazing.

However, mazing is indicative of more than competence, and the resolution of the maze, its position in the text and the maze type can also play a significant part. Resolution of mazing may result in an obvious improvement to the speech, as in the correction of a grammatical error or a move towards a greater degree of elaboration or specificity. The coding frame also includes a count of those mazings which result in an obvious weakening of the text.

The position of mazing in relation to units of information in the game structure is also important, since it can indicate the degree of difficulty the child finds in planning his instruction and ordering the information. Three maze positions have been isolated in the coding frame: (1) *pre-stage* mazing – at the beginning of the text before the game instruction has commenced; (2) *inter-stage* mazing – occurring at the boundaries of information units in the instruction; (3) *within-stage* mazing. The first two categories relate directly to the structuring of the answer and are associated with the child's ability to perform the task, whereas type 3 is more likely to concern grammatical detail or a move to greater elaboration.

For the purposes of this analysis five kinds of maze have been isolated, again reflecting the causes of mazing: (1) *backtracking* involves the abandonment of a sequence once initiated and a return to an earlier point either to redefine it or to add more information; (2) *verbal change* – includes any change in tense, mode, etc. in a verbal group; (3) *semantic confusion* – this is the most complex form of mazing and is characterised by complete breakdown in semantic content and abandonment of the sequence. It occurs most often at stage boundaries where the child is unsure of the structuring of the information he wishes to convey; (4) *hesitation/repetition* – the repetition, one or more times of a word or phrase, representing a 'stalling time' for extra thought; (5) *redefinition of role* – a common maze type relates to role definition. Two subgroups of this type can be important (a) when resolution of mazing corrects a role switch and (b) when resolution results in a move to a higher level of specificity.

Results

Before the major sections of the coding frame were applied, an analysis of variance was carried out on the total number of words in each script, since this could influence the number of occurrences of many categories. It was found that there was a significant class influence in the length of the instructions – working-class scripts tended to be longer – although there were no IQ or sex influences or interactions (see Table 3.1; $F = 5.65, p < 0.025$).

Table 3.1   Analysis of variance, total numbers of words

Source	df	ss	MS	F
A (class)	1	11 026		$5.65\, p < 0.025$
B (IQ)	1	42		
C (sex)	1	435		
AB	1	98		
AC	1	81		
BC	1	172		
ABC	1	5 279		2.09 n.s.
W cells	120	234 289	1952.4	

Out of the 128 scripts analysed, only four (two middle-class and two working-class) could not be categorised into one of the three basic mode types. All four of these children failed to give any instructional speech and instead produced a narrative description of a particular instance of the game. The remaining 124 scripts fell easily within the overall classification types and each of the two pure mode types A and B showed a significant association with class. Within the classes neither IQ nor sex appeared to be an influential factor in the choice of mode adopted.

Type A was the most frequently chosen mode used by well over half the total sample. It was, however, more closely associated with the middle class and was chosen by 46 in this group, compared with 34 in the working-class group (see Table 3.2). This difference proved to be statistically significant ($\chi^2 = 4{\cdot}03$, $p < 0{\cdot}05$), but what is especially interesting is the reversal of the pattern in mode B. Although this mode was adopted by fewer children, only 18 altogether, its use relates much more strongly to class. Three middle-class children used mode B and fifteen working-class ($\chi^2 = 7{\cdot}8$, $p < 0{\cdot}01$). There were no class differences in the number of children using mode C: thirteen from each class.

Table 3.2   Mode type as used by total sample

	Mode A	Mode B	Mode C
MC	46	3	13
WC	34	15	13

Mode A: class $\chi^2 = 4{\cdot}03$, $p < 0{\cdot}05$.
Mode B: class $\chi^2 = 7{\cdot}8$, $p < 0{\cdot}01$.
Association of mode type with social class: $\chi^2 = 8{\cdot}85$, $p < 0{\cdot}01$.

A χ^2 test on the distribution of modes A and B in working and middle class proved significant beyond the 0·01 level ($\chi^2 = 8{\cdot}85$, $p < 0{\cdot}01$). However, the figures given by the eleven E1 children appeared to complicate the picture since the distribution of their answers was atypical of their social-class group and more closely resembled the middle class (see Table 3.3). When these children were excluded from the total working-class sample, the significant relationship of modes A and B with middle and working class increased to give significance beyond the 0·001 level.

The sub-categories of role speech, narrative, meta-task speech and scene-setting, when looked at in conjunction with individual mode

Table 3.3 Mode type as used by the sample when E1 children are excluded

	Mode A	Mode B	Mode C
MC	46	3	13
WC (non-E1)	26	14	12
E1	8	1	1

Association of mode type with social class (excluding
E1 children): $\chi^2 = 10.09$, $p < 0.001$.

types, resulted in groups too small to offer significant counts. However, counts were possible if the sub-categories were summed across
the main mode divisions (see Table 3.4). Although there were indications that working-class children favoured the use of role speech,
only one category was statistically significant – the use of narrative
sequences showed a close relationship with class, being used by
twenty children in the working-class group and five in the middle-
class ($\chi^2 = 9.74$, $p < 0.01$).

Table 3.4 Orientation sub-categories

	(a) Role speech	(b) narrative	(c) meta-task	(d) scene-setting
MC	6	5	7	8
WC	9	20	7	8

Narrative: $\chi^2 = 9.74$, $p < 0.01$.

There were two possible ways in which the children could utilise
sub-categories (a), (b) and (d); sequences of role speech, narrative or
scene-setting could occur contained within the context of the chosen
mode, or the instructional mode could be abandoned as the child
moved exclusively into one of the sub-categories. Initially, the two
types were counted separately, but numbers obtained were very
small, and since combining the two varieties did not alter the pattern
of distribution it was felt that the subdivision was impractical. This
does not, of course, deny the importance of breakdown of mode,
which was analysed separately in part B of the orientation analysis.

Included in the second section was a brief examination of consistency in the way in which the subject referred to his participants,
although this was distinct from the more detailed analysis of reference
in the third part of the coding frame. An overall total, summed
across modes, showed that 52 children achieved consistent subject

Table 3.5   Consistent subject maintenance in total sample

MC	HIQ	G	8	WC	HIQ	G	6
MC	HIQ	B	9	WC	HIQ	B	6
MC	MIQ	G	10	WC	MIQ	G	3
MC	MIQ	B	7	WC	MIQ	B	3
			34				**18**

$\chi^2 = 7.3, p < 0.01$.

maintenance. Of these 34 were middle-class and 18 working-class, the difference being statistically significant ($\chi^2 = 7.3, p < 0.01$) (see Table 3.5).

Consistent subject maintenance was also examined in relation to each mode, although except for mode A the numbers achieved were too small to test statistically. In mode A consistency was counted as a proportion of the total number of children using the type (see Table 3.6), and although there were no differences between classes, indications in the previous table that high IQ children within the working class may be more successful at maintaining a consistent subject reference here reached significance ($\chi^2 = 6.1, p < 0.02$). IQ had little effect in the middle class.

Table 3.6   Consistent subject maintenance in children adopting mode A

MC	HIQ	G	7/12 ⎱ 14	WC	HIQ	G	4/6 ⎱ 10
MC	HIQ	B	7/12 ⎰ 24	WC	HIQ	B	6/10 ⎰ 16
MC	MIQ	G	8/12 ⎱ 12	WC	MIQ	G	2/9 ⎱ 3
MC	MIQ	B	4/10 ⎰ 22	WC	MIQ	B	1/9 ⎰ 18

Working-class/IQ. $\chi^2 = 6.1, p < 0.02$.

In a further sub-group, a count was taken of those children who adopted a single mode of instruction, i.e. without using narrative, role speech or scene-setting sequences. It was found that 51 middle-class children fell into this category and 39 working-class (a difference which suggested a trend but was not statistically significant). However, when the category was further limited by excluding subjects who did not achieve maintenance of a consistent subject the class difference reached significance beyond the 0.01 level (see Table 3.7). Again there was a slight trend towards an IQ difference within the working class, but the number of children involved was too small to reach significance.

Table 3.7   Adoption of single instructional mode, including maintenance of consistent subject

MC	HIQ	G	7	WC	HIQ	G	4
MC	HIQ	B	7	WC	HIQ	B	4
MC	MIQ	G	9	WC	MIQ	G	2
MC	MIQ	B	6	WC	MIQ	B	2
			29				12

$\chi^2 = 9\cdot2, p < 0\cdot01$.

The final part of this section of the analysis involved a count of those children who failed to maintain the mode they first adopted. At first counts made for each mode type gave very small numbers, and as these figures would also have had to be regarded as proportions of the total numbers using the mode it was decided again to collapse the mode-types distinction and give a total for all subjects (see Table 3.8). Among high-IQ middle-class children there were no examples of breakdown of mode, although there were four in the medium-IQ group. Four children in each of the working-class groups failed to maintain the mode chosen, giving a relationship with class significant beyond the 0·01 level ($\chi^2 = 8\cdot2, p < 0\cdot01$).

Table 3.8   Breakdown of mode

MC	HIQ	G	—	WC	HIQ	G	4
MC	HIQ	B	—	WC	HIQ	B	4
MC	MIQ	G	3	WC	MIQ	G	4
MC	MIQ	B	1	WC	MIQ	B	5
			4				17

$\chi^2 = 8\cdot2, p < 0\cdot01$.

In the section of the coding frame dealing with reference the initial count showed a significant relationship between the ability to maintain reference sets once initiated throughout the instruction and the middle-class groups ($\chi^2 = 6\cdot14, p < 0\cdot02$). Again there were no indications of IQ or sex influences (see Table 3.9).

The second general reference category of those children who gave the instruction within the confines of a single reference set was used by very few subjects, and a statistical test would not have proved worthwhile.

Table 3.9   Reference sets maintained through instruction

MC	HIQ	G	7	WC	HIQ	G	5
MC	HIQ	B	6	WC	HIQ	B	3
MC	MIQ	G	8	WC	MIQ	G	3
MC	MIQ	B	6	WC	MIQ	B	2
			27				13

$\chi^2 = 6.14, p < 0.02$.

Presence of role switch showed a strong association with class, the characteristic being associated mainly with working-class children (see Table 3.10). Twenty-seven working-class children gave instances of role switch in their instructions and only eight middle-class ($\chi^2 = 9.7, p < 0.01$).

Table 3.10   Presence of role switch

MC	HIQ	G	3	WC	HIQ	G	4
MC	HIQ	B	1	WC	HIQ	B	8
MC	MIQ	G	2	WC	MIQ	G	10
MC	MIQ	B	2	WC	MIQ	B	5
			8				27

$\chi^2 = 9.7, p < 0.01$.

In the sub-category of functionally defined subsidiary reference sets there was a high degree of variation in the number of users in each group, although this did not fall into a regular pattern (see Table 3.11). There was, however, a decided preference for the adoption of the category shown by middle-class children ($\chi^2 = 4.6$, $p < 0.05$).

Table 3.11   Secondary reference sets defined functionally

MC	HIQ	G	11	WC	HIQ	G	2
MC	HIQ	B	7	WC	HIQ	B	5
MC	MIQ	G	6	WC	MIQ	G	8
MC	MIQ	B	10	WC	MIQ	B	6
			34				21

$\chi^2 = 4.6, p < 0.05$.

Part B of this section of the analysis involved a study of the way in which the children set up their initial reference sets, the kinds of nouns or pronouns they applied to their imaginary players. The results of this analysis are given in full in Table 3.12. These are in some respects surprising, especially in the first group of categories which correspond with adoption of mode A. The initial 'functional definition' category was little used – only nine children out of the total sample – so that no statistical test was possible.

Table 3.12 *'One/one of'*

MC	HIQ	G	6	WC	HIQ	G	2
MC	HIQ	B	3	WC	HIQ	B	5
MC	MIQ	G	5	WC	MIQ	G	2
MC	MIQ	B	5	WC	MIQ	B	4
			19				**13**

Table 3.13 *'Someone/somebody'*

MC	HIQ	G	3	WC	HIQ	G	4
MC	HIQ	B	3	WC	HIQ	B	2
MC	MIQ	G	4	WC	MIQ	G	6
MC	MIQ	B	5	WC	MIQ	B	2
			15				**14**

The second and third categories 'one/one of' and 'someone/somebody' showed an even distribution through the factorial groups (Tables 3.12 and 3.13).

Table 3.14 *'Person/people'*

MC	HIQ	G	7	WC	HIQ	G	3
MC	HIQ	B	4	WC	HIQ	B	2
MC	MIQ	G	1	WC	MIQ	G	—
MC	MIQ	B	3	WC	MIQ	B	—
			15				**5**

IQ: $\chi^2 = 7 \cdot 2$, $p < 0 \cdot 01$.
Class: $\chi^2 = 4 \cdot 8$, $p < 0 \cdot 05$.

This, however, was not repeated in the fourth category of 'person/people' where both IQ and class influences were evident (Table 3.14). The IQ difference was more strongly marked within the working class, where the category was used by five children in the high IQ groups and none in the medium IQ group. The pattern was repeated, although less strikingly, in the middle class with eleven high-IQ children using 'person' or 'people' and four medium-IQ, giving a significant IQ difference over the two classes ($\chi^2 = 7\cdot2, p < 0\cdot01$). There was also a significant correlation between the use of the category and social class ($\chi^2 = 4\cdot8, p < 0\cdot05$).

Table 3.15   Third-person pronouns, exophoric reference

MC	HIQ	G	1	WC	HIQ	G	1
MC	HIQ	B	1	WC	HIQ	B	3
MC	MIQ	G	1	WC	MIQ	G	5
MC	MIQ	B	—	WC	MIQ	B	3
			3				12

$\chi^2 = 4\cdot8, p < 0\cdot05.$

Table 3.16   'You/I'

MC	HIQ	G	1	WC	HIQ	G	4
MC	HIQ	B	1	WC	HIQ	B	—
MC	MIQ	G	2	WC	MIQ	G	2
MC	MIQ	B	—	WC	MIQ	B	3
			4				9

Table 3.17   Other 'particular' definition

MC	HIQ	G	1	WC	HIQ	G	4
MC	HIQ	B	3	WC	HIQ	B	1
MC	MIQ	G	—	WC	MIQ	G	2
MC	MIQ	B	1	WC	MIQ	B	2
			5				9

Of the three 'particularistic' categories (see Tables 3.15–3.17) only one gave a statistically significant count.

The use of third-person exophoric pronouns in initial role definition, although not common, was largely restricted to working-class subjects, being used by twelve children in this group and only three in the middle-class group ($\chi^2 = 4\cdot8, p < 0\cdot05$). There was a trend within the working-class group for the category to be adopted more often by the medium IQ children although this was not significant.

Interesting class relationships were revealed when the first four 'universalistic' categories were collapsed. Fifty-three middle-class subjects gave examples drawn from one of these categories and forty working-class, giving a statistically significant correlation beyond the 0·02 level ($\chi^2 = 6\cdot1, p < 0\cdot02$). This pattern was mirrored in the adoption of items from the second group of categories – the 'particularistic' – by twenty-nine working-class subjects and only twelve middle-class. The association here proved to be significant beyond 0·01 ($\chi^2 = 9\cdot2, p < 0\cdot01$).

The final part of the coding frame involved the amount and type of mazing in each script. Significantly more working-class than middle-class children gave responses containing mazing ($\chi^2 = 10\cdot9, p < 0\cdot001$). An indication that more MIQ than HIQ children offer mazed speech proved to be non-significant (see Table 3.18).

Table 3.18 Presence of mazing: number of children

MC	HIQ	G	10	WC	HIQ	G	14
MC	HIQ	B	9	WC	HIQ	B	14
MC	MIQ	G	13	WC	MIQ	G	15
MC	MIQ	B	11	WC	MIQ	B	16
Total MC			43	Total WC			59

Whether or not a child used mazing was also related to the length of his answer. Thus of 18 WC and 10 MC children whose speech exceeded 110 words in length (a point determined by plotting a scattergram), only 2 children (1 MC and 1 WC) gave no instance of mazing.

Table 3.19 Presence of mazing related to length of script

	Long scripts	Average scripts	Total
MC	9/10	34/54	43/64
WC	17/18	42/46	59/64

As Table 3.19 indicates, the children least likely to give maze-free speech are MC children with average verbal output. While length of answer per se would appear strongly to influence the tendency to maze, this tendency is not independent of social class and, as will be seen below, is also associated with other aspects of the speech (see section on location of mazing).

Analyses of variance were carried out both on the total number of words mazed and on the number of occasions of mazing. In both cases, social class was an important variable ($F = 5.93, p < 0.05$; $F = 9.13, p < 0.05$ respectively) with WC children giving both more mazed words and more instances of mazing in their speech. However, since WC children tend to give longer answers (see Table 3.1), these results are compounded with verbal output. We know from Table 3.20 that mazing itself is compounded with length of response, but it is important to know also whether any one group of children gives a higher proportion of mazing than any other group or groups. A further analysis of variance was therefore made on the number of words mazed relative to the total number of words for each child. In this case there were no significant main effects but a class/sex interaction showing that WC boys maze more often than any other group ($F = 6.895, p < 0.01$).

Table 3.20 Location of mazing: numbers of children mazing at each stage

	Pre-stage	Inter-stage	Within-stage
MC	12	26	33
WC	25	45	33

Location of mazes within the scripts also gave some interesting figures. Table 3.20 shows the number of children in each social-class group who gave mazed speech at each of the three positions identified in the coding frame.

A difficulty arises in the analysis of these figures as to whether each category should be considered separately or as a subdivision of the supra-category 'mazing'. That is, do the categories have logically independent antecedents that happen to be realised in similar linguistic structures or is the similarity of the surface realisations of significant or even primary importance? It is impossible to give a definitive answer to this question, but there are both theoretical and empirical arguments which clarify the issue. Inter-stage mazing may be seen as related to the facility with which the child sequences his instructions, within-stage mazing may be seen as related to a conern with lexical and grammatical aspects of the text.

Corroborative evidence for the first proposition is fairly strong. Of 17 WC children who fail to maintain the mode, 14 give inter-stage mazing. Conversely, of 12 WC children who show maintenance of mode, and consistent subject maintenance, only 4 give inter-stage mazing. This difference is highly significant ($\chi^2 = 6\cdot95, p < 0\cdot01$). In the MC, only 4 children show breakdown of mode and 3 of these give inter-stage mazing, while only 12 of the 29 who maintain the mode with consistent subject maintenance do so. The MC figures may not be meaningfully subject to statistical analysis, but when the class distinction is collapsed we see that a comparison of those children who have most difficulty in structuring their answers with those who manifest least difficulty shows that children in the latter group are much less likely to show inter-stage mazing. These figures are summarised in Table 3.21.

Table 3.21   Mode maintenance and inter-stage mazing

	MC		WC		Total	
	Present	*Absent*	*Present*	*Absent*	*Present*	*Absent*
Breakdown	3	1	14	3	17	4
Maintenance and consistent subject maintenance	12	17	4	8	16	25

Further, there is an association between length of speech and breakdown of mode – 11 of the 17 WC children and all 4 of the MC children who fail to maintain the mode give long scripts. This association is highly significant in the WC ($p < 0\cdot01$) and significant in the sample as a whole.

There is thus a strong association between failure to maintain the mode, length of utterance and inter-stage mazing. This kind of mazing is one indication that the child is having difficulty in structuring his instructions and as such may be treated as a category on its own. Twenty-six MC and 45 WC children give inter-stage mazing, the difference being highly significant ($\chi^2 = 11\cdot4, p < 0\cdot001$). Independent of other factors, then, social-class membership influences the tendency to give structural mazes, and this may be seen as an additional indication that WC children are having greater difficulty in structuring their responses.

Pre-stage mazing was also originally supposed to be structural in nature but showed no association with any of the above variables; in fact, it is difficult to discriminate true pre-stage mazing from mazing within the first stage, and despite the significant class difference ($\chi^2 = 6\cdot4, p < 0\cdot02$) it would be unwarranted to draw any firm conclusion from the result.

The status of within-stage mazing is unclear. There is, for example, no inverse relationship with inter-stage mazing or breakdown of mode, such as might be expected if some children were sure of their organisation but concerned with its linguistic expression. Of the 43 MC children who maze, only 10 do *not* give intra-stage mazing, while of the 59 WC children who maze, 26 show no within-stage mazing (see Table 3.22).

Table 3.22   *Social class and intra-stage mazing*

	MC	*WC*
Intra-stage	33	33
Other forms of mazing	10	26
Total who maze	43	59

However, having argued for the independence of the inter-stage category it is hardly feasible to see within-stage mazing as a sub-category of mazing per se. We must therefore conclude that the meaning or cause of within-stage mazing is in some doubt and that social class appears not to influence its occurrence.

In the section devoted to the resolution of mazing, examination in terms of a resulting weakening or improvement in the text gave suggestive results, although it proved difficult to apply statistical tests. Numbers of children in each social-class group who showed any improvement as a result of mazing were very similar; 27 in the middle class and 32 in the working class, but there is again the confounding factor of the greater number of working-class children who mazed. If the proportion of actual mazes which result in improvement is considered the figures show that out of 112 total mazes in the middle class, 36 show improvement while the corresponding figures

Table 3.23   *Mazing resulting in improved text*

	No. of mazes	*Nos resulting in improvement*
MC	112	36 (proportion $= 0\cdot322$)
WC	198	46 (proportion $= 0\cdot232$)

for the working class are 198 and 46. Thus working-class children give a total of 86 more mazes than middle-class children and only 10 were improvements (see Table 3.23).

We would, however, be reluctant to base any strong arguments on such figures.

We turn now to the analysis of mazing types. Since many of these occurred only once in the speech of those children who used them, it was felt that, at least initially, χ^2 tests on presence and absence of each category were justified (see Tables 3.24a–e).

Table 3.24   Mazing types

(a) *Backtracking*

MC	HIQ	G	2		WC	HIQ	G	2
MC	HIQ	B	2		WC	HIQ	B	2
MC	MIQ	G	1		WC	MIQ	G	1
MC	MIQ	B	2		WC	MIQ	B	3
			7					8

(b) *Change in verbal group*

MC	HIQ	G	1		WC	HIQ	G	1
MC	HIQ	B	4		WC	HIQ	B	2
MC	MIQ	G	4		WC	MIQ	G	3
MC	MIQ	B	4		WC	MIQ	B	6
			13					12

IQ: HIQ = 8, MIQ = 17 ($\chi^2 = 3 \cdot 2$, $p < 0 \cdot 1$).

(c) *Semantic confusion*

MC	HIQ	G	2		WC	HIQ	G	6
MC	HIQ	B	4		WC	HIQ	B	4
MC	MIQ	G	2		WC	MIQ	G	5
MC	MIQ	B	2		WC	MIQ	B	7
			10					22

$\chi^2 = 5 \cdot 1$, $p < 0 \cdot 05$.

(d) *Hesitation/Repetition*

MC	HIQ	G	6	WC	HIQ	G	7
MC	HIQ	B	6	WC	HIQ	B	9
MC	MIQ	G	8	WC	MIQ	G	11
MC	MIQ	B	6	WC	MIQ	B	9
			26				36

$\chi^2 = 2 \cdot 7, p < 0 \cdot 1.$

(e) *Role definition*

MC	HIQ	G	7	WC	HIQ	G	6
MC	HIQ	B	3	WC	HIQ	B	9
MC	MIQ	G	6	WC	MIQ	G	9
MC	MIQ	B	6	WC	MIQ	B	8
			22				32

Not all categories showed significant differences, but in those which did class was the dominant influence. In category (a), 'backtracking', no differences at all were found, but in category (b), 'change in verbal group', there were indications of a part played by IQ, especially within the working class. Altogether seventeen medium-IQ children used this category, and only eight high-IQ ($\chi^2 = 3 \cdot 5, p < 0 \cdot 1$).

Category (c), 'semantic confusion', showed the strongest class influence and was used by more than twice as many working-class as middle-class, 22 in the former group and ten in the latter, giving a result significant beyond the 0·05 level ($\chi^2 = 5 \cdot 1, p < 0 \cdot 05$).

The 'hesitation/repetition' category was used by a large number of children from each group, but there was a strong trend towards greater use by the working class; 36 children from this group, compared with 26 middle-class children, made use of the category. A similar pattern was obtained from the final category, 'role definition', which was used by 22 middle-class children and 32 working-class, again giving a strong trend but again failing to reach significance.

Discussion

The speech context, though clearly defined in the interviewer's introduction, is undoubtedly one of the most difficult situations in the interview schedule, and it both demands and elicits the most complex linguistic structures from all groups of subjects. The fact that only four out of the 128 children in the study failed to give an answer relevant to the task instruction implies that the majority of the children are both familiar with instructional speech and able to manipulate it in an interview situation.

The major hypothesis put forward in the introduction was that differences in socialisation between the two class groups would result in differences in the way in which they conceptualised the demands of the task. It was expected that middle-class children would view the task as an opportunity to review the rules of hide and seek explicitly and with little reliance upon the conditions of the context – their approach would be universalistic. It was also predicted that working-class children would bring to their instructions characteristics peculiar to the situation and their approach would be embedded in the context.

The results do in fact show class to be the major determining factor in the choice of approach, or mode type adopted, and both modes A and B proved to be significantly related to class. Although mode A was by far the most popular method of approach, used by well over half the children in the sample, its association with the middle class was statistically significant, and this is emphasised by the strong reversal effect provided by the relationship of mode B with the working class. Tests on the distribution of these two categories also proved highly significant. However, when the E1 children were regarded separately the pattern of the distribution of their answers between modes A and B paralleled that of the middle-class children and not that of the children in their own social group. These children then were a disturbing influence on the normal working-class distribution and their exclusion reinforced the identification of mode type with class, increasing the association to the 0·001 level.

It would thus seem fair to conclude that the experimental language programme which these children received has altered the way in which they respond to the demands of the task. Eight out of the eleven children gave a response consistent with the universalistic, context-independent mode associated with the middle class, although their own social background was identical with that of the rest of the working-class sample. Yet if the analysis is regarded as having a dual approach – as both an examination of the children's approach to instructional speech and an evaluation of their ability to maintain it in a cohesive text – the limitations of the language intervention programme become clear. In spite of the strong identification with the middle-class orientation towards the context, in none of the evaluative categories either in this section or in the studies of mazing and reference did the E1 children behave differently from the rest of the working-class sample.

The conclusions concerning orientation of the children's speech are further strengthened by an examination of the sub-categories attached to mode type. Meta-task speech and scene-setting can be seen as additional ways of defining the context, and as such do not imply the use of a particularistic approach. The categories of role speech and narrative sequences, however, do relate instructional speech to the particular situation and they are used much more frequently by working- than middle-class children, although only the latter difference reaches statistical significance. In these categories the numbers of children involved were too small to allow the E1 children to be considered separately, but it is significant that only one child in this group gave any example of narrative speech. Again their orientation more closely resembles the middle than working class.

The result of the analysis of variance carried out on the total number of words in each script may also be relevant to the relationship of class with mode. This analysis showed that the main determining factor on the length of the text was the social-class rating of the child, and neither sex nor IQ had any appreciable influence. Since the middle class tend to use an objective mode, and also to say less than the working class, this suggests that a mode A approach to the instruction will be shorter. There is certainly no difference in the amount of information given as indexed by the number of stages relative to the different modes, and the differences in length must therefore be a function of the manner of instruction. Identification of length with method of approach is reinforced by the findings of the sub-categories above. These related the use of role-speech and narrative sequences, both of which would suggest a less constrained response to the task, to class influence and especially to a particularistic approach.

The second part of the orientation section of the analysis examines the competence of the children in maintaining and manipulating their chosen mode. All the evaluative categories in this section showed a strong association with class, and significantly the E1 children behaved in exactly the same way as the rest of the working class. Middle-class children proved better able to maintain a consistent subject throughout their instruction. Also, having defined the conditions in which they were operating – i.e. the mode type – they were more competent at remaining within those limitations and gave fewer examples of changes or breakdown of mode. Further, significantly more middle-class children maintained a single mode without the use of narrative, role-speech or scene-setting, while at the same time achieving consistency of subject.

Within the working-class groups there are indications of an IQ influence in some of the above categories, but except for one case these did not reach significance, and numbers involved were frequently too small for statistical analysis. In the light of other studies carried out in the SRU which also show IQ to be a more influential factor in the working-class score than in the middle-class, these results are interesting, but in the present context it is felt that no firm conclusion should be drawn from them.

The results of the orientation section indicate firmly that although many working-class children do aim at a mode A approach to the task, their approach relative to the middle class is more likely to be particularistic and context-dependent. Further, they are much less able than the middle class to manipulate instructional speech in a universal setting in the contexts of the interview. However, it is important not to confuse an assessment of efficiency of movement within the mode chosen with ability to manipulate the instructional context. For example, a child may attempt a universalistic mode, but does maintain it and move to a more particularistic approach in terms of mode and maintenance; his results would then show a lower score than a second child, who had adopted and maintained a particularistic mode. Ideally, in order to eliminate this possible source of ambiguity, the idea of mode type as an adopted sub-context could be developed further. Mode would then be regarded as a further variable, and each category examined in terms of mode as well as the other variables.

This is especially important in the evaluative categories, since the management of different modes presents a range of difficulties. Mode A is undoubtedly more difficult to manipulate than mode B, for example in the maintenance of reference sets. The participants in a mode A instruction are likely to have been defined by the use of universal nouns and pronouns, and maintenance of an explicit and consistent linguistic distinction between the roles in subsequent pronominal reference demands the manipulation of complex grammatical structures and anaphoric networks. In contrast, in a mode B approach some non-grammatical means of establishing the two necessary roles in the game can be employed, such as a definition in terms of sex – the boys hiding and the girls seeking – making later reference to the roles much simpler.

Some attempt was in fact made to examine results in relation to the mode used, by showing the numbers of children using a particular category in each mode as a proportion of the total number using the mode. However, this was rarely successful, since in many categories the number of users, when subdivided according to mode type, gave results too small to be important. The very small number of mode B users within the middle class was an additional complication. One proportional count which did prove possible was consistent subject maintenance within mode A, and Table 3.6 indicated that medium-IQ working-class children who moved to a context-independent mode are less likely to maintain this mode.

The next section of the coding frame relating to the construction and maintenance of reference networks was essentially designed as an indication of textual cohesion. Hasan identified two aspects of cohesion: external or situational cohesion and internal or linguistic cohesion (Hasan, 1968). The first of these, the 'context of situation', is given to the children in the interviewer's instructions. At its broadest level the context is the interview situation; within this the children are asked for instructional speech which is to be directed to an imaginary third person. The context then refers to all those extra-linguistic features which are responsible for fixing the language of a text. It is the establishment of the conditions for the realisation of a speech function. The way in which children respond to the context of situation results in groups of semantic and linguistic features characterising a speech variant.

The reference section of the analysis is concerned with the internal or linguistic aspects of cohesion. The situational criteria for the formation of a text have been defined for the child, and it is then his responsibility to shape his response into a structured and integrated piece of language. A collection of sentences elicited by a single context of situation will not necessarily form a text, internal linguistic features are also necessary to organise and integrate a succession of semantic units into a single body of speech. Such links may be grammatical, lexical – in the repetition of certain key words for example – or phonological, provided by intonation. The present study is concerned with the first of these, although it would also be possible to extend the coding frame to deal with other aspects of cohesion.

Hasan claims that 'the internal patterns of language are significant among other things because they embody, and impose structure on the speaker's experience of his environment; and conversely the linguistic patterns enable us to identify what features of the environment are relevant to, and thus enter into the "context of situation" of, linguistic behaviour'. Since middle-class children are more familiar with a form of structuring in the home which is similar to what is expected at school and their language shows a correspondingly high degree of control, ·their texts may be expected to show a more developed grasp of the notion of cohesion than the working-class texts in the context of the interview. If reference is accepted as an indicator of grammatical cohesion the results certainly confirm this.

The analysis of reference is concerned with the link provided by the way in which the child defines the role structure in his instruction and the consistency of his later pronominal reference to those roles. This was examined in terms of reference sets, since it was likely that most children would redefine the roles in the course of their instruction rather than maintain their original definitions only by pronominal reference.

The maintenance of reference sets throughout the instruction means that anaphoric reference to the original role definition must be clear and consistent, and that subsequent redefinition of roles is also consistent and does not result in 'role switch'. This was achieved by many more middle-class than working-class children, although the more universal mode adopted by most of the middle-class children made consistent reference much more complicated than it would be in the particularistic mode associated with the working class. One indication of inconsistency of reference is the presence of role switch, which as might be expected correlates highly with the working class.

A sub-category of the reference analysis deals with redefinition of roles, and is also relevant to orientation. Definition of secondary reference sets may be a repetition of the initial definition, especially in a particularistic instruction. For example, if primary role definition sets up the game with 'the boys' as hiders and 'the girls' as seekers, a secondary role definition could well be 'now it's the girls' turn to hide'. However, if the original definition speaks of 'someone hides' or 'some people have to look' redefinition must be more complex since a repetition of 'someone' will fail to make the role explicit. One way of doing this is to initiate a secondary reference set with a functional definition such as 'the one who finds him has to hide next'. This demands both long-term planning and structuring of the instruction and the handling of complicated linguistic construction, and is found very much more frequently among middle-class than working-class scripts.

The findings of the study of initial role definition are also relevant to orientation as well as to reference. Role definition is the way in which the child chooses to refer to the participants in his review of the game, and reflects his initial response to the context of situation. His focus is directed but not fixed by the interviewer's instruction and he can initiate his reference system in a number of different ways. Whichever way he chooses will be largely responsible for determining the mode type of his instruction. Thus the six categories identified for the purposes of the coding frame divide into two groups according to the mode type they suggest. The first four categories can be identified with a universalistic approach, although only one of these shows any significant relationship with class. The words 'person' or 'people' were used by significantly more middle-class than working-class children, but even more interesting is the association of this category with the high-IQ groups: of the twenty children who defined their participants in this way, sixteen were high IQ, eleven middle class and five working class. This result reflects the earlier study by Robinson of five-year-old children, in which he found that there was a strong relationship between his middle-class high-IQ group and the use of nouns as headwords as indicators of universality (Robinson, 1973). The tendency has now become more marked, and although still stronger among middle-class children it is also true of the working class. Significantly, among the latter group there were no examples of this category in the medium-IQ group.

Of the second group of categories the only one to show a statistically significant relationship with social class is the use of third-person pronoun with exophoric reference in role definition. Although not used by very many children, the category can be associated with the working class. This result is important because the use of exophoric third-person pronouns is a frequent characteristic of restricted speech variants, and in the present study there were a number of objections to making complete counts of exophoric pronouns throughout the texts.

In this instructional context identification of exophoric pronouns presents its own problems, since anaphoric and exophoric reference are not necessarily absolutes. In an extended reference set the network is complex, and it is possible for a pronominal head to rely both on the situation and on a distant linguistic referent for its meaning. When the links are thus attenuated definition of the kind of reference is difficult. This is particularly true of the present situation in which the cohesive element is especially important. The children have been given the opportunity to create their own texts and manage their own reference networks. A straight count of exophoric pronouns is here only likely to obscure inconsistencies in reference sets, such as role switch or inconsistent anaphoric reference. Children attempting to create a complex network of anaphoric reference in a universalistic setting are more likely to give examples of ambiguous reference than those who avoid the problem by the constant repetition of a generalised 'you'. In such a situation a hard classification of exophora would add nothing to the understanding of cohesive links or to the analysis.

The mazing section of the analysis may be regarded as giving additional information about the difficulties the child encounters in manipulating his context. A maze represents the inability of the child to give fluent linguistic expression to the meaning, it is a breakdown in semantic or linguistic planning. The degree of mazing, its location

and type, all explicate the extent and the kinds of problems encountered in the task. The initial count of presence or absence of
mazing in which 43 middle-class children gave examples compared
with 59 working-class provides strong grounds for concluding that
the working class are finding the task more demanding.

The association of mazing with length of script has many implications, one of which is to raise questions about the meaning of the
finding that working-class children tend to maze more frequently
than middle-class children. Since we suspect that this is not a simple
relationship whereby, on average, longer scripts lead to more mazing
but that there is some third factor which affects both mazing and
verbal production, then any attempt to 'control for' length must give
equivocal results. Such a frequency analysis was nevertheless carried
out and showed that, independently of length, working-class boys
give considerably more examples of mazing than any other group.
However, the numbers of children responsible for the mazes are no
greater than in any other working-class set. The reason for this sex
difference within the working class is not certain beyond the general
theoretical hypothesis that within the working class the speech
socialisation of girls is such that they have more experience with
some speech contexts than do boys. The instructional context may
be a significant one in this regard. There is, also, the question of the
sex of the interviewer (always female), a factor which has not been
examined as yet.

The analysis of location of mazing was treated in some detail in
the results section, where it was suggested that inter-stage mazing
could be seen as one component in a cluster that indexed difficulty
in structuring and sequencing speech. The tendency to give long
responses (often containing narrative or non-task speech), breakdown of the initially adopted mode and inter-stage mazing were
found to be interrelated in the sample as a whole.

Earlier studies have shown that both groups of children knew the
rules of the game and that the amount of information they communicate in their instruction is substantially the same. The presence
of the above features in a piece of instructional speech is not therefore
related to differential access to the material but must be a strong
indication of difficulty in the organisation of that material. The
results show that more working-class than middle-class children are
experiencing such a difficulty.

If it is possible to associate mazing with a failure of the planning
function then the present findings can be related to those of an earlier
study by P. R. Hawkins (1973) on pause location and hesitation
phenomena. Working again with seven-year-old children who were
on this occasion asked to tell a story, Hawkins demonstrated a

relationship between hesitation and clause and group structure. His results suggest that working-class boys spent a greater amount of time pausing at clause boundaries, whereas middle-class children used more of what he called the longest 'genuine' hesitation pause, many of which occurred within the clause.

If mazing and hesitation are accepted as evidence of where difficulties in planning occur and where most planning takes place then Hawkins's study gives some generality to the present suggestion that, at least in the interview setting, working-class children are less able than middle-class children to engage in long-term planning and structuring of material. His finding of a sex difference in the working class is consonant with the tendency of working-class boys to give more frequent mazing. It is readily seen that working-class girls rather than boys would have some experience with the narrative context, and we might speculate that while this could generalise to some extent to other contexts which demanded organisation of material, there would also be context-specific difficulties.

Our investigation does not, however, support Hawkins's suggestion that middle-class children more often engage in linguistic planning at the lexical/grammatical level. Nor does it oppose his conclusion. Rather, Hawkins's analysis argues for a more comprehensive study of such paralinguistic phenomena in all contexts in order to explicate the nature of within-stage/clause mazing in the speech and its social correlates.

The analysis of kinds of mazing gave one result which supports the identification of inter-stage planning and problems of structuring and the greater incidence of this in the working class. This group of children were more likely to use the 'semantic confusion' category than their middle-class counterparts. This type of mazing refers to complete breakdown in the organisation of material or information, and must of necessity occur at stage boundaries. In general, however, a greater amount of speech would be required before these categories could be fully explored.

The mazing analysis has three main findings. First, middle-class children are less likely than working-class children to show the phenomenon at all. Hawkins's analysis raises the question of whether planning activity in the middle class may typically have a different realisation – pausing, interjections such as 'mmm', etc. Second, working-class children were found to give more mazing which could reasonably be seen as generated by structural difficulties. And finally, such structural mazing was found to be associated with other indices of difficulty in organising the material. Hence we can give a fairly clear description of some of the surface realisations of problems in sequencing and structuring in instructional speech.

It remains to understand the origins of the structural difficulties which we suggest are at the root of mazed speech. The relatively formal nature of the interview context must have been important, but there is little evidence that working-class children were made more anxious than their middle-class peers. Indeed, the suggestion from other studies (Turner, 1973a; see also Bernstein, 1973b) is that it is the latter who are the more constrained. As has been emphasised throughout this paper, the interview setting is thought to be critical in the different communicative and cognitive orientations which it evokes in different children. This is not to discount motivational factors but to stress that the main source of variation lies, it is suggested, not here but in the children's varying sociolinguistic rule systems.

Concluding remarks

To summarise the results, it would seem that this instructional context evokes from the middle class an objective, universalistic orientation which they are able to maintain. They produce highly structured integrated texts with complex reference networks, and they are less likely than working-class children to show sequencing and structural mazes. Middle-class children are able to organise their information and to offer cohesive text in an experimental setting.

However, it is important that these results should not lead us to take a negative view of the working-class approach to the task. The context elicits from this group a far less homogeneous response – their answers are distributed more evenly through the mode types than in the middle class – but a typical working-class orientation is embedded in the situation and shows a particularistic approach to the problem. This means that a working-class child's instruction will be related directly to the conditions set out in the task instruction, but does not imply that it will convey any less information within those conditions. The working-class children are less able to maintain their orientation, and their mazing shows that they are less likely than the middle class to engage in long-term linguistic planning. This is also suggested by the reduced level of cohesion found in their texts.

The working-class children's response to the situation then can be seen as less highly structured and less formalised than that of the middle-class children. But because it is a freer and a less constrained approach, as we have already seen, the amount of information conveyed is not therefore any less. The imaginary child who is to be taught to play hide and seek does not need to be given a tightly structured, context-independent review of the rules to enable him to understand the game.

It is plain that two distinct responses to the demands of the situation have emerged from this analysis of the data, and that these responses can be associated with the social class of the speaker. In some of the evaluative categories, especially among the working class, there is some indication of an IQ influence, and there is one instance of a sex influence again in the working class, but social class is undoubtedly the major factor determining the type of approach to the demands of the context and the language used.

From these approaches, sets of semantic and linguistic characteristics can be identified as constituting the differing speech variants. As has been seen, the variants in this situation are strongly associated with the social class of the speaker. They should, however, be compared to the variants evoked by other contexts, since each set of linguistic characteristics is situation-specific and therefore unlikely to give us complete information about the code which generated them.

This paper has explored the nature of a particular language function – the instructional – in response to a particular eliciting context. From the study we have attempted a description of the characteristics of the elaborated and restricted variants generated. We might usefully identify the following sub-groups within the sample.

1 A group of children who are following a particular ground-rule in their interpretation of the context, i.e. children who adopt mode A.

2 A group of children who are following a similar ground-rule but who offer a different linguistic realisation, e.g. children who show less facility in mode maintenance or cohesion within a mode A approach.

3 A group of children who differ in their selection of the initial ground rule.

The final stage of the research will attempt to show the social antecedents of such variation, through an analysis of intra-class variation in types of families.

APPENDIX   CODING   GRID   AND   EXAMPLES

Orientation analysis

A. Mode type

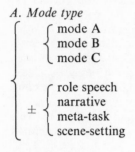

B

{ single mode maintained ± consistency of subject
  breakdown of mode

Examples

A. Orientation analysis

Mode A
(i) 'Well one person hides their eyes while the other person goes and hides and then when they're hidden themselves they shout out ready so the one who's hiding their eyes goes and finds them and when they've found them the person who was hiding hides their eyes and the other person goes and hides.'

Mode B
(ii) 'If you and your friend go behind the wall and me and my friend hide our eyes and when you're ready you say ready and we come and find you.'

Mode C
(iii) 'You hide your eyes the one who's on it then when we hide then when we say yes and ready you got to come and look for us, the first one to be found is out it . . .'

+ role speech
(iv) '. . . and he was looking to see where I'd gone and I said not that you have to hide your eyes and count up to ten and he said all right . . .'

narrative

(v) (continuation of example (iii))

'. . . and then he tries that and he forgot how to do it so we had to tell him again so we told him again and he kept on forgetting so this is the last time we told him then he forgot it so we never played hide and seek we played something else.'

meta-task

(speech addressed to the interviewer concerning the nature of the task).

(vi) 'I say it to you really' (Yes) 'You hide first . . .'

scene-setting

(vii) 'She says how do you play hide and seek and I tell her this is how you play it someone hides and the other people come and find you . . .'

B. Single mode maintained

+ subject consistency:

(see examples (i) and (ii))

− subject consistency:

(viii) 'You hide and they've got to find you when you've found *them* then *I* find *her*.'

Breakdown of mode

(ix) 'You hide and I've got to find you and if I find you I got to hide and you got to find me the boy closed his eyes and he went out in the kitchen and found him then I hided and he had to find me.'

(Abandonment of instructional mode and change to narrative.)

Reference

A

1 Reference sets maintained/non-maintained through instruction.
2 Instruction given using only one reference set.
3 Presence/absence of role switch.

(Number of scripts using 'functionally defined' secondary reference sets.)

B. *Role definition*

⎧ 1 Functional
⎪ 2 'one'/'one of'
⎨ 3 'someone'/'somebody'
⎩ 4 'person'/'people'

$\left\{\begin{array}{l} \text{5 3rd person pronoun with exophoric reference} \\ \text{6 'you'/'I'} \\ \text{7 (any other particular).} \end{array}\right.$

Examples

A. (1) *Reference set maintained*
(i) 'You have to cover your eyes and the others got to hide and you have to find them . . .' ('them' anaphoric reference to 'others').
Reference set non-maintained
(ii) 'One hide your eyes and the other three go and hide themselves when you say ready *the one who's hiding her eyes* has to go and find *you* . . .' (secondary reference sets defined inconsistently with role definition).

(2) *Instruction using one reference set only*
(iii) 'First one has to hide their eyes then the others go and find a place to hide then they have to look for them and when they find them they can change over.'

(3) *Presence of role switch*
(iv) 'One has to hide their eyes and the others have to hide and then when *she*'s got to have *them* . . .'

B. *Role definition*
(1) *Functional*
(v) 'Well there's *a girl who has to count* or *a boy who has to count* and you have to hide . . .'

(2) *'one'/'one of'*
(vi) 'Well *one* goes and hides and the other tried to find her.'

(3) *'someone'/'somebody'*
(vii) '. . . first *someone* goes to hide their eyes and then the other goes and hides.'

(4) *'Person'/'people'*
(viii) 'Well you say one *person* must hide and then the other *person* goes and hides . . .'

(5) *3rd person pronoun (exophoric)*
(ix) '*She's* got to hide her eyes while *they* run and hide . . .' (No referents given.)

(6) *'You'/'I'*
(x) 'You have to hide and when *I*'ve counted up to ten then I have to come and find you . . .'

(7) (*any other particular definition*)
(xi) '*If you and your friend* go behind the wall and *me and my friend* go and hide our eyes . . .'

Mazing

A
1 Number of children mazing
2 Number of words mazed
3 Number of occasions of mazing
  (a) number of occasions resulting in improvement (+ a move to greater specificity)
  (b) number of occasions resulting in weakening

B. *Location of mazing*
1 Pre-stage
2 Inter-stage
3 Within stage

C. *Type of mazing*
1 Backtracking
2 Change in verbal group
3 Semantic confusion
4 Hesitation/repetition
5 Redefinition of roles
  (a) correction of role switch
  (b) move to greater specificity

Examples

C. *Type of mazing*
  (1) *Backtracking*
(i) '. . . and then the people come along and try and find her and when they find her the person comes back with her *and then* to the other two people and then he has a go . . .' (Backtracking allows additional information to be added before the next information unit.)
  (2) *Change in verbal group*
(ii) '. . . then the person has to come *and have* and find you . . .'
  (3) *Semantic confusion*
(iii) '. . . *and/and then and he went* and he was looking to see where I'd gone.'
  (4) *Hesitation/repetition*
(iv) '. . . they may do it so you can stay in so you can stay in the game.'
  (5) *Redefinition of roles*
  (a) *correction of role switch*
(v) 'Well you've got to hide and I've got to go and find you and when I've found you *you've got to go and hide.* I've got to go and hide . . .'
  (b) *move to greater specificity*
(vi) 'first *you have to* one of you has to hide your eyes . . .'

Chapter 4   Code in Context

Diana Adlam and Geoffrey Turner

I   INTRODUCTION

A principal concern of the research reported in this volume has been the investigation of social-class differences in children's speech. In the preceding chapters it has been demonstrated that the general principle used by Bernstein to distinguish elaborated and restricted codes could generate contextually specific criteria to guide empirical analysis. These investigations showed that the children's speech, when understood as a realisation of orientation to code, was significantly related to the social class of their parents. WC children were much more likely to make restricted codings whereas MC children typically gave elaborated coding in the two contexts. However, the writers were at pains to point out the importance of comparing the speech of individual children across a range of situations. In order to infer orientation to code, it was stressed, we require information about a range of contextually specific codings. Drawing on the studies already reported, the present investigation looks at the speech of 180 children in a descriptive, an instructional and a control situation in order to test the hypothesis that children will be consistent in their coding orientation. Such a finding would suggest that the notion of a sociolinguistic code governing language use in a range of situations is a significant explanatory concept.

It should be immediately underlined that since code is defined as a general orientation to meaning and the form of its realisation, the prediction that children will be consistent in their contextually specific use of language is not self-evident. We are not asking, for example, whether the child who uses a high frequency of pronouns in the control task also does so in his instructional speech. Rather the central questions concern issues such as whether the child who makes explicit and specific descriptions of pictorial material also explains hide and seek in terms of a general rule system, both such responses being realisations of the semantic orientation of an

126

elaborated code. It is of course possible that both contexts (the descriptive and the instructional) will elicit, for example, a relatively frequent use of pronouns from one or another group of children. But the analysis does not begin from such features. Rather they are the speech (and therefore observable) indices of certain semantic choices. Any one speech characteristic may be relevant in one context and not in another, or it may be relevant in both but as an index in different semantic areas, or it may realise comparable semantic choices in both contexts. This is not to say that form and function are arbitrarily related, merely that the link between them is complex. The main point, as far as the present investigation is concerned, is that the contextually specific realisations of code need not be obviously related to one another at the level of lexical or grammatical choice. The central distinction in Turner's analysis is between control strategies which include information about what is being done or why it is being done and control strategies which are more exclusively concerned to direct, to encourage or to inhibit certain activities; the central distinction in Lineker's analysis is between children who explain the game of hide and seek in general terms and those who give a more context-dependent or particularistic instruction; and Adlam's analysis hinges on the notion that, at least in the context of an adult–child interaction, some children will give highly explicit and specific descriptions of picture postcards while others will be more inclined to make their descriptions verbally implicit. Nevertheless, all these analyses were carried out in terms of the children's *linguistic* constructions, the coding frames being derived directly and explicitly from the main theoretical distinctions. The lexical and grammatical features of speech that command attention differ considerably between contexts, and so the 'consistency' to which we alluded earlier refers to the underlying semantic and social orientation of the child, the key to which is his contextually specific speech.

The central aim of the investigation, then, is the empirical exploration of the notion that an underlying code governs language use in diverse situations; that a child's sociolinguistic code will point him towards, and in varying degrees, either a restricted or an elaborated coding of a wide range of communication situations. Nevertheless we do not expect all children to produce only restricted variants or only elaborated variants. Some children will do this, others may fluctuate in their approach. In any case, such a formulation implies discrete categories, whereas we are more often faced with data of a dimensional nature and a number of children will not be strongly oriented to either code. In general, however, it is expected that if a child offers a restricted variant in one context then he will tend to make restricted codings in other contexts also. Similarly, the child who is oriented to elaborated coding in one context will tend to offer elaborated variants in the other two contexts. The kind of result that would throw doubt on either the theoretical framework or the research methodology would be the finding of a considerable number of children who were strongly oriented to elaborated coding in two contexts and strongly oriented to restricted coding in the remaining situation.

It is clear that the analysis as outlined so far is to a degree independent of social class. The first question that will be put to the present data is not whether the child who gives restricted coding in context A is a working-class child but whether he also offers restricted coding in contexts B and C. Thus, for example, Lineker in Chapter 3 showed that a number of working-class children explained the game of hide and seek in a universalistic way. We are interested to know how these children respond in the descriptive and control tasks. Do they tend to give explicit descriptions of pictorial material; do they opt for more informative control strategies? Such questions demand that we look at the pattern of responses within social-class groups and attempt to establish how individual children respond.

However, our interest in the coding orientations of individual children as a means of throwing some light on what they are learning about communication and language use remains a part of the general question of social-class differences in code and in the structure of transmission. If our hypothesis that children will show consistency in their choice of either a restricted or an elaborated speech variant is confirmed then we expect also that the elaborated code will be typical of MC children, whereas WC children will be much more likely to employ the restricted code. In other words, we know that children differ in their contextually specific codings. The present analysis attempts to test the stronger statement that MC children have a *general* orientation to the selection of meanings and the form of their realisation that differs from the *general* orientation of many WC children. Should our findings conform to this thesis, one more question is raised. How do we account for those WC children who show a strong orientation to an elaborated code and also for those MC children whose codings are consistently restricted? This issue will not be explored empirically in the present paper but it is useful to anticipate future research.

In terms of Bernstein's thesis variation in coding orientation is causally linked to variation in the form of familial transmission. Previous work (Bernstein and Brandis, in Brandis and Henderson, 1970) has shown that there are indeed strong social-class differences in maternal patterns of communication and control. It is argued, then, that the crucial factor is not socio-economic status per se but the different transmission systems associated with MC and WC groups. It would therefore be expected that those WC children who are oriented to an elaborated code in the interview setting will have mothers whose patterns of communication and control are atypical for their group. And similarly with the mothers of those MC children whose coding orientation is restricted. A detailed analysis is currently in progress which is attempting to link variations in the children's sociolinguistic coding orientations with variations in the focus of familial communication and control and other demographic features of the family.

Characterising the children's speech

The present study, then, draws on the results of the two preceding chapters as well as on Turner's analysis of the regulative context. These investigations involved very detailed analysis of the children's speech but the present work is based on those features which theoretically and empirically appear as the most significant indices of coding orientation. Thus Adlam's original seventeen categories have been modified to yield five indices of descriptive speech; many of Lineker's more refined distinctions have been compressed, and six indices of instructional speech result.

The decision to operate with as few indices as possible is only partly a response to the need to keep data matrices to manageable proportions. More important was our conviction that the units of linguistic analysis should not be estranged from the social and semantic levels of investigation. The delicate linguistic distinctions had been important in showing where cruder divisions were sometimes masking important differences and also in suggesting modifications to the initial coding frames. But it was considered that for present purposes we were now in a position to build these distinctions into composite, harder indices. Thus, typically, four or five categories were constructed for each context and these in turn were used in order to arrive at a single, overall characterisation of the text of each child in each context.

This emphasis on textual description in sociolinguistic research has been recurrent in Bernstein's writings and in the authors represented in the present volume. The theoretical argument is presented in some detail in Chapter 1 (pp. 16–20). Its main thrust is that sociolinguistic research should not confine itself to lexical and grammatical frequency counts but should further use these to arrive at a theoretically relevant description of the text as a whole. The problem of operationalising this notion was not a simple one, neither do we pretend to have solved it. The chief difficulty, as will be seen below, is that a textual index is essentially qualitative but must, if it is to retain any degree of objectivity, be based on quantitative linguistic counts. The reader who has followed the argument in Chapter 1 will realise that an additive model is often quite inappropriate in constructing such a description. Eventually, however, a textual index was arrived at for each context, and so each is here described by four or five linguistic indices and an overall index, based on these and corresponding to the primary theoretical distinction.

The speech tasks

A word concerning the choice of speech tasks is appropriate at this point. In Chapter 1 this issue is the basis of extended discussion and so will merely be mentioned here. The tasks were chosen to represent three of the four socialising contexts which Bernstein has suggested are critical in familial transmission. The form of language use in the four generalised contexts called the regulative, the instructional, the interpersonal and the innovative is said to differ according to which code is dominant. Thus it is important to look at how subcultural differences in transmission in these four socialising contexts are reflected in the child's use of language in situations representing these contexts. Here we consider the child's orientation to language use in tasks designed to elicit instructional, regulative and descriptive speech.

Readers interested in more detailed explication of the notion of a generalised socialising context, as well as in the use of the interview situation as a vehicle for the investigation of coding orientation, are referred to Bernstein (1973b) and to Chapter 1 of this book.

Structure of the report

The report of this investigation falls into six sections. The first three are as follows: the descriptive context; the instructional context; the regulative context. In these three sections the coding frame used in the analysis of each context is described and the construction of a textual index is explicated in some detail. In these sections, too, social-class and sex differences are described and discussed, with particular emphasis on the relevance of these differences for the analyses which follow.

The second three sections of the report describe how the children's speech is related across contexts. In order to simplify the exposition the speech situations are treated in pairs as follows: description and instruction; control and description; control and instruction. There is a good deal of detailed discussion in these sections, and in order to avoid undue repetition the final section, entitled 'Evaluation', does not discuss the interrelationships of the three texts at length but rather attempts to draw out and summarise the main points from the preceding discussions. The relevance of the findings to the concepts of 'code' and 'context' is then suggested.

Subjects

The subjects for this analysis were chosen from those who had already participated in previous SRU investigations. Basically, two overlapping groups of subjects were available:
(1) those who had taken part in the descriptive and instructional analyses described in previous chapters of this book;
(2) those who had been used in Turner's inquiry.
We attempted as far as possible to amalgamate these two groups. Inevitably there were some gaps in the data and children had to be excluded for various reasons. We arrived at a sample of 170 children but, as is explained below, it was statistically impossible to include 3 of these children in the final analysis.

Of the children investigated 84 were MC and 87 (excluding the three mentioned above) were WC. The final sample had the composition shown in Figure 5.

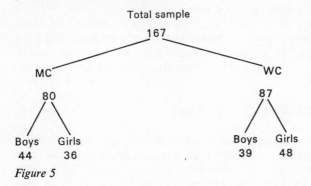

Figure 5

Statistics

In the light of the large sample we had analysed and the relatively large number of indices with which we were dealing, it was decided that the relationship between these indices should be examined using a correlational statistic. This posed many problems, since the distributions in some of the categories are extremely skewed. In some cases a category is not used at all by over three-quarters of the children. In others, a more nearly normal distribution is disturbed by the presence of one or two children who use a category far more frequently than any of the others. Clearly we could not make the necessary assumptions in order to use a parametric technique. It was decided that we use Kendall's Tau, which is a non-parametric correlational measure. This technique is much less strongly affected by skewed distributions although its use does not solve the problem completely.

We must admit to being less than satisfied with the statistical technique which we employed. However, to use more basically descriptive statistics was not feasible with such a large sample. We therefore decided to use Kendall's Tau, but with caution and referring back to the raw data in cases of extreme skewedness or where we were doubtful about the interpretation to be made from a pattern of results.

All the variables were inter-correlated for the sample as a whole and then separately for each social class sub-group. When it became apparent that sex differences were sometimes significant, four more matrices were run, viz. WC boys, WC girls, MC boys and MC girls. Not all of these results are reported in the main body of the paper. For example, in some parts of the analysis no significant sex difference emerged, and so the corresponding matrices are not printed in that section. However, all results that do not appear in the main body of the text may be found in Appendix 1.

Finally we should point out that this study is not using the correlational technique inductively. All the indices have been derived from theory and, working within a theoretical framework, it is possible to make quite firm predictions about how the results might be patterned.

II THE DESCRIPTIVE CONTEXT

In Chapter 2 Adlam reports an analysis of the speech of 128 children in response to a request to describe three detailed picture-postcard reproductions of work by the Belgian artist Hector Trotin. The linguistic indices used in the present study are based on the findings of that analysis. In addition these criteria form the basis of a textual description of the children's speech.

It was suggested in the original study that three broad approaches to the task of describing the pictures were distinguishable. One group of children, who on the whole were middle-class children, showed a strong orientation to context-independent speech; a second group, who were predominantly working class, were more oriented to a context-dependent description of the card; and a third group, who were almost exclusively working class, showed a tendency to move away from descriptive speech and use the pictures as springboards for 'narrative'. We may briefly describe these orientations, which are discussed at length in Chapter 2.

Context-independent speech may be described as speech that can be understood independently of the immediate setting that evokes it. The speaker makes very few assumptions about the listener's knowledge of the topic. Context-independence may be semantically based (Lineker, Chapter 3 and Section III below) but in the descriptive task the degree of context-independence is given more by the way in which meanings are realised than by variations in the meaning structure itself (the interdependence of these two levels is, of course, critical). Thus context-independent descriptive speech is explicit and highly specific, with a tendency to include more general statements where detail is not realised.

Context-dependent speech, by contrast, tends to implicitness in that more of the meaning is left embedded in the eliciting situation. The listener must have access to the picture postcard in order fully to retrieve the referents of the speech. Highly specific constructions are less common in the context-dependent descriptive variant and the child is less likely to provide more general or thematic statements about the content of the card. Some examples from the children's speech should help to elucidate the different orientations which these notions describe. Complete texts exemplifying the approaches may be found in Chapter 2.

The man in blue is pushing a trolley
he's pushing that

people are waiting for the train to go
she's waiting he is too

there are some flowers in a vase on top of the gate
that's one of those there

it's a street market picture
he's a seller

In making the distinction between context-independent and context-dependent descriptive speech, it was stressed that the child's actual utterances could be thus described only in terms of his understanding of the eliciting context and the orientation to meaning and speech which such an understanding includes. Thus it was argued that some children interpreted the task as calling for an explicit and accurate description of the card whereas others saw less need to explicate their meanings. It was further suggested that this difference in orientation leads to variations in what Hasan (1973) has called the text-wide semantic of the answer. For one set of children this difference was especially sharp since they used the setting to explore a rather different aspect of language use. These children offered narrative texts, and their basic orientation to the task was clearly very different from that of the children who framed their responses in descriptive speech. In discussing the speech of one such child (given in Chapter 2, p. 80) Adlam suggests:

> This child has moved into the narrative mode and never, in fact, gives a description as we would define it. Her speech devolves around her imagination and the card is relevant only in so far as it provides the protagonists, and a rudimentary basis for the action, of her story. Minimally, she has created her own linguistic context and thus gives a type of context-dependent speech rather different from that which we anticipated and described. For it is on the context as the child constructs it that our interpretation of his speech must depend and for some children this construction apparently diverges considerably from that of the researcher.

A principal aim of the present analysis is to construct a single index that will capture the degree of context-independence/depencence in the child's response. A separate index will represent the child's orientation to narrative. The index of text must, however, be based on the more detailed linguistic analysis described in Chapter 2. The speech offered in the descriptive context is too lengthy and unconstrained to allow us to 'read off' the basic orientations from the surface of the text. This is possible only in more tightly framed contexts such as Lineker examined. Our aim, then, is to synthesise the more micro categories (e.g. exophora, high specificity) into an index comparable with the one that Lineker managed to hold throughout her analysis.

The form of the analysis also permits us to make a more detailed empirical investigation of the notion that children do in fact differ in the kind of texts which they offer. We know that children vary in the extent to which they use the linguistic categories analysed in Chapter 2, and we have stressed that it is the pattern formed by their interrelationships rather than the incidence of any one feature individually that is important for the characterisation of a text as context-independent or context-dependent. But it has yet to be shown directly that these sub-indices are in fact patterned by speakers in a way which would permit a characterisation of their texts in context-independent/dependent terms. Indirect evidence exists. We know, for example, that one group of children make relatively frequent use of implicitness (exophora) and that these same children make relatively infrequent use of highly explicit constructions (indefinites and specificity). This has been shown by a comparison of means between the WC and MC groups. It is conceivable that such a comparison conceals large numbers of children who use as much (or as little) implicit as highly explicit realisations. In other words, it may be that the majority of children do not balance the two forms in the way we anticipate. It still has to be established directly that individual children who show a preference for the implicit forms will tend not to use the highly explicit forms; conversely, children who avoid the implicit forms must be shown to make relatively frequent use of the highly explicit categories.

Two aspects of the present analysis allow empirical investigation of this question. First, if individual children do not balance their linguistic usage according to the suggested context-independent/dependent patterns then we should have difficulty in constructing a textual index at all. Most children will be categorised as offering a 'mixed' text (see below). Second, and more stringently, the pattern of correlations between the linguistic indices will shed some light on whether, for example, measures of implicitness are negatively related to measures of explicitness in descriptive speech.

To some extent this investigation of the empirical validity of the concepts of context-independent and context-dependent descriptive texts can be seen as separate from, although embedded in, the wider analysis. The construction of the textual indices is critical to the question of consistency of coding orientation, but the relation of these indices to their components and of the components to each other is as much a continuation of Chapter 2 as it is a prelude to the main body of the present analysis. We say this in case the reader feels the main questions have been lost sight of in detail and digression. For those most interested in the children's responses across the different speech contexts, a reading of the final pages of this section will probably suffice. The analysis will comprise four sections, as follows.

1 The basic analysis and reduction of the original categories to yield three linguistic indices of the speech. Social-class differences in these indices.

2 The construction of a textual index based on these three sub-indices. Social-class factors in this analysis.

3 The inter-correlations of the sub-indices and the textual index in the descriptive context. Social-class and sex considerations in interpreting the correlations.

4 The role of narrative in the descriptive context.

(1)   The basic analysis

Coding categories

The descriptive speech of all the children was analysed according to the complete coding frame used in Chapter 2. Narrative speech was excluded from the analysis and merely coded for length. This constitutes a departure from the procedure followed in the original study, where narrative speech was analysed in the same way as descriptive speech. In this study narrative is considered separately in Section 4.

From the analysis of descriptive speech, categories representing critical features of context-independence and context-dependence were selected and combined to yield indices of exophora, indefinites and specificity. In the remainder of the paper, these will be referred to as the descriptive 'sub-indices' since they refer to aspects of the speech below the level of text.

(1a)   *A measure of exophora*
Exophoric pronouns and adverbs have their referents in the context of situation rather than in the linguistic context. All the pronouns and adverbs in the statement

he's kicking it down there

are exophoric so long as the statement has not been preceded by a statement such as

a boy is playing with his ball

in which case the referents of 'he' and 'it' in the first example may be retrieved from the previous utterance, whereas the referent of 'there' still needs recourse to the context of situation to be identified. Exophoric reference is a major way of implicitly realising meaning. Expressed as a proportion of the total number of headwords (roughly, nouns and pronouns), this index included the following components of the original coding frame: (a) exophoric third-person pronouns; (b) exophoric determiners and ordinators; (c) implicit location, i.e. exophoric adverbs of location.

(b)   *A measure of indefinite words*
This index is simply the number of indefinite words (e.g. someone, people, everything) expressed proportionally as above. The only modification from the corresponding category in the original coding frame is the inclusion of the initial pronoun in those statements identified as thematic in the original analysis, e.g.

it's a railway station
it's a wedding party

Indefinite words are the main means by which a child makes his description more general.

(c) *A measure of specificity*
This index, again expressed proportionally, included the following components of the original coding frame: (a) high specificity, location, e.g. the shop *on the other side of the street*; (b) high specificity, relation, e.g. the man *in the blue striped suit*; (c) high specificity, elaboration, e.g. grass *for the children to play on.*

The specificity index assesses the child's tendency to give highly detailed information about an object, person or event. Thus a statement such as

the shop on the street

is explicit but not highly specific. High-specificity constructions were relatively rare in the speech of most seven-year-olds.

Social-class differences on the descriptive sub-indices

Table 4.1 shows the average proportional use of exophora, indefinites and specificity for the total sample, the MC sample and the WC sample.

Table 4.1 Mean proportional use of the three linguistic sub-indices for the total sample, the MC sub-sample and the WC sub-sample

	Exophora	Indefinites	Specificity
Total sample	0·146	0·123	0·042
MC	0·111	0·153	0·054
WC	0·175	0·098	0·033

The social-class differences confirm those found in the initial study. We must note that, for all groups, more than two-thirds of the total speech is unaccounted for by these categories. This is consonant with the suggestion made in the initial study that all children give a great deal of basic descriptive speech in the form of unmodified nouns and simple verb constructions. Most of this 'core' speech is categorised as 'explicit, low specificity' and was omitted from this anslysis, since theoretically its contribution to relative context-independence is not great. What matters more is what the child does when he moves outside this core. Does the child move towards implicitness? Does he/ she move towards a higher level of generality? Does the child increase the level of specificity in his speech by the use of modifications and qualifications? These three features were chosen as the critical indices for the characterisation of texts, since their relative use appeared to be the major means of realising the two orientations to descriptive speech. Children from the two social-class groups differ in their use of these features in the predicted way. That the children do differ in this way causes some problems in the construction of the textual index and to this we now turn.

(2)   The textual index

The three indices described above were further combined to yield a characterisation of the text constructed by each child. A context-independent text, for example, would be one scoring low on the exophoric index and high on the indices of generality and specificity. The converse pattern would indicate a context-dependent text. However, these are only two of a possible eight configurations of the three measures, and all eight are set out in Table 4.2. A plus sign indicates an above-average score, a minus sign indicates a below-average score.

Table 4.2   Possible combinations of the three linguistic indices of descriptive speech

	Exophora	Indefinites	Specificity		
Context-dependent	+	—	—	(i)	1
	+	+	—	(ii)	2
	+	—	+	(iii)	2
	+	+	+	(iv)	3
	—	—	—	(v)	3
	—	+	—	(vi)	4
Context-independent	—	—	+	(vii)	4
	—	+	+	(viii)	5

It is of course expected that the three indices will not be unrelated and that therefore few children will fall in categories (iv) and (v). We would, however, expect quite a number of children to fall in categories (ii), (iii), (vi) and (vii). In terms of speech, what sort of texts do these patterns describe? The combination —exophora, +indefinite, —specificity may serve as an example. This was a fairly frequent configuration among middle-class girls, who tended to give very short, constrained responses with practically no exophoric reference, a number of thematic as well as general statements and very little detailed realisations. An example of such a response follows:

it's a train station
people are waiting for the train
some people are standing
other ones are sitting on the seat
smoke is coming out of the chimney
a café is there

This child is quite explicit but never raises the level of specificity in her description. It is apparent that this response is still context-independent just as it was apparent in the original study that the child cited on p. 80 was constructing a relatively context-dependent text, despite a comparatively high incidence of specificity. This, then, is the main problem in assigning children to groups. It remains necessary to arrive at explicit criteria for so doing.

Our first attempt at a solution consisted in constructing a five-point scale as shown in Table 4.2. This presupposes that a child who satisfies all the criteria for context-independence is necessarily more strongly oriented to such speech than is a child who meets only two criteria. And similarly with context-dependence. Intuitively, this was unsatisfactory. Other factors besides coding orientation contribute to the index configuration of any child, and it was clear to us that one such significant factor was sheer length of utterance. This in turn appeared to be a function of the degree of constraint felt by the child (cf. Bernstein, 1973b; Turner, 1973a).

It was therefore decided that only a three-category index be constructed (context-independent, context-dependent and mixed). Thus any child who satisfied two criteria for allocation to one of the extreme groups was allocated to that group provided that his score on at least one of the relevant indices was 0·5 of a standard deviation away from the sample mean. Thus all children originally assigned to group 1 remain in this group. Some children in the original group 2 are re-allocated to group 1 (i.e. context-independent), while others join the mixed group, etc.

This method of allocation is not without difficulties, the most important of which concerns the social-class differences on the linguistic sub-indices shown in Table 4.1. The system is clearly a relative one – children are assigned to groups on the basis of how they speak relative to the others in the sample, i.e. relative to the group means. If the children are scored in terms of the total sample, then it is likely that most of the context-independent group will be middle class and most of the context-dependent group will be working class. Children were allocated on this basis, however, and Table 4.3

confirms that a child's orientation to context-independent speech relative to the total sample is very strongly related to the social class of that child.

Table 4.3   No. of children in each sample classified as giving context-independent, mixed and context-dependent texts when the total sample means are used as the basis for allocation

	Context-independent	Mixed	Context-dependent
Total sample	56	60	51
MC	43	32	5
WC	13	28	46

In view of our interest in variation within social-class groups as well as between them, this raises some difficulties. The middle-class group, being more homogeneous in their orientation to language use in the descriptive task, are especially difficult to investigate as to the cross-context response of individual children. It was therefore decided to score each child twice. First, as above, in relation to the total sample means and secondly in relation to the mean scores of their own social-class groups. Table 4.4 shows that when children are classified according to the mean sub-index scores of their *own social group*, a more even distribution results.

Table 4.4   No. of children in each sub-sample classified as giving context-independent, mixed and context-dependent texts when the sub-sample means are used as a basis for allocation

	Context-independent	Mixed	Context-dependent
MC	28	41	11
WC	27	31	29

To summarise the investigation so far, we can underline the following points:
1   There are large social-class differences in all three sub-indices.
2   Thus most MC children are found at the context-independent end of the total sample textual index and very few MC children are found at the context-dependent end. The distribution in the WC sample is the converse of this, but is rather more even

3   The two class-specific textual indices allocate children more evenly across the categories, although in the MC there is still a skew
towards the context-independent end. This raises the question of
whether the allocation of children on a relative basis is always
appropriate. Specifically it must be asked whether the notion of
relative context-dependence can be maintained within a group of
children who use implicit realisations as infrequently and explicit
realisations as frequently as the present MC sample. It is likely that
the large majority of these children are oriented to context-independent speech (as conceived in Bernstein's theoretical writings) and
that the variation in their language use will be in terms of different
ways of realising this common orientation.

Notwithstanding these reservations concerning the MC sample,
the fact that approximately two-thirds of the children can be characterised as showing either a context-independent or a context-dependent orientation provides some support for the empirical validity of
the concepts. A more stringent test is to examine the inter-correlations of the sub-indices and the textual indices described above. Such
an analysis, carried out for the total sample, the two social-class sub-
samples and the two sex groups within each social-class sub-sample,
is described in the next section.

(3)   The inter-relationship of the sub-indices and textual indices in the descriptive context

In this section we shall investigate more directly the hypotheses that
children who offer a relatively high proportion of implicit realisations
(exophora) will tend to avoid more explicit realisations and will therefore create a context-dependent text: children oriented to context-
independent speech will show the converse patterning of sub-indices.
More specifically, we expect the following pattern of correlations
between the sub-indices: a negative correlation between exophora
and indefinites: a negative correlation between exophora and
specificity: a positive correlation between indefinites and specificity.

Precisely because our central concern is with the patterning of these
sub-indices, however, the correlations are not expected to be very
strong. As was shown in the coding frame, it is the way these three
indices pattern together rather than the proportional use of any one
of them that determines the allocation of a text to the general categories. In computing a correlation coefficient, however, only nu-
merical value is important, and so we can expect only relatively weak
correlations between any two of these indices.[1] The following predictions are more strongly asserted: a positive association between

exophora and the textual indices (N.B. a high score on the textual index denotes a context-dependent text); a negative association between indefinites and the textual indices; a negative association between specificity and the textual indices. These relationships are, of course, partly induced by the method of construction of the textual indices. Further, since we know that the majority of children were clearly identifiable as oriented to either context-independent or context-dependent speech, partial confirmation of these hypotheses already exists. Had most of the children been classified as 'mixed' in orientation then the hypothesis of differential orientations to context-independent speech would have been seriously questioned. Since we already have evidence that the theoretical categories do indeed have counterparts in the speech of children, the correlations involving the textual indices are more of a check that a critical test.

Findings

Table 4.5 shows the pattern of relationships between the descriptive indices for the total sample. In the total sample matrix all the predicted relationships appear and all except one are significant at the 0·001 level. The association between indefinites and specificity is significant at the 0·05 level. The strongest correlations obtain between the sub-indices and the index of text. These correlations are

Table 4.5   Tau coefficients between the descriptive indices for the total sample

	Exophora	Indefinites	Specificity	Text
Exophora		−0·152***	−0·161***	0·480***
Indefinites			0·094*	−0·561***
Specificity				0·323***
Text				

consonant with the notion that there are two broad approaches to this descriptive task: a context-independent approach which yields a text low on exophora (implicitness) and high on indefinite statements and highly specific statements (explicitness), and a context-dependent approach which yields a text that relies more heavily on implicit than highly explicit description.

We shall now give the pattern of relationships within the WC group and within the MC group. Table 4.6 shows that the pattern of correlations in the WC sub-sample is very much a reflection of that

Table 4.6   Tau coefficients between the descriptive indices for the WC sub-sample

	Exophora	Indefinites	Specificity	Text
Exophora		−0·118*	−0·114*	0·516***
Indefinites			0·138*	−0·532***
Specificity				−0·281***

found in the total sample matrix. Highly significant relationships obtain between the general index and the linguistic sub-indices, and the associations between the three linguistic sub-indices are all as predicted although the significance levels are on the whole lower than is the case for the total sample matrix. Overall the results suggest that the dimension of context-independence/dependence has a validity in this sub-sample. WC children are differentially oriented to context-independent speech in the descriptive task.

The WC sub-sample was split by sex to see if any strong differences emerged. The results of this analysis may be found in Appendix 1. The boys and girls separately considered very much reflect the total sample pattern except that the positive correlation between indefinites and specificity is very strong for the boys and weak for the girls. Thus boys may be clearer in their orientation than girls. This may be because of the tendency of a group of WC girls to move to narrative, and will be discussed in the next section.

Table 4.7   Tau coefficients between the descriptive indices for the MC sub-sample

	Exophora	Indefinites	Specificity	Text
Exophora		−0·154*	−0·066	0·419***
Indefinites			−0·154*	−0·517***
Specificity				−0·131*
Text				

In the MC sub-sample only three of our six predictions are confirmed and one rather puzzling result emerges (Table 4.7). As expected, there is a highly significantly positive correlation between exophora and the general index and a highly significantly negative correlation between indefinites and the general index. Further, the correlation between indefinites and exophora is negative and significant. However, the expected negative correlation between specificity

and exophora does not reach significance and the negative association between specificity and the general index is only weakly significant. The truly puzzling correlation is that between indefinites and
specificity. Instead of being positively associated, as was predicted
and found both in the total sample and in the WC sub-sample, these
two linguistic indices correlate negatively. How might this result be
interpreted?

It is likely that we are here faced with empirical evidence that the
decision to characterise texts in relative terms was not wholly appropriate. For whilst it is the case that MC children do vary in their proportional use of exophora, indefinites and specificity in the Trotin
task, it may also be the case that they are, as a group, rather homogeneous in their orientation to context-independent speech. Such an
assertion has a ring of paradox and so demands expansion.

In coding the data as we did, and particularly in the construction
of the textual indices, we were making a basic assumption. This is
that the main source of variation in the speech of the children is in
terms of their orientation to context-independent speech, and that
this dimension will usefully discriminate texts. In terms of the total
sample and the WC sub-sample, the correlation matrices provide
rather strong support for this assumption. But it appears that the
distinction has less validity in the MC sub-group. We suggest that
this is because practically all MC children are oriented to context-
independent speech in this situation and that children in this group
vary principally in the *kind* of context-independent text which they
construct. Specifically it is suggested that some children will make
very general descriptions, some will make very explicit and detailed
descriptions and some will construct texts including both general and
detailed information. All will tend to avoid implicitness. If this is
the case then our attempt to categorise MC children in terms of
relative context-dependence was not appropriate. We shall now consider in some detail whether in the case of the MC group the variation between the children is in terms of different ways of realising a
context-independent text. A number of findings throw light on the
matter.

First, the negative correlation between indefinites and specificity
suggests the distinction between general and detailed descriptions.[2]
Second, when children's texts were classified according to mean
scores based upon the total sample, this produced a very uneven
distribution of types of texts within the MC. Only 5 MC children
were classified as creating context-dependent texts, whereas 13 WC
children were classified as producing context-independent texts. If it
is accepted that the total sample textual index more nearly corresponds to an absolute index (such as might be constructed had we a

very large sample on which to establish criteria) then there is little variation in orientation to context-independent speech in the MC, whereas the variation in the WC is greater. Even when the children are allocated relative to their own social group, only a small number of MC children are classified as context-dependent; instead, the number of children in the 'mixed' group is increased.

A third finding consonant with the notion that MC children vary principally in the kind of context-independent text which they construct concerns social-class differences in the use of the sub-indices. If most MC children are oriented to context-independent speech then they should be very low on implicitness. The mean score of the MC group on the exophoric index is 0·111 (i.e. 1 exophoric word in every 10 headwords) and in fact there exists a skew towards low scores, as

Table 4.8   Number of MC children giving each of five proportional uses of exophora

	> 0·05	0·05 — 0·100	0·100 — 0·150	0·150 — 0·200	< 0·200
Number of children	26	22	10	9	13

Table 4.8 shows. Thus approximately two-thirds of the MC sample realise implicitly less than 1 in 10 of their headwords. Since the average number of headwords per child is around 60, we are talking about whether the child gives 1, 2, 3 or 4 instances of exophora. Such variation contributes little to an increase or decrease in the context-independence of the text. Such children may vary along this dimension by increasing their use of indefinites and specificity. *We suggest, however, that the frequency and patterning of these two variables will principally contribute to the kind of context-independent text which the children create.*

Separate matrices were run for MC boys and MC girls. No strong pattern of differences emerged, but the negative correlation between indefinites and specificity is stronger for girls than for boys. This may reflect the tendency of some girls to give constrained general texts, as was discussed above. The results may be found in Appendix 1.

Conclusion

The pattern of relationships found in the total sample matrix and the WC sub-sample matrix provide rather strong support for the notion that the texts children offer in the descriptive task may be differentiated in terms of relative context-independence/dependence. The sample as a whole and the WC children as a separate group may meaningfully be said to differ in the extent of their orientation to context-independent descriptive speech.

In the MC sample we have argued and shown that the majority of children are oriented towards producing a context-independent text. It is not suggested that MC children do not differ at all in the extent to which they make their descriptions context-independent but that variation on this dimension is greatly reduced. Far more important, according to the data presented above, is variation in the *kind* of context-independent text created by MC children. The problem, of course, is that the general index was constructed specifically to handle only the theoretical dimension which we assumed would predominate in all groups; that of relative context-dependence. Because of our central concern with the context-independent/dependent dimension, we robbed ourselves of the opportunity to discriminate different ways whereby context-independent texts are produced. Thus in the case of the MC children the indefinite index may tell us something about children who approached the task with a highly general perspective, whereas the specificity index may tell us something about children who approached the same task from a perspective which created very detailed analytic description. However, since some children include both kinds of information in their speech such inferences must be treated very cautiously.

(4) Narrative speech

The number of headwords (i.e. nouns and pronouns) realised in narrative speech was counted for each child and excluded from the analysis to which descriptive speech was subject. Any statements going beyond what was given in the card were counted as narrative and four proportional categories were established as follows:
(1) no narrative speech whatever;
(2) two or three statements of a hypothetical nature;
(3) more than minimal narrative but less than half of the speech realised in this mode;
(4) at least half of the speech realised in the narrative mode.

Category (4) accounts for most of those children who wove complete imaginative stories around a card. One-half was chosen as the cut-off point for this category because three cards were given to the children and any child who gave more than half of his speech as narrative tended to have used at least one card as a basis for storytelling.

It should be noted that very few children gave *only* narrative speech since practically all began with two or three statements about the contents of the cards and then began their imaginings from these statements. These first few utterances were subject to the descriptive coding frame. Thus, almost all children (only three WC girls are exempt) are included in the analysis of non-narrative descriptive speech.

Table 4.9   Number of children in each social-class group using each of the four degrees of narrative

	1 (*no narrative*)	2	3	4 (*maximal narrative*)
MC	64	10	5	1
WC	45	13	9	23[3]

Table 4.9 shows the numbers of children in each social-class group using each of the four categories.

Thus more than three-quarters of the MC sample use no narrative speech at all. Further, since level 2 represents less than ten headwords of such speech, only 7 MC children can be described as adopting a story-telling mode in this task. These results reflect the finding in the original study that very few MC children show a move to narrative. With a distribution as uneven as this, we can conclude very little about how MC children who have moved to narrative respond in other contexts. Any correlation is bound to be extremely unreliable. For this reason we shall not discuss such relationships for the MC sub-sample. The correlations were run, however, and may be found in Appendix 1.

The use of narrative in the WC sub-sample is sufficiently evenly balanced to allow consideration of the relation between the use of narrative in this context and other modes of language use both in this and the other tasks. Before investigating the relation of narrative to other indices in the descriptive context we should take note of the marked sex difference found in the original study. In Chapter 2 it was shown that far more girls than boys were oriented to narrative. Is this the case for the present sample also? Table 4.10 presents the results.

It is clear, then, that an orientation to narrative speech is much more marked amongst WC girls than amongst any other group. For this reason discussion about the meaning of narrative will be largely confined to this group of children. We turn now to an examination of the relationship between narrative and the various measures of

Table 4.10   Narrative usage by WC boys and girls

	1	2	3	4
Boys	22	6	7	4
Girls	23	7	2	19

descriptive speech used in this context. As noted above, the enquiry is restricted to the WC sample, with particular emphasis on the speech of the girls.

Expectations

In the original study of the children's responses to the Trotin cards, it was suggested that those children who introduced narrative speech were offering a context-dependent variant that depended on the child's constructing a different context which then provided the frame for his or her speech. We might then expect that such a child will also be context-dependent (i.e. implicit) in his purely descriptive speech. One possibility militates against such a prediction being confirmed within the Trotin analysis. If these two variants of a context-dependent orientation to description are distinct (i.e. implicit speech within the frame of the interviewer's probes and narrative speech that constructs a different frame) then if a child is strongly oriented to one of them, she may avoid the other. The children most strongly oriented to narrative will give very little straight description (three of them give absolutely none) and those children who show a strong preference for implicit description may give no narrative at all. What we do expect is that if a child is strongly oriented to context-independent speech then he will avoid narrative. But it may be necessary to look at the correlations of narrative in description with the measures of context-dependence in other contexts in order to investigate more reliably the hypothesis that the use of narrative in the Trotin task realises a context-dependent orientation.

With these reservations in mind, a relationship is expected between context-dependent description and the introduction of narrative in the Trotin task.

Findings

Table 4.11 gives the correlations for the total WC sub-sample and the sex-specific sub-samples between the narrative index and the indices of descriptive speech.

Table 4.11 Correlations between the narrative index and the descriptive indices in the Trotin task for the WC sample

	Total WC sample	Boys	Girls
Exophora	0·252***	0·195*	0·293*
Indefinites	0·034	0·227*	0·116
Specificity	0·208**	0·369***	0·081
Text	0·080	−0·027	0·124

The pattern of relationships shown by the girls provides some support for our hypotheses. Narrative shows a significant positive correlation with exophora, and the correlations with indefinites and the textual index are in the expected direction. Narrative is thus associated with a high degree of *implicitness* but is not so strongly associated with low scores on the measures of *explicitness*.

In the sub-sample of boys narrative correlates positively with all the indices and particularly strongly with specificity. These relationships are reflected in the pattern of relationships revealed in the total WC sample. Since so few children are involved these correlations are likely to be very volatile and so will not be discussed further.

The pattern of relationships shown by the girls is not strong enough definitively to support the idea that children who give narrative also give context-dependent descriptions. Do these correlations obscure a substantial number of WC children who offer relatively context-independent descriptive speech and then introduce long stretches of narrative? The correlation with exophora denies this, but the possibility directly contradicts our predictions and so demands careful investigation. We look first at how children moving to the two strongest levels of narrative fall on the general indices of context-independence/dependence. This information is presented in Tables 4.12 and 4.13.

Table 4.12 The textual descriptive index (total sample) and narrative for WC girls

	Maximum narrative (4)	Intermediate narrative (3)	Others (1, 2)
Context-independent	0	0	6
Mixed	3	1	12
Context-dependent	10	2	13

Table 4.13 The textual descriptive index (WC) and narrative for WC girls

	Maximum narrative (4)	Intermediate narrative (3)	Others (1, 2)
Context-independent	1	0	11
Mixed	5	2	9
Context-dependent	7	1	11

The clearest thing to emerge from these tables is that if a child moves to narrative then her descriptive speech is very unlikely to be context-independent. This is true whether texts are categorised relative to the total sample or the WC sub-sample itself. When the sub-sample means are used as the basis of categorisation, however, it is clear that those children who introduce narrative are just as likely to be mixed as to be strongly context-dependent in their purely descriptive speech. Thus the situation anticipated above has arisen; many of the children most strongly oriented to context-dependent descriptive speech (boys as well as girls) tend not to move to narrative.

In conclusion, the results reported above show that those children, predominantly girls, who move to narrative in the Trotin task tend to implicitness in their descriptive speech. This finding lends support to the notion that narrative is a form of context-dependence that relies on a subjectively constructed context for its production and comprehension. When the children who move to narrative are seen in terms of their own social group, the results also suggest that there is a distinction to be drawn between the orientation that is realised in narrative and that which leads to the construction of a highly implicit text within the frame of the interviewer's probes. The data presented above also show quite clearly that both these orientations are distinct from that which is realised in context-independent speech.

Summary

The analysis of the kinds of texts produced by children when asked to describe the Trotin cards suggests that the dimension of context-independence/dependence discriminates well between children but that there are some further important differences. It seems likely that the majority of MC children show a context-independent orientation and that within that group the chief variation lies in the *way* this orientation is realised. Some children construct general texts, others move towards detail and some include both kinds of information in their response.

Within the WC group, three orientations are identifiable: one group of children, relatively small in number, oriented to context-independent speech, a larger group oriented to context-dependent speech and cutting across the latter but also somewhat separate from it, a group of children who move towards narrative speech in the formal interview context.

It has yet to be suggested exactly why those children who move to narrative are in some respects different in their purely descriptive speech from those children who do not. But precisely because the two forms of context-dependence are assumed to realise distinct sociolinguistic orientations it will be useful to look outside the Trotin task to how the two groups of children respond in other contexts in order better to understand how they differ. We might also reiterate that despite the differences found here it is still the case that these two groups have far more in common with each other than either does with the group of children who are oriented to context-independent speech in the Trotin task. This is the case whether the total sample or the WC sub-sample is taken as the basis for comparison.

Summary of indices constructed for the Trotin task

The following indices, described in detail above, describe the speech of children in the Trotin task and will be used in subsequent analyses to investigate the question of consistency of coding orientation. It should be remembered that considerable social-class differences exist in all these measures.

Exophora indicates the frequency of implicit realisations used in the text.
Indefinites indicates the frequency of general realisations used in the text.
Specificity indicates the extent to which the child makes very detailed realisations.
Textual index: an overall index, based on the above three indices, to indicate the extent to which the child is oriented to context-independent or context-dependent speech. The index is a relative one and each child is scored twice, once in relation to the total sample and once in relation to his social-class sub-group.
Narrative indicates the extent to which the child moves to the narrative mode. Since very few MC children do this, only the data for WC children will be discussed in the main body of the text.

III THE INSTRUCTIONAL CONTEXT

Of the three investigations on which the present inquiry is based, Lesley Lineker's analysis of the instructional context requires the least procedural modifications in order to yield a small number of critical indices that will describe the children's speech according to socially relevant distinctions. In this case, the children were asked to explain the game of hide and seek to a hypothetical listener who is ignorant of the rules. Lineker distinguished three broad approaches to this task and her classification is here retained unchanged. This part of Lineker's analysis is significant in that the linguistic analysis remains firmly grounded in the sociological level of inquiry. Thus the problem of 'reconstructing' a textual from a lexical or grammatical analysis is minimal. This was made possible partly because the context for the instruction put heavy restraints on what could be realised. Explaining a specific game is a more strongly bounded activity than describing a picture. It is also the case, however, that the classification in terms of orientation resulted from a conscious attempt not to attenuate the relationship between the social, the semantic and the lexico-grammatical levels of analysis. For these reasons we consider this context to be of special significance.

Lineker did in fact carry out some more detailed linguistic analyses, and these are used as the basis for two further categories included in the present study. These categories describe the extent to which the child managed to maintain his initially adopted instructional mode, and therefore entail an analysis of reference and cohesion. The child's use of narrative in the instructional context was also considered in the original study.

Thus the indices in the instructional context fall into three groups: those describing the child's basic orientation to explanation, those concerning mode maintenance and cohesion and, finally, those concerning the index of narrative. We shall consider each set of indices in turn and will report how MC and WC children vary in their use of the options described. A separate section will deal with the inter-relationships of indices within the instructional context.

(1)   The orientation indices

The three approaches to instruction identified by Lineker are described at length in Chapter 3. They may be summarised as follows.

(1) *Mode A*
Ideally, this approach to the explanation of hide and seek is a realisation in the instructional context of Bernstein's notion of 'universalistic' meaning. The child selects and organises his meanings in terms of general rules which would apply to any instance of the game. In terms of lexes and grammar the approach is characterised by the use

of universal nouns and pronouns and, particularly if the mode is maintained throughout the instruction (see category 5), by the use of relative clauses. The latter have a cohesive function (e.g. the one *who was hiding their eyes* goes and looks) and are a chief means of making the instruction explicit. This approach to the explanation of hide and seek is exemplified by the following child.

> Well one person hides their eyes while the other persons goes
>   and hides
> and then when they've hidden themselves they shout out ready
> so the one who's hiding their eyes goes and finds them
> and when they've found them the person who was hiding hides
>   their eyes
> and the other person goes and hides.

(2) *Mode B*
This mode of instruction incorporates the main characteristics of a 'particularistic' semantic. The game is described in terms of particular players, places and instances. Often allusion is made to events occurring in the course of a game in which the child has participated in the past. In terms of its realisation in speech, this mode may refer explicitly to people and places (e.g. little girl goes and hides in the kitchen) or may include a good deal of exophoric reference (e.g. she has to hide there). The following child offers a relatively particularistic instruction:

> if you and your friend go behind the wall
> and me and my friend hide our eyes
> and when you're ready you say ready
> and we come and find you.

(3) *Mode C*
Lineker characterises this third approach as a 'mixed' mode but stresses that while including features of both the other orientations, it is distinct from either and also from those texts which begin in one mode and then, failing to maintain it, switch to another approach. Lineker describes this orientation as follows:

> The identification of the mode, usually in the initial definition of the roles, frequently contains characteristics of universal and particular instructional methods, for example in the use of universal nouns in the identification of one role, while the speaker and hypothetical listener are also involved in the activity. The principles of the game are frequently given universally but the instruction will then include some personal application.

Lineker gives the following example of this method of instruction.

> You hide your eyes the one who's on it
> then when we hide
> then when we say yes and ready you got to come and look for us
> the first one to be found is out it

(4) *A textual index*

In the instructional context, the coding of speech in terms of semantic orientation to instruction in fact constitutes a textual characterisation of each child's response. However, in terms of the statistical analysis employed in this investigation, it is advisable to find some way of expressing these individual categories as points on a single index. That is, each child now has a score of either 'present' or 'absent' for each of the three modes. But in correlating these indices with other measures it is as important to know what a child does not do as it is to know what he does do. We may (or rather, the computer may) know that an individual child did not make a universalistic instruction. But we need recourse to another index to find what kind of instruction he did make. Correlative techniques cannot make use of this information unless it is all contained in a single index. We therefore quite simply constructed a scale as follows: mode A, 1; mode C, 2; mode B, 3. It should perhaps be noted that this is in no way an evaluative scale. The instructions did not differ in terms of efficiency. The index is an attempt to put all the information about each child's orientation into one statistical category. The individual measures are retained as separate indices in order that we may see whether one or another group of children is particularly important in establishing a relationship with indices from the other contexts.

Social-class differences in the orientation indices

Table 4.14 shows the number of children in each social class who adopt each of the three modes. As we might expect from Lineker's analysis, most MC children adopt a context-independent approach to instruction. There is very little variation in this group in terms of orientation to instructional speech, whereas in the WC sample there

Table 4.14 Distinction of children according to social class and mode type

	Mode A	Mode B	Mode C
MC	54	11	15
WC	37	37	13

is much more variation. Clearly the correlations of mode B in the MC must be interpreted in the light of the above distribution. The responses of two or three children might lead to a high level of statistical significance but it would be unwarranted to attach very much empirical or theoretical significance to such a result.

The mode-maintenance and cohesion categories

Two mutually exclusive indices deal with the extent to which the child maintains both the mode of his instruction and the reference sets within the mode.

Mode breakdown

In all the examples of instructional speech given in the previous section, the mode of explanation initially adopted is maintained throughout. If the child begins in the universalistic mode then the universalistic mode is held to the end. And similarly with the particularistic mode. Some children have difficulty in maintaining the role definitions and reference sets with which they begin their instruction and the initially adopted mode may then be abandoned altogether. Either the child moves to a different mode or else he moves into narrative. The child who does this is scored as showing mode breakdown. An example follows.

> You hide and I've got to find you
> and if I find you I got to hide
> and you got to find me
> the boy closed his eyes and he went out in the
> kitchen and found him
> then I hided and he had to find me

Mode maintenance

Children who maintain their initially adopted mode may again be divided into two groups on the basis of linguistic cohesion. Thus some children give their entire instruction within a single mode but their nominal and pronominal reference sets are incongruent. Lineker writes: 'This is felt to be important since while an inconsistency in the number or sex of one group of players or the presence of role switch does not indicate a change in mode, it does point to a weakening in the child's ability to hold the mode.' One group of children both maintain their initially adopted mode *and* are consistent in referring to participants. It is this group that are scored on the present index. Children who maintain their mode but are inconsistent in referring to participants are scored neither on this index nor on the 'mode breakdown' category.

Social-class differences on the mode-maintenance and cohesion categories

Table 4.15 shows how MC and WC children respond in terms of these coding categories. From Table 4.15 it can be seen that approximately 50 per cent of each social-class group maintain their initially adopted mode but do not achieve consistency of reference sets. There are, however, social-class differences in the numbers of

Table 4.15   Distribution of children by social class on the mode-maintenance and mode-breakdown categories

	Mode maintenance	Mode breakdown
MC	29	9
WC	19	27

children who achieve such consistency in their reference sets and, at the opposite pole, who show mode breakdown. More MC than WC children are found in the former category; more WC than MC children show breakdown of mode. In fact, almost all MC children maintain the mode with which they began, the chief distinction in this group being whether or not the child manages to maintain consistency of reference sets. The WC children are distributed more evenly across the mode-maintenance categories.

We now turn to a consideration of the inter-relationships of indices within the instructional context. The following points, summarising the above analyses, should be underlined before proceeding.

1   Most MC children are oriented to a context-independent mode of instruction. WC children are as likely to take up the context-dependent option as they are to take up the context-independent option. The very skewed distributions in the MC mean that correlations involving mode B in the MC should be treated with caution.

2   Most MC children maintain their initially adopted mode. The correlations in the MC involving the mode-breakdown category will be unreliable. Since WC children are more evenly represented in the mode-maintenance and mode-breakdown categories, correlations involving these categories in the WC are more reliable.

Inter-relationships of indices in the instructional context

The indices in the instructional context fall into two distinct groups. First there are the four indices describing the child's orientation to instructional speech. Three of these indices correspond to the three mode types of universalistic (mode A), particularistic (mode B), and mixed (mode C) while the fourth is the composite index of text that summarises the first three within a single measure. Correlations between those four categories are uninteresting since they are induced by the method of scoring. If a child adopts mode A then he adopts neither mode B nor mode C. Thus the three mode types are mutually exclusive categories and are inevitably negatively correlated. The second group of indices in this context concerns the extent to which the child maintains his initially chosen instructional mode. The two indices in this group are mode maintenance and mode breakdown. Again, correlations between these indices are induced and so not important. The relationships of interest in this context are those between the indices in the first group and those in the second group. Our central question is whether a child's tendency to maintain or break down his instruction is related to the mode type which he initially adopts. For example, is the child who gives a universalistic, or more context-independent instruction likely to maintain that instruction, or is he more likely to abandon that instruction in favour of another mode or narrative? We shall, therefore, present and discuss only correlations between the two groups of indices.

Findings
Table 4.16 shows the pattern of correlations between the instructional indices for the total sample of children. For the total sample,

Table 4.16   Inter-relationships of instructional indices in the total sample

	Mode A	Mode B	Mode C	Text
Mode breakdown	−0·166***	0·352***	−0·122***	0·179***
Mode maintenance	0·343***	−0·189***	−0·187***	−0·284***

the pattern of relationships is very clear. Children who adopt mode A tend to maintain that mode and to show consistency in their reference sets. Children opting for a context-dependent instruction are more likely to breakdown in that instruction and, where mode maintenance is achieved, reference sets are unlikely to be consistent. The mixed mode C shows a negative correlation with both mode maintenance and breakdown of mode. This suggests that while children who offer the mixed mode do maintain this approach, they are less likely also to keep their reference sets consistent.

Table 4.17   Inter-relationships of instructional indices in WC sub-sample

	Mode A	Mode B	Mode C	Text
Mode breakdown	−0·074	0·337***	−0·241***	0·197**
Mode maintenance	0·316***	−0·076	−0·234***	−0·303***

Are these results repeated in the sub-sample matrices? Table 4.17 shows the pattern of correlations for the WC sub-sample. The WC sub-sample is almost a direct replica of the total sample matrix. The description given above applies to this sample also and we shall not repeat it. Separate analyses were run for boys and girls and the patterns were found to be similar for both sexes.

Table 4.18   Inter-relationships of instructional indices in MC sub-sample

	Mode A	Mode B	Mode C	Text
Mode breakdown	0·308***	−0·199***	−0·158***	−0·318***
Mode maintenance	−0·132*	0·276***	0·064	0·188**

Table 4.18 shows the pattern for the MC group. The correlations in the MC group are again very like those yielded by the two previous samples. We should, however, remember the caution previously invoked when interpreting the matrix. We know that very few MC children offer a mode B instruction and also that very few MC children break down their instruction. If we then examine the distribution of this latter group according to mode type (see Table 4.19) we can begin to see that some of the correlations in Table 4.18 should be treated with caution.

Table 4.19   Proportion of MC children using each mode type who show mode breakdown

	Mode A	Mode B	Mode C
Children who break down	3	4	2
No. in each category	54	11	15

The number of children who abandon their initially adopted mode in each category is constant. In proportional terms, however, there are very great differences, and so very high correlations are computed between mode breakdown and the orientation categories. To draw any firm conclusions on the basis of such small numbers is unwarranted. Clearly we need information about far more MC children who are oriented to a context-dependent instruction. This does not mean that we must therefore totally ignore the children who do this in the MC sample, but it would be more reliable in considering relationships involving mode B or mode breakdown to base any inferences upon an analysis of the total sample and the WC subsample.

What, then, is it permissible to say about the matrix yielded by the MC sub-sample? We know that the chief distinction in the MC is not between mode maintenance and mode breakdown. Almost all children in this group show mode maintenance, but while some also keep their reference sets consistent, others become confused in the handling of reference. As far as the MC sub-sample is concerned, then, we can say that those children who adopt mode A in the MC are more likely to show mode maintenance with consistency of reference sets than they are to be inconsistent in their reference sets. Children who do not adopt mode A are more likely to become confused in their handling of reference.

As with the WC sub-sample, no difference emerged between boys and girls in the relation of the orientation indices with the mode-maintenance indices in this context.

Before summarising our findings for the instructional context, we shall consider the use of narrative in this task.

4 Narrative

As in the descriptive task, narrative speech is an interesting phenomenon since it represents a weakening of the frame set up by the interviewer's probes. We were interested to know whether the same children moved to narrative in the two tasks and whether our conception of narrative as a variant of context-dependent speech is supported by the descriptive and instructional coding orientations of children who move to the narrative mode. In the Trotin task our hypothesis was borne out in that children introducing narrative tended to implicitness in their purely descriptive speech. In the present task we might expect children who move to narrative to give a particularistic instruction.

In the hide and seek task, narrative was not coded for length. Presence or absence only was noted. This was done because children did not vary extensively in their use of narrative as was the case in the descriptive context. However, on reflection, some measure of length should have been noted. Lack of this information will prove to be a limitation on the inferences we can make in some of the analysis which follows.

Findings

As we might expect, there are fairly marked social-class and sex differences in the numbers of children who introduce narrative in this task. These are shown in Table 4.20. More WC than MC children move to narrative in this task, and the group most strongly represented is WC girls. This pattern is very like that found in the Trotin task although here the class and sex differences are less marked. It is likely that the figures in Table 4.20 mask differences in the length of narrative given by the children. This possibility becomes even

Table 4.20 Social-class and sex differences in the numbers of children moving to narrative in the instructional context

	MC	WC
Boys	6	12
Girls	5	20
Total	11	32

greater when it is realised that of the children represented in Table 4.20, 8 give no purely instructional speech and frame their response entirely in the narrative mode. Of these 8, 5 are WC girls, 1 a WC boy, 1 a MC boy and 1 a MC girl. These children have the same narrative 'score' (i.e. 'present') as children who, for example, give only one narrative sequence. For this reason, correlations involving the narrative index must be treated cautiously. We can, of course, separately consider the children who respond entirely in the narrative mode.

We now turn to a consideration of the relation of narrative to the other instructional indices for the total sample, the MC sub-sample and the WC sub-sample. The eight children who give only narrative have been excluded from this analysis (Table 4.21). These results show clearly that only children who choose a particularistic instruction are likely to introduce narrative in that instruction. Children choosing the mixed mode, as well as those adopting the more context-independent approach, tend to stay within the frame of instructional speech. The suggestion that narrative speech in such a situation

Table 4.21   The relationship of narrative in instruction to other instructional indices for the total sample, the WC sub-sample and the MC sub-sample

	Total sample	WC	MC
Mode A	−0·236***	−0·175**	−0·232***
Mode B	0·418***	0·393***	0·343***
Mode C	−0·202***	−0·288***	−0·087
Text	0·317***	0·285***	0·284***

realises a context-dependent orientation receives considerable support from these data. A consideration of the cross-context speech of children orientated to narrative in both the instructional and the descriptive contexts should further illuminate the question.

Table 4.22   The relationship of narrative in instruction to other instructional indices for WC boys and WC girls

	WC boys	WC girls
Mode A	−0·220*	−0·127
Mode B	0·418***	0·368***
Mode C	−0·250*	−0·323***
Text	0·314***	0·254**

Only one sex difference emerged when boys and girls were considered separately. This was in the WC, and the full set of correlations is given in Table 4.22. Thus while the strong positive correlation between mode B and narrative still obtains in both groups, the negative association between mode A and narrative is no longer significant for girls. This means that some WC girls introduce narrative into a predominantly context-independent instruction. The correlation still has a negative sign and it would be unwise to attach too much significance to the result. The finding should, however, be borne in mind in interpreting future matrices.

Summary of the analysis of the instructional context

The picture emerging from this analysis is of three distinct orientations to instructional speech. One group of children adopt a context-dependent or particularistic approach to instruction and are also quite likely to abandon this approach in favour of another or for narrative speech. And whether or not the child who explains the game in terms of particular people and places manages or decides to complete the instruction, he is more likely than other children to move away from instructional speech altogether and relate an event or story unconnected with the game itself. Perhaps there is some underlying relationship between context-dependent meanings and narrative which facilitates such a shift. It is possible that the task was somewhat difficult for these children and so became a trigger for story-telling. These two tentative suggestions are not mutually exclusive.

Children choosing the more context-independent approach are more likely to complete their explanation within this mode and maintain consistency in their reference sets. Further, such children do not on the whole include narrative speech in their answers. Children opting for the mixed mode also tend not to weaken the instructional frame by the introduction of narrative and they tend to stay within a single mode. However, their ability to manage consistent reference is less stable.

These three orientations are distinguishable within the WC group as well as in the total sample. The pattern of correlations in the MC group is also consistent with the total picture, if somewhat unreliable in places. This suggests that we are dealing with something other than individual correlates of social class. That is, it could be argued that MC children have learned that what adults want in a situation such as this is a neat review of the rules given without interruption, and that they have also learned to manage this without becoming linguistically confused or losing interest. We would suggest that the class-specific intercorrelations argue that a large group of children are orientated in this situation to a context-independent mode of instruction, and that this entails an explicitness that fosters a cohesive text. Another group, smaller but still substantial in number, are orientated to a more context-dependent mode of explanation that is often realised implicitly in speech and may easily be abandoned in favour of an alternative mode or narrative. Now we know that most MC children are orientated to the first kind of instruction. But a substantial number of WC children also adopt this approach. And although the large majority of children who give the context-dependent type of explanation are WC, there are a few MC children who do so. It becomes a matter of some interest as to how those WC children who are orientated to context-independent instructional speech and those MC children who are not so orientated respond in other contexts, both within the interview and outside it.

IV THE REGULATIVE CONTEXT

The linguistic indices for the regulative context are derived from previous analyses of this context by Cook-Gumperz (1973) and Turner (1973a; and in press); detailed reference is made to this work in Turner (in press). Here it is sufficient for our purposes to summarise the main points concerning the task used to elicit regulative speech, Cook-Gumperz's analysis of this speech, and the later analysis of it by the present researcher.

The task was essentially a role-play task. The child was invited to make a model room, using various articles of living-room furniture: table, chairs, television and so on. He was then given several doll figures, clearly representing members of a family: father, mother and children. With the help of these props, several conflict situations were set up and described to the child. The child was invited to say what the main participants in the situations, the mother and her child, would say or do. Here is an illustration of one of the situations and a child's response to it.

> Mummy says it's time to go to bed and the little girl cries because she wants to watch something on TV.
> What does mummy do about that?
> (Child) I'd just smack her and just say Go up to bed.
> What does mummy say?
> (Child) You must come up to bed straightaway otherwise I'll call up Daddy and he'll smack you and he'll take you straight up.
> What will the little girl do then?
> (Child) She'll disobey him I should think.

There were six conflict situations in all.

The analysis performed by Cook-Gumperz (1973) used a detailed coding frame for social control designed to operationalise Bernstein's concepts of imperative, positional and personal control (Bernstein, 1971, ch. 9; Bernstein and Cook, 1965). This analysis revealed a pattern of social-class differences, but it was suggested that a greater focusing on the linguistic aspects of the children's use of language in the regulative context might reveal a stronger pattern of differences.

The re-analysis of Cook-Gumperz's data (Turner, in press) had two thrusts: one, to make finer discriminations within some of the earlier categories in order to capture variation previously missed; and, two, to use elements of this additional information to build up higher-order indices of the children's use of language in the regulative context. The analysis, then, was at once more detailed than that of Cook-Gumperz, with a greater focusing on linguistic features of the children's speech, and yet more general, in that new, higher-order groupings of categories were made. An earlier example of this approach is to be found in the analysis of the children's 'social control' responses to a picture-story task (Turner, 1973a); here features of the children's use of language in this context were summarised in terms of a distinction between 'forceful' and 'less forceful' options.

The four indices of the children's regulative speech to be described shortly have points of contact with the 'punishment' and 'child-oriented reasoning' indices constructed for the mothers' social control data (Bernstein and Brandis in Brandis and Henderson, 1970) and with the 'forceful' and 'less forceful' indices constructed for the children's responses to a picture-story task (Turner, 1973a). The modifications we made in the indices were necessitated by the age of the subjects, and by differences in the speech-eliciting contexts. A full account of the points of similarity and dissimilarity, and the reasons for the modifications, is given by Turner (in press).

The plan for the treatment of the regulative context is as follows.
1   The basic analysis and the construction of the four indices of the children's regulative speech. Social-class differences in these indices.
2   The attempt to construct a textual index, using the above indices as sub-indices. Social-class differences.
3   The inter-correlations of the sub-indices and the textual index in the regulative context.
4   Sex differences in the regulative context.

(1)   The basic analysis

Coding categories

The regulative speech of the children was first analysed according to the coding frame described in full in Turner (in press). Taking Bernstein's distinction of three types of control – imperative, positional and personal – as the starting point, fine discriminations were made within strategies of control, representing choices relevant to the distinction of code in terms of universalistic and particularistic meanings. In a sense, then, the aim was to explore Bernstein's theory of control and his theory of code at the same time. This was made possible through the application of Halliday's (1973) concept of language as 'meaning potential'.

The four indices of regulative speech which summarise aspects of the basic analysis are now described.

(1) *Punishment*

Under 'punishment' are grouped the most extreme strategies of imperative control used by the children: physical punishment, verbal punishment and threat of punishment. Frequent choices here, at the expense of others, are thought to indicate a relative preference for hierarchical control, based upon power at its most explicit. Here the social relationship is strongly asymmetrical and the child is accorded little discretion, little hope of negotiation. The categories, with examples, are now listed.

(a) physical punishment, e.g. She smacks him.

(b) verbal punishment, e.g. She tells him off.

(c) threat of punishment, e.g. You must go to school or I'll smack you.

If you stay at home, you're going to get told off by the school-board man.

(2) *Contingencies, backings and affect*

Under this heading are grouped those choices in positional and personal control where explicitness and specificity are at a premium. An important consideration is: how are rules and decisions communicated to the child? Are situational contingencies mentioned? Are reasons given? The relevant categories are now listed.

(a) Concessions: conditional, partial or delimited. For example:

If he's a good boy and helps her to wash up the tea things, he can look at it.

If you go to bed as soon as the programme's finished, you can watch it.

You can only watch half of it.

I'll let you stay up till the film has gone off and if the film goes off too late you'll have to go up in between the film.

You can stay up until it ends.

(b) Extenuating conditions, reasons, warnings of consequences or recognition of intent, associated mainly with commands and rules. For example:

You mustn't pick flowers from other people's gardens unless you ask for them.

You mustn't take things out of a shop without paying for them.

You must go to school because you can get very clever.

You must go to school because you're not ill.

You must go to school because if you don't you won't learn.

You must go to school or else you won't learn your lessons right or cross the road properly.

. . . says that she must go to bed because if she doesn't go to bed then she won't have a good night's sleep.

If you don't go to bed you'll be too tired to go to school in the morning.

Thank you very much but you really aren't allowed to pick other people's flowers.

(c) Qualified disapprobation

We also included in the index instances of qualified disapprobation, where the child distinguished between the misdemeanours across the contexts in terms of their relative severity. The category is exemplified below:

You're a very naughty boy.

The aim of including this category was to capture an aspect of situationally contingent control, and it is important to note that if a child mentioned disapprobation with reference to more than one of the six conflict situations but did not distinguish between the situations, this was not counted as contingent control.

(d) Affective state of mother

Finally, we included in the index reference to the affective state of the mother. Here the child makes explicit one of the consequences of the offence, its effect on the mother's feelings. We now give examples:

She's very cross about it.
Oh well I suppose she's rather cross.
She's angry.
I would say she would be angry with me.

(3) and (4) *Directive: imperative and Directive: modified*

The final two indices are concerned with relatively simple directions on the part of the mother, that is, those instances where the mother tells the child to do something, but does not, on the one hand, reinforce the direction with a threat, or, on the other, qualify it in terms of some situational contingency or offer some justification for it. The 'directive' indices are concerned with 'bare' directions given to the child. In a way, one could regard the control captured by these two indices as lying midway between the control captured by the 'punishment' and the 'contingencies, backings and affect' indices, but that is perhaps too simple. The 'directive' indices cut across certain categories of imperative control, particularly commands and loss of privilege, and certain categories of positional control, particularly rules and reparation seeking. (As discussed in Turner (in press), the distinction between commands and rules is not easy to make in the case of children of this age, but this does not affect the directive indices, since these cut across the categories, ignoring the distinction.) For all these directions a distinction was made between what we called the 'directive: imperative' type and the 'directive: modified' type. In the case of the first type the directive is given by means of an imperative, e.g.

Go and talk to Daddy.
Start talking at once.
Don't do it again.
Don't spill the tea again.
Don't nick no flowers again.
Wipe it up.
Go to bed.
Go to school.
Take it back.

By contrast, in the case of the second type the directive is given by means of a declarative with relevant propositional content, and 'modulation', to use Halliday's (1973) technical term. Here the obligation or prohibition is made explicit by means of a modal auxiliary (must, ought to, should), a semi-auxiliary (be to, had better/best have to, have got to) or a lexical verb (allow), e.g.

You must talk to Daddy.
She should look what she's doing.
You'll have to help me put another tablecloth on it now.
You're not to pick flowers from other people's gardens.
You shouldn't pick them from other people's gardens.
You've got to go to bed.
You must go to school.
You can't stay at home.
You ought to take it back.
You have to take it back.
You'd best take them back.

A small number of children gave directives indicating the controller's decision, e.g.

You're going to bed.
You will go to school.

These were included under the 'directive: imperative' type.

It needs no emphasising that the distinction between the two types of directive is not great. Furthermore, the distinction is of much less theoretical interest than the distinction between the 'punishment' and the 'contingencies, backings and affect' indices. Nevertheless, it is thought that the distinction could throw some light on how authority relationships are mediated through language. We would interpret the 'directive: imperative' type as the more direct, probably more abrasive type. Here the controller is simply telling the controlled what to do; there is direct person-to-person pressure. The 'directive: modified' type is the more indirect type. Here the controller tells the controlled what he has to do, what he ought to do, what he should do, etc. The making explicit of the obligation gives these directives an objectivity not found in the other type. It is possible that these directives are more challengeable and open to discussion than the others, e.g. Why is it best to . . . ?, Why do people have to . . . ?

The notion of an elaborated variant in the regulative context

In any attempt to characterise speech in the regulative context as an elaborated or restricted variant relatable to code, it is essential to remember Bernstein's basic contention that it is the form of social relationship – relevant meanings in the context and the mediating language – that gives rise to different codes. A critical question for Bernstein concerns how the power that is at the back of all parent–child relationships is realised. How naked is the power? How much discretion is accorded to the child, and on what terms? What is salient for the controller, the child's formal status or his individual qualities? Are principles and decisions made explicit and explained, made objective and potentially open to discussion? Is the child encouraged to think about his intentions in committing certain acts and the consequences of his actions for himself and others? Is the child encouraged to be aware of his own feelings and sensitive to the feelings of others? Essentially, for Bernstein speech in the regulative context can be characterised as an elaborated variant when there is an attenuation of the relation of the latent power of the controller and the control that is exercised. Such matters as the explanation of rules and the making explicit of situational contingencies when decisions are made are regarded as being crucial matters in determining whether a variant is elaborated or restricted. Here power is in the background; explanations, reasons and conditions, by being made explicit, are in the foreground, and are potentially available for discussion. Of the four indices we have constructed for the children's data the one that is crucial for determining whether the speech is elaborated or restricted, bearing in mind the age of the subjects, is the 'contingencies, backings and affect' index. The significance of the other three indices derives largely from the relationships they enter into with this critical index. The 'contingencies, backings and affect' index is to be regarded as the cornerstone for the construction of an overall index of text in the regulative context.

Social-class differences on the regulative sub-indices

Table 4.23 shows the group means for punishment, contingencies, backings and affect, directive: imperative and directive: modified for the total sample and the two area sub-samples. The social-class differences confirm those found in Turner (in press). The middle-class children move to contingencies, backings and affect rather than

Table 4.23   Group means for the four sub-indices of control for the total sample, the MC sub-sample and the WC sub-sample

	Punishment	Contingencies, etc.	Dir.: imp.	Dir.: mod.
Total sample	1·337	1·124	1·172	0·882
MC	0·827	1·531	0·988	1·049
WC	1·807	0·750	1·341	0·727

punishment, whereas the reverse is true in the case of the working-class children; they opt for punishment rather than the other choices. The pattern is clear. The middle-class children's mean score for contingencies, backings and affect is twice the working-class children's score for contingencies, etc. The reverse of this pattern for these variables is found in the working-class sample. Turning to the two directive indices, a different pattern is apparent here. The middle-class children have a lower mean score for the imperative directives than the working-class children. The striking thing, however, is the evenness of the two types of selection in the middle-class sample and their unevenness in the working-class sample. In the case of the middle-class sample there is very little difference between the means, but in the working-class the mean score for the imperative directives is almost twice that for the modified directives.

Table 4.24 gives the number of children scoring on the four measures of control. The table shows that, as far as the total sample goes, each variable is used by roughly half of the children. The patterning of the distribution of the children in the sub-samples to a large extent 'echoes' the pattern given in Table 4.23, though it is clear that taking into account *relative frequency* of use (as in Table 4.23) gives a stronger pattern of class differences.

The critical question that we must now face concerns the way in which the scores of individual children are distributed across the four types of control. For example, do the children who score for punishment tend to avoid contingencies, backings and affect, and show a preference for imperative directives? This type of question

Table 4.24   No. of children in each sample using any punishment, contingencies, etc., directive: imperative and directive: modified

	Punishment	Contingencies, etc.	Dir.: imp.	Dir.: mod.
Total sample	96 (56%)	85 (51%)	95 (56%)	83 (49%)
MC	33 (41%)	45 (56%)	41 (51%)	40 (49%)
WC	63 (72%)	40 (45%)	54 (61%)	43 (49%)

must now be explored. For unless we can show a pattern of relationships between the four sub-indices of control, any attempt to construct an overall textual index based upon the sub-indices will face great difficulty.

(2)   The textual index

Before presenting the inter-correlations for the four sub-indices of control, we shall state our expectations. We have stated earlier that the crucial variable, from the point of view of determining whether a speech variant in the regulative context is elaborated or restricted, is the contingencies, backings and affect index. We would expect that children who obtain relatively high scores on this index would tend to obtain low scores for punishment. We would expect them, too, to show a preference for modified directives rather than imperative directives. More specifically, we would expect the following pattern of correlations between the sub-indices:
   a negative correlation between contingencies and punishment;
   a negative correlation between contingencies and directive: imperative;
   a positive correlation between contingencies and directive: modified;
   a positive correlation between punishment and directive: imperative;
   a negative correlation between punishment and directive: modified;
   a negative correlation between directive: imperative and directive: modified.
The predictions concerning correlations involving the punishment index are made with less confidence than the others, simply because we are dealing with young children. Cook-Gumperz (1973) reported large differences between the responses of the children and those of their mothers. Relative to their mothers, the children revealed a strong trend towards imperative-positional control. It is possible that

children of this age might tend to see some of the control situations in terms of punishment, irrespective of whether they mentioned contingencies, backings and affect or chose modified directives at other times.

Table 4.25   Inter-relationships of sub-indices of control for total sample

	Punishment	Contingencies, etc.	Dir.: imp.	Dir.: mod.
Punishment		−0·053	0·042	−0·078*
Contingencies, etc.			−0·180***	−0·002
Directive: imp.				−0·093*
Directive: mod.				

Table 4.26   Inter-relationships of sub-indices of control for MC sub-sample

	Punishment	Contingencies, etc.	Dir.: imp.	Dir.: mod.
Punishment		0·069	0·004	0·027
Contingencies, etc.			−0·132*	0·007
Directive: imp.				−0·143*
Directive: mod.				

Table 4.27   Inter-relationships of sub-indices of control for WC sub-sample

	Punishment	Contingencies, etc.	Dir.: imp.	Dir.: mod.
Punishment		0·034	−0·011	−0·158*
Contingencies, etc.			−0·170**	−0·051
Directive: imp.				−0·045
Directive: mod.				

Tables 4.25, 4.26 and 4.27 present the pattern of relationships between the sub-indices of control for the total sample and the sub-samples. The first thing to note about the correlations presented in these tables is the very weak relationship between the punishment index and the contingencies, backings and affect index. This immediately suggests that it is inappropriate to characterise the texts the children create in the regulative context in terms of a

punishment *v.* elaboration dimension. (Brandis (in Brandis and Henderson, 1970, pp. 141–2), in the case of the *maternal* data, was able to identify a general dimension 'dominated by punishment at one end and child-orientated personal appeals at the other'.)

The correlations generally are not high. In each set of six, two reach significance; all of the significant correlations are consistent with our expectations. There is a significant negative correlation between contingencies, backings and affect and imperative directives for the middle-class sub-sample, the working-class sub-sample and the total sample; a significant negative correlation between punishment and modified directives for the working-class sub-sample; a significant negative correlation between imperative directives and modified directives for the middle-class sub-sample. Parts of the expected pattern are there, and parts are missing. But it is of interest to note that where there are gaps, the correlations are very weak. There are no significant correlations that conflict with our expectations.

It needs no emphasising that the pattern of the correlations and their strength do not provide strong statistical grounds for constructing a single index based on the sub-indices. Nevertheless, we constructed a textual index which we thought was of some theoretical interest and which respected the pattern of correlations observed. We concentrated on the relationship between contingencies, backings and affect and imperative directives (a negative correlation, significant for the total sample and both of the sub-samples). We have stressed previously that we regard the contingencies, backings and affect index as our best single measure of an elaborated variant in the regulative context. We attempted to strengthen this measure by adding to it a measure of the child's relative preference for modified directives rather than imperative directives; we obtained a difference score for these two indices. The formula for the textual index can be stated thus:

regulative text index = contingencies, backings and affect
+ (modified directives—imperative directives).

To avoid negative numbers, a constant was added to each difference score.

It is worth pointing out that, in practice, it is not just a matter of taking the child's score for contingencies, backings and affect and increasing it. For, if the child's score for imperative directives is greater than that for modified directives, the difference score effectively reduces the child's score for contingencies, backings and affect. So, from this point of view, the regulative text index can be seen as a more stringent measure of elaboration than the contingencies, backings and affect index alone. But from other points of view it can be viewed as less stringent. It is possible, for example, for a child with a low score for contingencies, backings and affect still to score relatively high on the textual index if his score for modified directives is greater than that for imperative directives. A central concern, when we examine the correlations between the three types of context, descriptive, instructional and regulative, will be the assessment of the power of the regulative text index as a discriminator of texts, particularly its power as compared with the contingencies, backings and affect index alone.

Table 4.28 gives the group means for the textual index for the total sample and the two sub-samples. The means for the contingencies, backings and affect index are included for comparison. We have previously noted the large class difference in the selection of contingencies, backings and affect. Table 4.28 shows that, when this scale

Table 4.28   Group means for the regulative text index and the contingencies, etc. index for the total sample, the MC sub-sample and the WC sub-sample

	Text	*Contingencies, etc.*
Total sample	0·834	1·124
MC	1·593	1·531
WC	0·136	0·750

is combined with the other two scales, in a way that captures relative preference, the class difference is increased.[4] The middle-class children's score for the textual index is very similar to their score for contingencies, backings and affect, but the working-class children's score is much lower, reflecting their preference for imperative directives.

(3)   The inter-relationships of the sub-indices and the textual index in the regulative context

In this section we set out the correlations between the sub-indices of control and the textual index we have constructed. We have given the correlations between the punishment index and the textual index, even though the punishment index was not used in the construction of the textual index. It is of some interest that the correlation between the two indices reaches significance for the total sample and is negative in sign. That is, children who score high on the measure of elaboration tend to score low on the measure of punishment. The

Table 4.29   Inter-relationships of the sub-indices of control and the textual index for the total sample, the MC sub-sample and the WC sub-sample

	Punishment	Contingencies, etc.	Dir.: imp.	Dir.: mod.
Total sample	−0·097*	0·521***	−0·620***	0·413***
MC	0·054	0·548***	−0·530***	0·474***
WC	−0·052	0·426***	−0·693***	0·360***

correlations between these variables for the sub-samples, however, are very weak.

The correlations between the other three sub-indices and the textual index are as we would expect them to be, given the way that the textual index was constructed. Imperative directives correlate negatively with the textual index, whilst modified directives and contingencies, backings and affect correlate positively with it. All the correlations are highly significant.

Conclusion

The chief aim of this section was to explore what we mean by an elaborated variant in the regulative context. We have described the four basic indices we used to characterise the children's control, and we have examined the relationships between the indices, to see how we could combine them in a way that respected these relationships and gave us an accurate overall characterisation of the children's regulative texts. Our conclusions concerning this analysis can be stated succinctly:

1   There is little support for constructing two higher-order indices, contrasting punishment and contingencies, backings and affect.
2   There is little support for constructing one higher-order index which includes punishment.
3   What the evidence does support, albeit not strongly, is the construction of an index derived from the other three indices – contingencies, backings and affect, imperatives and modified directives.

We can meaningfully talk about verbal elaboration in the regulative context either in terms of the contingencies, backings and affect index or in terms of the textual index. We have stressed that the contingencies, backings and affect index is our best single index of elaboration in this context. The question to be explored in later sections of this paper is whether the combined index is a more effective discriminator of texts than the single index alone.

(4) Sex differences in the regulative context

The study by Turner (in press) revealed certain sex differences in the children's speech in the regulative context. As a check on possible sex differences in the present sample, we give in Table 4.30 the means for the control indices for the sub-groups of children, controlling for social class and sex. The first thing to notice is that there is sex variation associated with all the variables, except contingencies, backings

Table 4.30   Group means for the sub-indices and the textual index for boys and girls for the MC sub-sample and the WC sub-sample

| | MC | | WC | |
	B	G	B	G
Punishment	0·909	0·728	2·050	1·604
Contingencies, etc.	1·568	1·487	0·750	0·750
Dir.: imp.	1·068	0·892	1·525	1·188
Dir.: mod.	0·955	1·162	0·575	0·854
Text	1·455	1·757	−0·200	0·417

and affect, but this variation is much less than that associated with social class (see Table 4.23). The second thing to note is that the sex variation is much more marked in the working-class sample than in the middle-class, although the same basic pattern is common to both: the boys show a preference for punishment and imperative directives, whereas the girls are more likely than the boys to choose modified directives. Although there is virtually no sex variation in the selection of contingencies, backings and affect, the boys, particularly in the working-class sample, obtain lower scores on the textual index because of their relative preference for imperative directives, whereas the girls, again particularly in the working-class sample, obtain higher text scores because of their relative preference for modified directives. The size of sex difference in the working-class sample suggests that it may be necessary to control for sex when examining the relationships between the indices of control and those of description and instruction for this sample of children.

V   DESCRIPTION AND INSTRUCTION

The primary question with which this section of the analysis is concerned is whether a child's orientation to instructional speech can predict his orientation to descriptive speech and vice versa. Are the same children orientated to a more context-independent use of language in the two tasks? Concretely, do those children who give a universalistic instruction tend to make more explicit descriptions of the Trotin cards? Do those children who explain hide and seek in terms of particular players and places tend to be more implicit in their descriptive speech? At a superficial level, there seems little reason why this should be the case. The prediction derives directly from Bernstein's thesis of distinct sociolinguistic coding orientations and just because it is a non-obvious prediction it is particularly important to the analysis.

The relationships between the instructional and descriptive contexts fall into three groups. First, is the pattern of relationships between the mode type measures in instruction and the four indices of context-independence/dependence in description. These relationships are most relevant to the question of consistency of coding orientation. Second, the descriptive indices can be considered in relation to the measures of the child's tendency to produce a cohesive text in the instructional context. Finally, the pattern of relationships involving the two narrative indices warrants attention. These three groups of correlations will be dealt with separately.

(1)   Orientation to instruction and context-independence/dependence in description

Expectations

The central prediction in this analysis is that the index of text in description will correlate positively with the index of text in instruction. This association most directly tests the basic question of consistency in coding orientation. In addition we expect:
(1) indices of context-independence in the two tasks to be positively associated, i.e. mode A will correlate positively with indefinites and with specificity;
(2) indices of context-dependence in the two tasks to be positively associated, i.e. mode B will correlate positively with exophora and the textual index in description; the textual index in instruction will correlate positively with exophora;
(3) indices of context-independence is one task to be negatively

associated with indices of context-dependence in the other, i.e. mode A will correlate negatively with exophora and with the textual index in description; mode B will correlate negatively with indefinites and specificity; the textual index in instruction will correlate negatively with indefinites and specificity.

In all cases we expect the correlations involving the textual indices to be the most informative. Finally, given the conclusions reached in the two previous sections we may expect some difficulties in interpreting the results of the MC sub-sample.

Findings

Table 4.31 shows the inter-relationships of the relevant indices for the total sample. The pattern of correlates yielded by the total sample

Table 4.31   Tau coefficients between the orientation indices for instruction and the context-independent/dependent indices for description for the total sample

	Exophora	Indefinites	Specificity	Text
Mode A	−0·087*	0·144**	0·018	−0·203**
Mode B	0·044	−0·144**	−0·061	0·143**
Mode C	0·003	0·055	0·053	−0·026
Text	0·144**	−0·162***	−0·019	0·219***

is largely in accordance with our predictions. Most importantly, the text summary indices for instruction and description have a strong positive correlation. The textual index in description correlates negatively with mode A and positively with mode B. The textual index for instruction correlates positively with exophora and negatively with indefinites. All these correlations are significant and as predicted. The correlations between the individual mode-type categories and the sub-indices in description follow the same pattern but are somewhat weaker. Exophora correlates negatively with mode A at a weak significance level and the correlation with mode B is not significant. Indefinites correlate significantly with both modes and in the predicted manner. The one descriptive sub-index that fails to show significant correlations is that of specificity.

In terms of the total sample, we find that children are consistent in their coding orientation across these two tasks. The correlation between the two summary indices is the strongest in the group but all the correlations are in the predicted direction and most reach statistical significance. The status of the specificity index will be considered presently.

Table 4.32 shows the pattern of relationships within the WC sub-sample. In the WC sub-sample, like the total sample, the strongest correlation is between the two textual indices. Context-independence

Table 4.32 Tau coefficients between the orientation indices for instruction and the context-independent/dependent indices for description for the WC sub-sample

	Exophora	Indefinites	Specificity	Text
Mode A	−0·037	0·086	0·070	−0·225**
Mode B	0·009	−0·052	−0·066	0·110(*)
Mode C	−0·090	0·006	0·045	0·021
Text	0·092(*)	−0·088	−0·064	0·236***

in instruction is associated within context-independence in description. In fact the correlations in the WC sample largely repeat those found in the total sample although now most of the relationships

Table 4.33 Tau coefficients between the orientation indices for instruction and the context-independent/dependent indices for description for WC boys

	Exophora	Indefinites	Specificity	Text
Mode A	−0·182*	0·229*	0·024	−0·357***
Mode B	0·257**	−0·094	−0·041	0·262**
Mode C	−0·163	−0·206*	0·088	0·061
Text	0·230*	−0·171*	−0·055	0·362***

Table 4.34 Tau coefficients between the orientation indices for instruction and the context-independent/dependent indices for description for WC girls

	Exophora	Indefinites	Specificity	Text
Mode A	0·042	−0·024	0·092	−0·097
Mode B	−0·194*	−0·009	−0·091	−0·030
Mode C	0·026	0·164*	−0·024	−0·060
Text	−0·050	−0·043	−0·082	0·118

have fallen below the level of statistical significance. The text summary score in description remains significantly associated with mode A and weakly so with mode B, but the individual linguistic measures no longer show significant correlations with the individual mode types. The patterning of signs is as predicted, however.

The results for the WC sub-sample suggest that this group of children are consistently context-independent or consistently context-dependent in their coding orientation in the descriptive and instructional contexts. In fact, the picture is not as clear as it looks at first sight. When boys and girls are considered separately, it is apparent that the results in Table 4.32 reflect only the speech of the boys. Girls respond somewhat differently. Tables 4.33 and 4.34 give the relevant findings.

The WC boys present a very clear picture of consistency in coding orientation. The correlations involving the textual indices are strong and many of the sub-index relationships are also significant. The matrix describing the pattern of responses among WC girls, however, lacks definition. Most of the results are well below the level of significance, and of the two that reach significance one directly contradicts our predictions. Mode B is negatively associated with exophora. In terms of this matrix there is apparently no relationship between how WC girls respond to the task of explaining hide and seek and how they respond to the task of describing picture postcards. We know, however, that children in this group vary considerably in their approaches to both these tasks, and the remaining two sections may shed some light on how they relate the two contexts in their speech.

Table 4.35   Tau coefficients between the orientation indices for instruction and the context-independent/dependent indices for description for the MC sample

	Exophora	Indefinites	Specificity	Text
Mode A	−0·037	0·054	−0·161*	−0·111*
Mode B	−0·064	−0·090	0·148*	0·128*
Mode C	0·109	0·060	0·051	−0·020
Text	0·041	−0·070	0·128*	0·122*

Table 4.35 shows the pattern of relationships within the MC sub-sample. There is little difference between girls and boys in the MC as to their speech across the two contexts and so the separate matrices will not be discussed here. These matrices may be found in Appendix 1.

The MC sample yields a pattern of correlations that is not as clear as that found in the total sample and the WC boys sample. The two textual indices show the expected positive correlation but the level of significance is reduced compared to the other two matrices. The index of text in description correlates negatively with mode A and positively with mode B but the former association is only weakly significant. The other relationships in the matrix either fail to reach acceptable significance levels or in fact contradict our expectations. In particular, the correlations involving the specificity index run contrary to what we predicted. Mode A shows a significant negative correlation with specificity while mode B correlates positively as does the composite index. Thus, relative to their own social group, those children who use highly specific constructions in the Trotin task tend to give more context-dependent explanations of hide and seek. This tendency is peculiar to the MC sub-sample and so demands closer inspection.

It will be remembered that in both the instructional and the descriptive contexts, MC children show less variation in their approaches than do WC children. Very few MC children adopt a context-dependent instructional mode and the great majority opt for the most context-independent form of explanation. In the descriptive task too, it is argued, very few MC children are orientated to context-dependent speech. The principal variation in this group appears to be in terms of different kinds of context-independent texts. The nature of this difference in MC children's responses to the Trotin task may shed some light on the unexpected findings in the present section of the analysis. In the MC sub-sample there exists a negative correlation between the use of indefinites and the use of specificity in descriptive speech. It was suggested that some MC children offer very constrained descriptions, others are much more specific and detailed in their approach while still others give descriptions including both general and specific information. We argued that these three response types are different realisations of a context-independent orientation. It would appear from the present matrix that the children who give more general descriptions also give more general instructions. This does not mean that only the children who give this type of description also give a mode A instruction – there are too many of the latter for this to be so. Rather it suggests that if a child gives a general description[5] then he will also give a general instruction.

But children orientated to other variants of context-independent descriptive speech will also give explanations in terms of general rules. The converse of the above argument would be that those MC children who adopt a particularistic instruction will include children conforming to a descriptive response that is low on implicitness, and low on generality but high in the explication of detail. In fact, 6 of the 9 mode B children can be thus characterised, and we might predict that their instructional speech although context-dependent in terms of semantic orientation will be linguistically explicit. The pattern of correlations for WC children who give a mode B instruction suggests that a substantial proportion of this group will, on the other hand, make their response relatively more implicit in speech. There is no way of testing this, however, and since the numbers are small and we are arguing across contexts, the suggestion is made very tentatively.

Summary

The results reported here for the total sample and the WC boys offer considerable support for the hypothesis that children will be consistent in their coding orientation in contexts of description and instruction. WC girls differed sharply from the boys in the sample in that no consistency, between situations in terms of our coding categories, was evident in their speech. The tendency of a substantial number of WC girls to move to narrative in both these contexts may have influenced the results, and this possibility will be discussed in the section on narrative below.

The results concerning the MC group are weaker than those for the total sample of the WC boys, and two reasons for this are suggested. First, there is very little variation in this group in terms of choice of instructional mode. Secondly, the variation in approach to the descriptive task is largely in terms of different context-independent variants rather than differential orientation to context-independent speech. When such reduced variation occurs in both contexts then the correlational technique, as well as the coding categories, inadequately reveal the structure of speech in different tasks.

(2) Mode maintenance in instruction and context-independence/dependence in description

We turn now to those instructional indices concerned with mode breakdown and mode maintenance. We had no strong prior expectations as to how these categories would relate to the descriptive indices and so shall turn directly to the findings.

Findings

Table 4.36 shows the pattern of correlations for the total sample. Breakdown of mode in the full sample is positively related to the two indices of context-dependence in the Trotin task (the textual index and exophora) and negatively related to the two indices of

Table 4.36 Tau coefficients between the mode-maintenance categories in instruction and the context-independent/dependent indices in description for the total sample

	Exophora	Indefinites	Specificity	Text
Mode breakdown	0·180***	−0·137**	−0·035	0·161***
Mode maintenance	−0·117*	0·115*	0·039	−0·174***

context-independence (indefinites and specificity). Apart from those involving specificity, all these correlations are significant. Thus those children who give context-dependent descriptive texts are inclined to have difficulty in completing an explanation of hide and seek. Those children who give context-independent descriptive texts are more likely to offer a cohesive text in the instructional task. Of course these correlations are influenced by the fact that both sets of indices correlate independently with the mode-type categories in instruction. The strength of the present correlations is interesting, however, particularly in the finding that the sub-indices of exophora and indefinites correlate consistently and quite strongly with the two mode-maintenance categories. We shall return to this after consideration of the two sub-sample matrices.

Table 4.37 Tau coefficients between the mode-maintenance categories in instruction and the context-independent/dependent indices in description for the WC sub-sample

	Exophora	Indefinites	Specificity	Text
Mode breakdown	0·093	−0·094	0·057	0·133*
Mode maintenance	−0·114**	0·189**	−0·012	−0·220***

Table 4.37 shows that the pattern for the total sample is repeated for the WC sub-sample although the significance levels are on the whole reduced. The correlations involving the mode-maintenance categories suggest rather strongly that those WC children who give a context-independent description will tend to give a complete instructional text in which the initially adopted reference sets are maintained

throughout. When the WC boys and girls are investigated separately we see that this pattern is more marked among the girls. Tables 4.38 and 4.39 give the relevant figures.

Table 4.38   Tau coefficients between the mode-maintenance categories in instruction and the context-independent/dependent indices in description for WC boys

	Exophora	Indefinites	Specificity	Text
Mode breakdown	0·092	0·000	−0·019	0·122
Mode maintenance	−0·088	0·112	0·070	−0·219*

Table 4.39   Tau coefficients between the mode-maintenance categories in instruction and the context-independent/dependent indices in description for WC girls

	Exophora	Indefinites	Specificity	Text
Mode breakdown	0·083	−0·181*	0·096	0·112
Mode maintenance	−0·157*	0·215*	−0·079	−0·222*

In the previous section there was no consistent pattern for WC girls between the mode type adopted in the instructional context and the degree of context-independence/dependence in their descriptive speech. It appears now that such consistency as this group of children did show is at the level of linguistic cohesion rather than semantic orientation. WC boys, too, show some consistency in the extent to which they create cohesive texts across the two contexts, but the pattern is less marked for the boys and certainly not as strong as the consistency shown by them in their semantic orientation. Before discussing these results more fully we shall consider the results for the MC sub-sample.

Table 4.40 reveals that only two of the relationships found in the total sample matrix are in evidence when the MC sub-sample is separately considered. These correlations do, however, suggest that those MC children who are orientated to implicit descriptive speech are more likely to break down in their construction of an instructional text. Such inferences are nevertheless tempered by the unreliability of

Table 4.40   Tau coefficients between the mode-maintenance categories in instruction and the context-independent/dependent indices in description for MC sub-sample

	Exophora	Indefinites	Specificity	Text
Mode breakdown	0·179**	−0·079	−0·043	0·215**
Mode maintenance	−0·016	−0·068	−0·040	−0·061

correlations involving the mode breakdown category in the MC sub-sample. Because of the small number of MC children using this category, separate analyses for boys and girls were not carried out. In general, the patterns of relationships described above suggest that those children orientated to context-dependence in description will show mode breakdown in instruction and those children oriented to context-independence in description will tend to maintain their initially adopted instructional mode and be consistent in their reference sets. An explanation for this pattern suggests itself.

The implicit realisation of meanings in description results in a series of individual statements whose referents are embedded in the eliciting context. The instructional context demands the construction of a text whose reference sets are internally, linguistically consistent. Cohesion in the instructional context must be achieved purely verbally, through anaphoric reference. The child whose orientation to language use results in a high frequency of exophora will find it more difficult to handle such cohesive devices since he/she tends to rely on the social and material situation to carry some of the burden of reference. Thus a context-dependent orientation is more likely to lead to the breakdown of reference sets, since these have to be wholly carried in the verbal system. In a sense the explanation of hide and seek is the most context-independent task the child is asked to complete, since it is the only task that includes no extra-verbal material. Children orientated to context-independent speech in a range of situations are more likely to manage the handling of a complex system of reference once this becomes obligatory. What is unclear is why the relationship between context-independence in description and linguistic cohesion in instruction should hold most clearly for WC girls, the group who show the least tendency to be consistent in their basic approaches to the two tasks. Since WC girls are also more likely to introduce narrative in both contexts, a consideration of the role of narrative may illuminate the issue.

(3) The two narrative indices

In both the descriptive and the instructional tasks we saw that narrative is more likely to be introduced by children showing a relatively context-dependent orientation. However, not all children who are orientated to context-dependent speech move to narrative in their responses. In the instructional task many children gave a context-dependent explanation without the inclusion of narrative. And among girls, although the use of narrative was strongly positively associated with the use of the particularistic mode, it was not strongly negatively associated with the use of the universalistic mode. Again, in the Trotin task many children gave an implicit description without moving to narrative. Indeed, the findings from the descriptive task suggest that such children are more strongly orientated to implicit description than are those who embed narrative within such a description. The picture concerning narrative is not altogether clear. Perhaps an analysis of how the different speech patterns are related across contexts will clarify their meaning in each.

Expectations

Three general predictions may be made in this analysis.
1 The same children will move to narrative in the two tasks.
2 Children who move to narrative in the descriptive task will tend to be particularistic in their instructional speech. Narrative in the Trotin task will correlate negatively with mode A, positively with mode B and positively with the general instructional index.
3 Children who move to narrative in the instructional task will tend to be context-dependent in their descriptive speech. Narrative in instruction will correlate positively with exophora, negatively with

Table 4.41 Tau coefficients between narrative in instruction and description and all other indices in these contexts for the total WC sample

	Narrative	Exophora	Indefinites	Specificity	Text
Narrative	0·381***	0·134*	−0·065	0·139*	0·196**
Mode A	−0·050				
Mode B	0·008				
Mode C	−0·062				
Text	0·075				
Mode breakdown	0·176**				
Mode maintenance	−0·150*				

indefinites and positively with the textual index. A negative correlation with specificity is less likely to appear, given the findings of the descriptive context.

As before, the analysis of narrative is confined to the WC sample, with particular emphasis on the girls.

Findings

Table 4.41 shows how the narrative in the two tasks correlates with the remaining indices in those tasks for the total WC sample. Before discussing this matrix we shall present the analyses for boys and girls separately considered (Tables 4.42 and 4.43).

Table 4.42   Tau coefficients between narrative in instruction and description and all other indices in these contexts for WC boys

	Narrative	Exophora	Indefinites	Specificity	Text
Narrative	0·127	0·088	0·075	0·085	0·129
Mode A	0·016				
Mode B	0·029				
Mode C	−0·099				
Text	0·019				
Mode breakdown	0·236*				
Mode maintenance	0·000				

Table 4.43   Tau coefficients between narrative in instruction and description and all the other indices in these contexts for WC girls

	Narrative	Exophora	Indefinites	Specificity	Text
Narrative	0·542***	0·162*	−0·194*	0·157*	0·215*
Mode A	−0·090				
Mode B	−0·001				
Mode C	−0·033				
Text	0·105				
Mode breakdown	0·504***				
Mode maintenance	−0·331***				

From these tables it can be seen that the results for the total WC sample are largely a reflection of the girls' patterns of language use.

In the boys' sample there are few significant correlations, and we consider this to be due to the small number of boys who move to narrative in either task, but particularly in the Trotin task. The finding that the tendency to move to narrative is not consistent across tasks is unexpected, however. It suggests that not only do boys as a group avoid the use of narrative but that individual boys who do adopt this mode are not strongly orientated to its use.

Girls, on the other hand, tend to be consistent in their use of narrative. If it is used in one context then it is highly likely to be introduced in the other. Further, the use of narrative in instruction is associated with a context-dependent orientation in description. Interestingly, of the five WC girls who gave only narrative speech in the instructional context, two gave a 'mixed' response in the Trotin task and three gave the most implicit level of descriptive speech. The children identified in the analysis of the descriptive context as offering implicit speech combined with a substantial amount of narrative apparently also move to narrative in the instructional context. Further they show a strong tendency to breakdown in their instructional speech, and even where this does not occur they are not consistent in the handling of reference. However, there is no evidence that such children are more likely to adopt one approach to instruction rather than another. Narrative in description is only very weakly associated with orientation to instruction. This result confirms many of the other findings in the analysis of the descriptive and instructional contexts. Although patterning is evident across the tasks in some aspects of the speech of WC girls, whether mode A or mode B is adopted is unrelated to the remaining speech categories. This finding is puzzling in the light of the very strong relationship between the instructional and descriptive categories found for WC boys.

VI DESCRIPTION AND CONTROL

So far we have examined the relationships between description and instruction, considering the extent to which the child's linguistic orientation in one context can predict his orientation in the other. The results show that this can be done with considerable success for these two contexts. In the present section we are concerned with the relationships between description and control. Here we consider such questions as the following. Do children who offer relatively explicit descriptions of the Trotin cards tend to choose the more verbally elaborate methods of control? What is the relationship between a move to narrative in the descriptive task and type of control? Does the pattern of correlations between control and description support the interpretation made in the preceding section that within the middle-class group there are children who are orientated to specificity and children who are orientated to generality in their linguistic usage?

The relationships between the descriptive and regulative contexts are handled in two groups. First, the pattern of relationships between the five indices of control and the four indices of context-independence/dependence in description is examined. Second, for the working-class sample, the relationships between the indices of control and the narrative index are given close attention. As only six middle-class children can be described as adopting a story-telling mode in the Trotin task, the correlations between the indices of control and the narrative index for the middle-class sample are unreliable; these correlations are given in Appendix 1.

(1)   Orientation to control and context independence/ dependence in description

Expectations

The central prediction in this analysis is that the index of text in the regulative context will correlate negatively with the index of text in the descriptive context, i.e. high elaboration in control correlating negatively with low elaboration (context-dependence) in description. This association directly tests the basic question of consistency in coding orientation. A second important prediction is that the contingencies, backings and affect index will correlate negatively with the descriptive text index. Taking into account the other sub-indices we would expect the following pattern of associations:

(a) In the case of contingencies, backings and affect, modified directives and the regulative text index, a positive correlation with indefinites and specificity, and a negative correlation with exophora and the descriptive text index.

(b) In the case of punishment and imperative directives, a negative correlation with indefinites and specificity, and a positive correlation with exophora and the descriptive text index.

These predictions were made with certain reservations. One, there was some doubt about whether the regulative text index would emerge as a more effective discriminator than the contingencies, backings and affect index, particularly in view of the sex variation in the working-class sub-sample. Two, it was thought that the contingencies, backings and affect index was a measure of specificity as well as explicitness, and that, therefore, whilst its correlation with specificity in the descriptive context can be expected to be relatively high, its correlation with indefinites (highly general, non-specific choices) can be expected to be lower. Three, it was not thought that punishment would give as clear a pattern of results as the other indices.

Findings

Table 4.44 shows the interrelationships of the relevant indices for the total sample. The pattern of correlations for the total sample is to a large degree in accord with our predictions. The regulative text index correlates negatively with the descriptive text index, and the correlation is significant at the 0·001 level. The regulative text index also has significant positive correlations with indefinites and specificity,

Table 4.44   Tau coefficients between the indices of control and the context-independent/dependent indices for description for the total sample

	Exophora	Indefinites	Specificity	Text
Punishment	0·079(*)	−0·084*	−0·120**	0·170***
Contingencies, etc.	−0·093*	0·180***	0·235***	−0·181***
Directive: imperative	−0·003	−0·130**	−0·043	0·154***
Directive: modified	−0·072(*)	−0·018	0·035	−0·036
Text	−0·053	0·159***	0·135**	−0·180***

but the negative correlation with exophora is not significant. The contingencies, backings and affect index reveals the same pattern of relationships, but here the correlations with the descriptive sub-indices are higher, and all are significant. The correlation between contingencies, etc. and the descriptive text index is almost exactly the same as that between the regulative text index and the descriptive text index, −0·181 as compared with −0·180. So, as far as the crucial correlations with the descriptive text index go, the power of the regulative text index and the contingencies, backings and affect index is about equal. Punishment, we may note, gives a clear but not strong pattern of correlations in the expected manner. The other two indices, imperative directives and modified directives, yield some very weak correlations, but imperative directives has a significant negative correlation with indefinites and a significant positive correlation with the descriptive text score.

Table 4.45 shows that when we control for social class, and look at the correlations for the working-class sub-sample, the number

Table 4.45   Tau coefficients between the indices of control and the context-independent/dependent indices for description for the WC sub-sample

	Exophora	Indefinites	Specificity	Text
Punishment	0·059	0·045	−0·060	0·007
Contingencies, etc.	0·084	0·083	0·206**	−0·031
Directive: imperative	0·002	−0·207**	0·054	0·069
Directive: modified	−0·031	−0·012	−0·024	−0·042
Text	0·059	0·170**	0·030	−0·045

of significant correlations is sharply reduced. The correlations between the regulative text index and the descriptive text index are both low. There is, however, a significant correlation between the regulative text index and indefinites, which reflects the significant negative correlation between imperative directives and indefinites. There is also a significant correlation between the contingencies, backings and affect index and specificity.

Previously we drew attention to the sex variation in the working-class sample. The question to be considered here is: are there conflicting tendencies in the working-class sample, differences between boys and girls, which reduce the correlations between the descriptive text index and the indices of elaboration in the regulative context?

Table 4.46   Tau coefficients between the indices of control and the context-independent/dependent indices for description for the WC boys' sub-sample

	Exophora	Indefinites	Specificity	Text
Punishment	0·219*	0·123	−0·148(*)	0·081
Contingencies, etc.	0·018	0·258***	0·351***	−0·176(*)
Directive: imperative	0·138	−0·310**	0·046	0·190*
Directive: modified	−0·119	0·053	−0·121	−0·138
Text	−0·122	0·339***	0·041	−0·228*

Tables 4.46 and 4.47 give the pattern of relationships within the sample of working-class boys and the sample of working-class girls respectively. The tables show that, when sex is controlled for

Table 4.47   Tau coefficients between the indices of control and the context-independent/dependent indices for description for the WC girls' sub-sample

	Exophora	Indefinites	Specificity	Text
Punishment	−0·043	−0·024	0·016	−0·055
Contingencies, etc.	0·138(*)	−0·082	0·090	0·075
Directive: imperative	−0·108	−0·131(*)	0·076	−0·024
Directive: modified	0·026	−0·079	0·010	0·005
Text	0·215*	0·010	–0·019	0·107

in the working-class sample, there is an increase in the number of significant relationships between control and description – in the case of the boys. By and large, the relationships are very different in the two groups, and this explains why, for example, the relationship between the two textual indices was so weak. The patterning in the boys' sample is very clear and is closely in accord with our expectations. There is a significant correlation between the two textual indices, and the correlation between contingencies, backings and affect and the descriptive text index almost reaches significance. There are four other correlations to note. Contingencies, backings and affect, besides having a significant correlation with specificity also has a significant correlation with indefinites, though the latter correlation is a little lower. Imperative directives has a significant negative correlation with indefinites and a positive one with the descriptive text index. Finally, interestingly, punishment has a significant positive correlation with exophora, and an almost significant negative correlation with specificity. The patterning in the girls' sample is less clear and less in accord with our expectations. Here there is an almost significant positive correlation between contingencies, backings and affect and exophora, and a significant positive correlation between the regulative text index and exophora – correlations which, according to our predictions, should be negative. It is chiefly these correlations which weaken the pattern of results for the total working-class sample.

Who are the girls who score relatively high on the regulative text score (because they opt for contingencies, etc. and avoid imperative directives) but who also score relatively high for exophora in the descriptive context? A clue is given in the earlier study by Turner (in press). It was observed that working-class girls were more likely than the boys to mention qualified concessions (in the 'bedtime' and 'school' situations), for example, 'You can stay for a little while until this is over', 'All right. You can watch a little bit of it'. To the extent that they made such selections they would avoid imperative directives in these situations, for example, 'Go up to bed at once', 'Get to bed'. It seems likely that it is chiefly the girls who are contributing to the positive correlations between contingencies, etc. and exophora, and between the regulative text index and exophora, and the negative correlation between imperative directives and exophora.

Table 4.48 Tau coefficients between the indices of control and the context-independent/dependent indices for description for the MC sub-sample

	Exophora	Indefinites	Specificity	Text
Punishment	−0·065	0·014	0·005	−0·028
Contingencies, etc.	−0·108(*)	0·100(*)	0·169**	−0·200**
Directive: imperative	−0·117(*)	0·042	−0·068	−0·128*
Directive: modified	−0·102(*)	−0·070	0·065	0·062
Text	−0·020	0·012	0·132*	0·001

Table 4.48 shows the pattern of relationships between control and description in the middle-class sample. The pattern of relationships demonstrated here is in certain respects the predicted one. The contingencies, backings and affect index has a very clear set of relationships with the descriptive indices. Children who mention contingencies, backings and affect show a preference for specificity in the descriptive context. They also tend, to a lesser extent, to choose indefinites and to avoid exophora. There is a significant correlation between contingencies, backings and affect and the descriptive text index. Reflecting these relationships, there is a significant correlation between the regulative text index and specificity. Where the pattern of relationships departs from expectation is in the case of the correlations between imperative directives and exophora and imperative directives and the descriptive text index. Here the signs are reversed. Children who mention imperative directives tend to avoid exophora and context-dependence. It is chiefly these two correlations that 'upset' the correlation between the two textual indices, which is very weak. When interpreting these correlations, it is important to bear in mind that there was relatively little variation in the middle-class sub-sample on the context-independent/dependent dimension; most of the children offered responses of the context-independent type.

In Appendix 1 we present the correlations between the indices of control and the context-independent/dependent indices for description for the MC boys and the MC girls separately. These are included for comparison with those for the WC boys and girls (Tables 4.46 and 4.47). They are not discussed here as, unlike in the working-class sample, there was no strong pattern of sex difference in the middle-class sample.

Summary

The results for the total sample and to a degree the results for the sub-samples offer support for the hypothesis that children will be consistent in their coding orientation in contexts of control and description. There are two main factors which complicate the picture for the middle-class and the working-class sub-samples. In the case of the middle-class group it is the fact that there is relatively little variation on the context-independent/dependent dimension. So, to a certain extent, no matter what type of control the children opted for in the regulative context, they tended to choose context-independent description in the descriptive context. It had previously been suggested that the variation in approach to the descriptive task, in the case of the middle-class children, is largely in terms of different context-independent variants, describable in terms of a specificity v. generality dimension, with specific detailed description at one pole (that is, low on indefinites, high on specificity) and general description at the other (high on indefinites, low on specificity). Our results in this section lend some support to the view that within the middle-class group there are children who are orientated to specificity in their linguistic usage and others who are orientated to generality. We regard the contingencies, backings and affect index as a measure of specificity as well as explicitness, and it is the case that the correlation between contingencies, etc. and specificity in the descriptive context is higher than that between contingencies etc. and indefinites; this pattern is also apparent in the working-class sample. In other words, children who give specific references in the descriptive context are more likely to mention contingencies, backings and affect in the regulative context than are children who make references of the indefinite kind.

Turning to the working-class group, here there is a different factor which complicates the picture. For this sample there is sufficient variation on the context-independent/dependent dimension. The problem lies in the sex variation in the selection of certain control options. There are conflicting tendencies in the boys and girls, with the result that the relationships between the descriptive text index and the indices of control are weak. When sex of child is controlled for, a very strong pattern of relationships is apparent in the case of the boys. For these children there was evidence of a relatively high degree of consistency in their responses to the two contexts; the children who obtained high scores for elaboration in the regulative context tended to obtain *low* scores for restriction (context-dependence) in the descriptive context. The picture was less clear in the case of the girls. Here there were children who obtained relatively high scores for contingencies, backings and affect and the regulative text index but who also tended to score high for exophora in the descriptive context. We associated this result with a preference on the part of working-class girls for mentioning concessions (of the contingent kind) in two of the control situations, particularly the 'bedtime' situation. Although the girls' linguistic usage was explicit and specific, chiefly with respect to this control function, their linguistic usage in the descriptive context was not.

On the question of which index of elaboration in the regulative context – the regulative text index or the contingencies, backings and affect index – is the more powerful discriminator of texts, our answer at this stage in the analysis must be that they have both proved their effectiveness, but that the contingencies index would appear to have the edge on the textual index. It was only in the case of working-class boys that the textual index was noticeably more powerful than the contingencies, backings and affect index alone.

(2)   Orientation in control and narrative in the descriptive context

Expectations

It has been suggested elsewhere that a move to narrative in the descriptive context or in the instructional context can be viewed as a form of restricted coding. Narrative speech in these contexts is 'context-dependent' in the special sense that the child constructs a context somewhat different from the one offered to him, and it is in terms of the modified context that the speech is to be understood. Concerning the descriptive context, it was noted that the children (chiefly working-class girls) who offered narrative tended to be children who were context-dependent or mixed in their description, but it was also noted that the children with both narrative and context-dependent description were somewhat less implicit in their description than were the children who offered only context-dependent description and did not move to narrative. So, whilst narrative in the descriptive context did not go with context-independence in description, there is a sense in which it went with a certain amount of explicitness in description. The correlations between the indices of control and narrative in the descriptive context enable us to explore a little further the relationship between narrative and explicitness.

Our predictions concerning the relationships between the indices of control and narrative in the descriptive context are based upon the assumption that narrative is a form of context-dependent coding. It is expected, therefore, that the indices of elaboration in the regulative context will correlate negatively with the index of narrative in the descriptive context.

Findings

Table 4.49 gives the correlations for the total sample, the working-class sub-sample and the working-class boys' and girls' sub-samples. (As only 6 middle-class children adopted a story-telling mode in the descriptive context, the correlations for the middle-class sub-sample are unreliable. They are given in Appendix 1.)

Table 4.49   Correlations between the indices of control and the narrative index for the total sample, the WC sub-sample and the WC boys' and girls' sub-samples

	Total sample	WC	WCB	WCG
Punishment	0·156***	0·060	0·099	0·050
Contingencies, etc.	0·094(*)	0·167**	0·123	0·198*
Directive: imperative	0·026	0·018	0·116	−0·035
Directive: modified	0·049	−0·099(*)	−0·084	−0·142(*)
Text	0·041	0·008	−0·077	0·047

Table 4.49 shows that for the total sample there are two significant relationships between the indices of control and narrative, one in the expected direction, the other not. Punishment has a positive correlation with narrative, but so has contingencies, backings and affect, though to a lesser degree. In the working-class sub-sample there is just one significant relation: contingencies, backings, and affect correlates positively with narrative. Children who use modified directives also tend to avoid narrative. When sex of child is controlled for, it can be seen that the correlation between contingencies, backings and affect is positive in each sub-group, but that it reaches significance in the case of the girls. The negative association between modified directives and narrative is also stronger in the case of girls.

The significant positive correlation between contingencies, backings and affect and narrative is in line with the positive correlation between contingencies, backings and affect and exophora in the case of working-class girls (Table 4.47). We know from Table 4.11 that there is a significant positive correlation between narrative and exophora in the case of working-class girls. The picture is, then, that the children who move to narrative in the descriptive context tend to take up the more elaborate methods of control in the regulative context. This is the case, even though in the descriptive context they opt for context-dependent rather than context-independent description.

Summary

The investigation of the relationships between control and narrative in the descriptive context provides some support for the interpretation that the working-class children who move to narrative in the descriptive context are less implicit in their linguistic usage than their counterparts who do not move to narrative.

VII INSTRUCTION AND CONTROL

In the previous two sections we have considered the relationships between description and instruction and between description and control, looking for patterns of consistency in the children's coding orientations in different contexts We have shown that one can predict with some success from the children's usage in one context to their usage in another, though we have encountered some problems. In this final section we consider the remaining set of relationships, those between instruction and control. The basic question we seek to answer is: do those children who give a universalistic instruction of how to play hide and seek tend to use verbally elaborate methods of control, and, conversely, do the children who explain the game in terms of particular people and places tend to use the less verbally elaborate methods of control? We are also interested in the relationship between control and narrative in the instructional context.

We now give the relationships between the instructional and the regulative context which are to be analysed. First, there is the pattern of relationships between the mode type of instruction and the indices of control. Second, there is the pattern of relationships between the indices of control and the measure of narrative in the instructional context. A third possible set of relationships, those between the indices of control and the measures of the child's tendency to produce a cohesive text in the instructional context, is not examined,

as we held no hypotheses about the relationships, though the correlations are given for interest in Appendix 1. The questions put to
the child in the regulative context in general produced short answers,
in which breaks in cohesion were unlikely. We had no measure of
cohesion in the five control indices, nor any strong reasons for
expecting a clear pattern of relationships between choice of control
in the regulative context and cohesion in the instructional context.

(1)   Orientation to control and mode of instruction

Expectations

The central prediction is that the index of text in the regulative context will correlate negatively with the index of text in the instructional context. In more detail we expect:
(a) In the case of contingencies, backings and affect, modified
directives and the regulative text index, a positive correlation with
mode A instruction and a negative correlation with mode B instruction and the instructional text index.
(b) In the case of punishment and imperative directives, a negative
correlation with mode A instruction and a positive correlation with
mode B instruction and the instructional text index.

No predictions were made about the relationships between the
indices of control and mode C instruction, that is, the mixed mode
of instruction. The above predictions were made with a certain
reservation. It was known that there was relatively little variation in
mode of instruction in the middle-class sub-sample; very few middle-
class children offered a mode B instruction. Clearly this fact would
be reflected in the pattern of correlations.

Findings

Table 4.50 shows the interrelationships of the relevant indices for
the total sample. The pattern of correlations is to a large extent
in accordance with our expectations. The contingencies, backings
and affect index reveals a strong set of relationships, correlating
positively with mode A instruction and negatively with mode B
instruction and the instructional text index. A similar set of relationships is revealed by the requlative text index, but these are a little less
strong, reflecting, to a certain extent, the weak relationships between
the directive indices and mode of instruction. Punishment correlates
negatively with mode A and positively with mode B, but contrary to
expectation its correlation with the instructional text index is negative.

Table 4.50 Tau coefficients between the indices of control and the orientation indices for instruction for the total sample

	Mode A	Mode B	Mode C	Text
Punishment	−0·095*	0·141**	−0·105*	−0·097*
Contingencies	0·135**	−0·211***	0·095*	−0·174***
Directive: imperative	−0·051	0·087*	−0·022	0·060
Directive: modified	0·030	−0·018	0·010	−0·035
Text	0·115*	−0·139**	0·034	−0·134**

Table 4.51 Tau coefficients between the indices of control and the orientation indices for instruction for the WC sub-sample

	Mode A	Mode B	Mode C	Text
Punishment	0·028	0·026	−0·049	−0·052
Contingencies, etc.	0·171**	−0·243***	0·123*	−0·214**
Directive: imperative	−0·067	0·067	0·027	0·056
Directive: modified	−0·042	0·023	0·100(*)	0·005
Text	0·069	−0·113(*)	0·075	−0·102(*)

Table 4.51 shows the pattern of relationships within the working-class sub-sample. In this sub-sample the contingencies, backings and affect index shows a very clear pattern of significant relationships, but otherwise the relationships between the two sets of indices are weak. The correlation between the textual indices does not reach significance (−0·102*).

Tables 4.52 and 4.53 show the pattern of relationshps within the working-class sub-sample when we control for sex of child. Perhaps the first thing to notice is the increase in the number of significant results when compared with Table 4.51. This is a clear indication that taking the working class as a group masks intra-group variation associated with sex. We shall now consider the boys and girls in turn. In the case of the boys the pattern of correlations is very largely the predicted one. What is most impressive in the matrix is the pattern of correlations between the instructional text index and the two key indices of elaboration in the regulative context. Both relationships

Table 4.52   Tau coefficients between the indices of control and the orientation indices for instruction for the WC boys' sub-sample

	Mode A	Mode B	Mode C	Text
Punishment	0·062	−0·089	−0·073	−0·042
Contingencies, etc.	0·249***	−0·220*	0·000	−0·252**
Directive: imperative	−0·270**	0·123	0·221*	0·207
Directive: modified	−0·057	−0·085	0·246**	−0·026
Text	0·225**	−0·203*	−0·013	−0·231*

Table 4.53   Tau coefficients between the indices of control and the orientation indices for instruction for the WC girls' sub-sample

	Mode A	Mode B	Mode C	Text
Punishment	−0·128	0·121	−0·030	0·141(*)
Contingencies, etc.	0·112	−0·267**	0·233*	−0·199*
Directive: imperative	0·109	0·022	−0·158(*)	−0·042
Directive: modified	−0·006	0·105	−0·009	0·010
Text	−0·072	−0·030	0·163*	0·006

are significant, but the correlation with the contingencies, backings and affect is slightly higher, −0·252** as opposed to −0·231*. Turning to the mode types, there are three significant correlations with mode A, involving contingencies, backings and affect, imperative directives and the regulative text index, and two significant correlations with mode B, involving contingencies and the text index. When we look at the matrix for the girls, there are only two points of close similarity with the correlations for the boys; there is a significant negative correlation between contingencies, backings and affect and mode B, and also a significant negative correlation between contingencies, etc. and the instructional text index. It is of interest to note that the correlation between the contingencies, backings and affect index and mode A is much lower for the girls than for the boys. In addition to this weaker relationship, there is also a *positive* relationship between imperative directives and mode A, though this relationship is not significant; whereas, in the case of the boys, the relationship is negative, as we should expect, and is significant. These factors have to be borne in mind when considering the weak relationship between the regulative text index and the instructional text index in the case of the girls.

Table 4.54 shows the pattern of relationships within the middle-class sub-sample.

Table 4.54 Tau coefficients between the indices of control and the orientation indices for instruction for the MC sub-sample

	Mode A	Mode B	Mode C	Text
Punishment	0·024 ,	0·078	−0·158*	0·010
Contingencies, etc.	0·001	−0·009	0·024	−0·006
Directive: imperative	0·066	−0·008	0·061	−0·058
Directive: modified	0·060	−0·017	−0·074	−0·049
Text	0·009	0·004	−0·016	−0·007

The table shows that for the middle-class sub-sample the relationships between control and instruction are very weak. Neither the regulative text index nor the contingencies, backings and affect index shows any relationship with the instructional text index. It seems clear that these results reflect the relative lack of variation in the middle-class children's selection of mode of instruction; most middle-class children gave instructions of the mode A type.

In Appendix 1 we give the correlation matrices for the middle-class boys and girls separately, for comparison with those for the working-class boys and girls. These correlations revealed no strong patterns of sex difference, and need not be discussed here.

Summary

The results for the total sample in large measure support our predictions based upon the hypothesis that children would be consistent in their coding orientation in the regulative and instructional contexts. To a degree the results for the sub-samples support the hypothesis, but there are a number of factors which complicate the picture. In the case of the middle-class children the chief problem seems to be the lack of variation on the context-independent/dependent instruction dimension. Most middle-class children chose the universalistic context-independent mode of instruction, so, to a certain extent, no matter what type of control the children opted for in the regulative context they tended to choose context-independent instruction in the instructional context. In the case of the working-class children there was greater variation, and the pattern of correlations between control and instruction was much clearer. But here the picture was complicated by the sex variation within the working-class group. The working-class boys, it was revealed, were relatively consistent in their coding orientation, with the children who scored high for elaboration in the regulative context tending to opt for universalistic, context-independent instruction in the instructional context. The working-class girls provided less evidence of consistency across contexts.

Throughout the analysis it was clear that the contingencies, backings and affect index was a more powerful discriminator of texts than the regulative text index.

(2) Orientation to control and narrative in the instructional context

Expectations

It has been stressed throughout the paper that a move to narrative in the descriptive context or the instructional context can be regarded as a form of context-dependence. Bearing this in mind, we would expect the indices of elaboration in the regulative context to correlate negatively with narrative in the instructional context.

Findings

Table 4.55 gives the correlations between the narrative index and the indices of control for the total sample and the sub-samples. (The middle-class sub-sample is included but it should be borne in mind that only 11 middle-class children gave narrative speech in the instructional context.) The table does not show a very clear pattern of relationships. For the total sample there are three significant correlations between control and narrative: a relatively strong positive correlation between punishment and narrative, and two rather weak negative correlations between modified directives and narrative and the regulative text index and narrative. The correlation involving punishment reflects a relationship in the middle-class sub-sample, and the other two correlations largely reflect a relationship in the working-class sub-sample, namely that those children (particularly the boys) who use modified directives tend to avoid narrative.

Table 4.55   Correlations between the narrative index and the indices of control for the total sample, the MC sub-sample, the WC sub-sample and the WC boys' and girls' sub-samples

	Total sample	WC	MC	WCB	WCG
Punishment	0·197***	0·040	0·303***	0·047	0·071
Contingencies, etc.	−0·038	0·018	0·076	−0·018	0·033
Directive: imperative	0·009	0·038	−0·151*	0·032	0·066
Directive: modified	−0·091*	−0·134*	−0·008	−0·242**	−0·109
Text	−0·084*	−0·079	0·069	−0·120	−0·060

Summary

The use of narrative in the instructional context is not strongly related to type of control in the regulative context. The results do not throw any further light on the interpretation of narrative as a form of context-dependent speech.

VIII   EVALUATION

The aim of this study is to investigate empirically the notion that children acquire, through the transmission system of the home, a code or set of ground rules by means of which they can create texts in a range of speech situations. It is proposed theoretically that the code acquired differs according to the principles of transmission and that sub-cultural or social-class differences in the transmission code may be found in this country. Specifically it is suggested that most middle-class children are orientated to an elaborated code through which they will create texts of a certain kind – universalistic in meaning and explicit in speech – across a range of contexts, whereas many WC children are orientated to a restricted code whose ground rules provoke the creation of more context-dependent texts in similar situations.

In this paper we looked at acquisition and realisation – at the child's ground rules or code as realised in three contexts. A further SRU publication will embed this analysis in the question of the transmission system which provokes the different acquired codes which we have identified.

We sought, then, to answer two related questions. One, whether the concept of an underlying principle or code is tenable in the light of empirical data. Our unit was the text or coding, and an attempt was made to see whether sufficient consistency in coding existed in order that an underlying code could be postulated. The second question concerns social-class differences in coding orientation – do the social classes differ in the way postulated in Bernstein's theory of cultural transmission?

In fact the hypotheses of social-class differences were affirmed so strongly that we found ourselves in considerable difficulty in analysing the finer points of our second question, that of consistency of coding orientation. We shall proceed in our discussion by looking first at the sample as a whole in order to throw light on both questions and we shall then examine the two social-class groups in order to deal more intensively with the question of consistency in coding orientation but against a background of our knowledge of how the two groups differ. In the WC sample we found considerable sex differences at various points. For this reason, boys and girls in the WC will be considered separately.

Before continuing with our discussion, however, it will be useful to remind the reader of our reasons for laying emphasis on the experimental context.

The experimental context

To our knowledge, no previous research has attempted to examine the consistency shown by individual children in their responses to different speech situations. From the point of view of Bernstein's thesis it was important to create an overall eliciting context which would provoke elaborated coding from children orientated to its use and restricted coding from children who had acquired a restricted code. By this we do not mean that the context was arranged so that MC children would speak fluently and WC children would be constrained. On the contrary, we often found the opposite to be the case. The parameters of the context were theoretically derived, particularly in the nature of the social relationship which pertained. Children interpreted this relationship very differently. Some MC children were very hesitant in responding until absolutely sure of what was required of them, others treated the situation as one of equality. On the other hand, some WC girls seemed to 'make' the relationship by talking fluently and telling stories. The issue is a complex one and is gone into in more detail in Chapter 1 as well as being taken up again at the end of this evaluation. For the moment let us stress that the nature of the experimental context is of theoretical importance (Bernstein has called it a 'context-independent' setting) in this, we believe, first attempt to relate children's speech patterns across situations.

We proceed now with the discussion.

The total sample

We may begin by looking at how our three indices of text correlate (Table 4.56). Is the text a child creates in one context related at the level of sociolinguistic code to the text he creates in another? Since in the regulative context it was unclear whether the index of text discriminated more powerfully than the index of contingencies, backings and affects, we shall here include results for both indices.

Table 4.56   Tau correlations between the indices of text in the descriptive, instructional and regulative contexts

	Trotin	Instruction	Regulative	Contingencies
Trotin		0·219***	−0·180***	−0·181***
Instruction			−0·134***	−0·174***
Regulative				
Contingencies				

From Table 4.56 we can say that a sample composed of both middle- and working-class children provides us with evidence that children differ and that they differ consistently in the principles they use to create texts in a range of situations. We consider this table to be evidence in support of Bernstein's notion of sociolinguistic code.

We have, however, stressed throughout this paper that it is important to examine consistency *within* social-class groups in order further to substantiate that children are in fact consistent in their sociolinguistic codings. Before doing this let us turn to the related question of social-class differences in the children's texts.

In all three contexts, large social-class differences were evident in the responses of the children to the speech tasks. In the descriptive task we found many WC children to be orientated to context-dependent speech whereas almost all MC children showed a context-independent orientation. We suggested, however, that this latter group differed in how they realised their elaborated code. In the instructional task again, the great majority of MC children were orientated to context-independent explanation although there was some variation in the extent to which reference sets were cohesively maintained. In the WC sample, on the other hand, as many children gave context-dependent instructions as context-independent ones. In the regulative context too, considerable social-class differences were evident. WC children were more orientated to punishment and not as inclined to give rationales or make contingent statements, whereas MC children showed the opposite pattern. In all contexts, in other words, it was possible to establish a dimension (represented by the textual indices) which corresponded to the theoretical dimension of coding orientation, and in all three contexts children differed in this dimension according to their social background, WC children tending towards restricted coding, MC children being more orientated to elaborated coding. These social-class differences are summarised in Table 4.57.

Table 4.57   Distribution of types of text in three contexts

| | The descriptive context (total sample means) | | |
	Context-independent	Mixed	Context-dependent
MC	43	32	5
WC	13	28	46

| | The descriptive context (class-specific means) | | |
	Context-independent	Mixed	Context-dependent
MC	28	41	11
WC	27	31	29

| | The instructional context | | |
	Mode A	Mode C	Mode B
MC	54	11	15
WC	37	37	13

| | The regulative context (distribution of scores on the sub-indices) | | | |
	Punishment	Contingencies	Dir.: imp.	Dir.: mod.
MC	0·827	1·531	0·988	1·049
WC	1·807	0·750	1·341	0·727

The study does, then, provide substantial support for Bernstein's theory that a child's social background or, more precisely, the structure of transmission in which he participates, will influence his orientation to language use. The differences also pose a methodological problem, however. We stressed in the introduction that a definitive analysis of our other fundamental question, that of coding orientation, requires that we look at patterns of language use within social class as well as between classes. This we did, and the results have been presented and discussed at length. The methodological problem posed by the social-class differences in the speech measures is that once we begin to look within social class the variability is very much reduced. The fact that the distribution of scores on our measures is so skewed makes it extremely difficult to carry out a meaningful analysis. In several cases basic adjustments were made in the scoring, at other points this was impossible. The kinds of adjustments we made were to exclude the narrative indices from the MC analysis – it did not make sense to correlate within this group since less than 10 per cent of the children used narrative at all. We also excluded the MC children's scores on the 'breakdown of mode' index since so few children showed such a pattern. Another way of dealing with the skewed distributions was to re-score the indices relative to the child's own social class, and this was done in the Trotin analysis. However, we saw that such a technique is not wholly appropriate. The MC children appeared to be so strongly orientated to context-independent speech that re-allocating the children according to the context-independent/dependent dimension had little meaning and in fact we were rather unsuccessful in capturing the variability in response to the Trotin task for the MC group.

Keeping in mind these problems we shall now examine the evidence for consistency of coding orientation within social class. Making the analysis independent of the child's social class means that we can ask more fundamentally the question whether or not children are consistently restricted or consistently elaborated in their coding of our three speech situations. Since there were a number of sex differences in the WC, we shall treat boys and girls separately in this group. It should be noted that such a procedure reduces the numbers of children in each sample (and in some cases reduces variability as well). Thus the tau coefficients must be fairly high in order to reach statistical significance.

Working-class boys

The picture for WC boys (Table 4.58) is very much that of the sample as a whole. Amongst these children, consistency in coding orientation is evident and this consistency is quite independent of social class. For WC boys, if a child is orientated to restricted coding in one context then he is likely to be similarly orientated in the other two.

Table 4.58   Tau coefficients between the indices of text in the descriptive, instructional and regulative contexts for WC boys

	Trotin	Instruction	Control	Contingencies
Trotin		0·362***	−0·228*	−0·176*
Instruction			−0·231*	−0·252*
Control				
Contingencies				

Those children who could be characterised as showing a relatively context-independent orientation do so in all the three contexts.

Working-class girls

The pattern of correlations for the sample of WC girls (Table 4.59) is very unlike the two matrices examined so far. The only evidence for any consistency in coding orientation is that the kind of instruction a child gives is weakly related to her use of contingent statements and rationales. Girls who give context-independent instructions are more likely to use the latter forms of control than are their contemporaries who give context-dependent instructions. For the rest, the WC girls show little evidence of consistency in coding orientation.

Table 4.59   Tau coefficients between the indices of text in the descriptive, instructional and regulative contexts for WC girls

	Trotin	Instruction	Control	Contingencies
Trotin		0·118	0·107	0·075
Instruction			0·006	−0·199*
Control				
Contingencies				

We do, however, have evidence of a different kind of consistency amongst WC girls. Those girls who move to narrative in the Trotin situation also tend to move to narrative in the instructional situation. Further, we have evidence that these are the children who are most strongly orientated to restricted coding in these two contexts. In order to try to elucidate further the meaning of this move to narrative we decided to pre-empt the forthcoming SRU study, which relates the children's speech to their mother's orientation to communication and control. This study is not yet complete but certain results are available. We decided to examine the correlations between a general index of communication and a general index of control and our two indices of narrative. The two background indices used are as follows.

A general index of communication

This index is a composite of schedules designed to measure the extent to which the mother relies on verbal communication in the socialisation of her child. It includes questions about the mother's inclination to avoid discussion, and to avoid answering fantasy questions as well as her views on the best way to define words (see Appendix 2 for the schedule).

The positional/personal index

This index is designed to measure the family's orientation towards 'personal' forms of control or 'positional' forms of control (see Bernstein, 1971). The former indicates a loose family structure where individuals are accorded a considerable degree of discretion over their own experience and practice, the latter points to a structure where the roles are more tightly defined (see Appendix 2 for the schedules).

Table 4.60 Tau coefficients between the two narrative indices and the two background measures

	Trotin narrative	Instructional narrative
General Communication	0·225**	0·401***
Positional/personal	0·183*	0·198*

The correlations between these two indices and our measures of narrative for WC girls are shown in Table 4.60. This table suggests that those children who move to narrative tend to have mothers who put less emphasis on verbal communication in the socialisation of their children. Further, the transmission systems in which the children participate tend to positionality, i.e. a tight role structure. In so far as positional families tend to differentiate more between boys and girls than personal families, these results go some way to explaining why it is the girls in the WC who move to narrative.

It is a matter of some interest that a relationship exists between the distribution of mothers' ticks on an interview schedule and the speech behaviour of children in contexts very different from the ones presented to the mothers. We therefore have some confidence in the possibility of finding a relationship between variations among mothers as measured by interview schedules and variations in the speech behaviour of children. We might interpret the above findings that WC mothers who report positional forms of control, who are less likely to move to explanation, who are less responsive to their children's attempts to initiate communication, who prefer context-dependent definitions of words (for these relationships are inter-correlational) in the following way. Such mothers, relative to those who are more person-focused and more communicative, may have a tendency to adopt a narrative style; that is, they may be more likely to report experiences than to reflect verbally upon the significance of their experiences, whereas person-focused mothers who create and are likely to be a part of a less-defined role structure may be more likely to reflect upon and evaluate verbally their experiences. Very tentatively we are hinting that the relationship between the communication measures and the narrative style of girls is an indirect one. Our suggestion is that these mothers have a preference for a narrative style in the home to which the girl is more exposed than the boy and which she is more likely to take over. The fact that the researchers who collected the speech were all women may have increased the probability of a narrative response from the girls. Hawkins (1973) found that when he examined the hesitation phenomena of a large sample of MC and WC children (which included the children in our sample) obtained from a context where the children created a spontaneous story, the articulation rate (which measures fluency of speech) of WC girls was the highest of any sub-group. In a number of cases, the texts of WC girls are longer than those of WC boys, and this is possibly because of their move to a narrative style.

We are still faced with the inconsistency in the coding orientation of WC girls despite their consistency in the use of narrative. Bernstein (1971) has suggested that the role relationship of the WC girl in the family and the differences in her peer-group attachment activities compared to the boy may affect the girl's coding orientation, particularly as this relates to her preferred control strategies. Brandis and Bernstein (1974) found that teachers tended to rate girls more favourably than boys at the end of their second year in school. It would not be unwarranted to assume that girls are more likely to be responsive to what the primary school offers. It is possible that the girls are subject to a variety of influences in their coding orientation and that these influences work in somewhat opposing ways.

It is not clear whether the existence of a large group of girls orientated to narrative had any effect on the correlations used to consider other aspects of consistency in coding orientation amongst WC girls. All we can say at present is that while there is considerable evidence that these girls are consistent in their ability to handle linguistic cohesion (p. 158), the basic semantic orientation evident in the boys is not revealed in our analysis of the girls. This may, however, be due to the consistently narrative children confounding the rest of the results.

The middle-class sample

Since there were no major differences between boys and girls in the middle class, the sample can be taken as a whole (Table 4.61). The results for the MC are rather weak. It is with this group that the problem of reduction in variability is most acute. As we pointed out,

Table 4.61   Tau coefficients between the indices of text in the descriptive, instructional and regulative contexts for MC children

	Trotin	Instruction .	Control	Contingencies
Trotin		0·122*	0·001	−0·200***
Instruction			−0·007	−0·006
Control				
Contingencies				

almost all MC children are orientated to context-independent speech in both the descriptive and the instructional task and so the association between these two contexts can only be weak. The correlation between context-independence in description and the contingencies index is strong but control and instruction do not at first appear to relate in the children's speech. These relationships have been discussed at length in other parts of the paper. Here it is only necessary to re-emphasise the problems posed by reduced variability when a correlation technique is being used. The MC are better seen in terms of the total sample in order that such consistency as they do show is adequately revealed.

In general, although not without reservations, this study provides support for the notion that children have a basic orientation to meaning and its realisation, and it is this orientation that is realised in their speech over a range of contexts.

Throughout this book the relevance of context has been stressed. We turn now to a discussion of the significance of context in the present study.

Why code and not context ?

In the introduction to this volume it was argued that any consistency in coding orientation shown by children in the three speech situations we are considering points to an underlying code through which the child interprets and realises the context. It was argued that the interview situation is one that will evoke elaborated coding from children orientated to its use, since the social relationship is such as to provoke elaborated coding from such children. We argued that consistency in coding orientation could be attributed to the child's sociolinguistic code precisely because of the structured nature of the interview setting. In this paper we have demonstrated, albeit not without problems and qualifications, that children are consistent in the codings they make across the three contexts. From this we have argued that one can talk meaningfully about different sociolinguistic codes (strong version) or coding orientations (weak version).

Perhaps at this point we should anticipate and discuss a possible question, the kind of question that might be put by students of contemporary sociolinguistics. To put the question as starkly as possible: supposing some children do consistently offer a restricted or an elaborated variant over a range of contexts, how do we know that the inference of radically different orientations to meaning is justified and that the variants we observe are not a direct function of the contexts we have created? It may be that the variants we have described are less a reflection of code and more a response to context. In other words, if children from different social backgrounds do show a consistent patterning in their speech over a range of situations it becomes important to explicate the critical sources of such patterning. There are two basic possibilities, the first more 'contemporary' and the second more 'historical' in perspective.

It has been suggested that the differences we observe exist squarely at the level of clashes in patterns of appropriate speech; that all observed variation in child speech can be explained through consideration of contextual variables. By manipulating features of the context – listener, topic, setting, instructions – it may prove very easy to change or even reverse the present pattern of results. It may, in other words, be quite wrong to talk of a general orientation to context-independent or context-dependent speech use, the real issue being to describe which contexts evoke which kinds of codings in which groups of children. We may have fortuitously chosen contexts which provoke elaborated coding from most MC children and more restricted coding from many WC children. What a MC transmission system may be achieving is success in orientating the child to context-independent speech use in just those contexts which the educational system generally, and researchers into speech use specifically, deem relevant. If this is the case then it is clearly important in the classroom but implies that ways of speaking are, first, unimportant in themselves – becoming problematic only when different rules for use result in lack of comprehension between speakers; and, second, that although different ways of speaking may be heavily invested with social meaning and are therefore potential instruments of control, the meaning is largely evaluative and the control external to the person. Hymes (1972), in a most considered piece, tends sometimes to this view, which is held in far stronger form by others:

> The problem is not in the existence of multiple varieties of language, nor even in the stratification of these varieties from locally to nationally acceptable, from least to most present elaboration for literature and technical discourse. The problem is in the attitude held towards the varieties. Is it one of approval or disapproval? Are the several varieties judged in terms of appropriateness to situation, or categorically (bad or good per se)?[6]

It may be, however, that a child's orientation to speech use – his notions of appropriate speech – does not only realise or, better, mark social contexts but also in part defines them. It is possible that a description of how context and speech co-vary for different groups of speakers will not, in fact, explain all differences in the ways in which children use language; that the child's communicative history cannot be fully understood by a description of what he says and how, to whom, where and when unless this includes also a distinction in terms of a general semantic orientation which has its basis in the social structure. If this is so then social control exists as much in the child's consciousness as in the action of others on him.

In Bernstein's writings code refers not to the decision whether to speak or stay silent, whether or not to drop the post-vocalic 'r', whether to use 'tu' or 'vous', but rather to the underlying system of rules which generates both these kinds of choices and, for example, the focusing on particular rather than general features of a game or a toy or a machine, the perception of and response to transgressions as absolute rather than arbitrary or contingent, the analytic rather than metaphoric communication of a picture, etc. All of these tendencies, competencies and skills can be seen as socially based, as founded on particular kinds of role experiences and acquisitions, but the phenomena on which they bear are not only social, and their psychological consequences may, according to theory, be profound.

The problem can be put differently. Communicative competence may be characterised as involving three interlocking levels. First, the child's understanding of aspects of the situation – what he takes to be his role in the context and how he does this. Second, his more specific orientation to meaning, that is, how he interprets the topic, given level one. And third, the rules for speaking which govern his realisation of that meaning. Clearly the second and third aspects presuppose the first, but they can be analytically separated from it. The issue is whether or not an understanding of socially based differences in the ways in which children use language has any need of the second aspect. Would the children in the present study who opted for imperative forms of control have switched to more informative strategies involving rationales and contingent statements if the listener had not been a strange adult and the physical setting had been different? Or is there a sense in which the meanings they offered are independent of the social meanings of that particular situation and dependent on the ongoing experience of contexts that constitutes socialisation?

In the last analysis the problem reduces to the validity of inferring different coding orientations in children of different social backgrounds, such orientations being definitely semantic in nature. Two strands of evidence would support this theory, and we suggest that one of these has been elucidated in this paper – the nature and consistency of children's coding orientations. It is important also to embed such a study in an analysis of the nature of the transmission systems in which these children participate. This is the subject of the final SRU monograph, and while not without its problems the study reveals interesting and theoretically relevant relationships between patterns of maternal communication and control and the children's coding orientations. Indeed, we anticipated this report in our discussion of those WC girls who are orientated to a narrative mode in the interview context. The very existence of a relationship between reported modes of communication and control and the actual speech of children makes us reluctant to accept that the variation in the children's speech can be adequately explained purely in terms of contextual variables.

But even confining our argument to the finding of consistency in coding orientation we suggest that there is support for the notion of code. Again, we would stress that the stability in orientation in this study is stability at the level of the selection and realisation of meanings rather than at the level of grammatical constructs or of lexes. This kind of consistency is difficult to explain in terms of the eliciting context. The social and psychological orders of meaning which the variants realise suggest a difference in basic orientation to meaning on the part of the speaker and some concept of code or coding orientation seems critical for an adequate understanding of the reasons behind and consequences of this difference.

We do not pretend that this is the whole story. We have been at pains to stress that, at the empirical level, this study has been concerned with speech use, with what is acquired and how it is realised. The question of transmission, in which this analysis must be grounded, has been brought in only at the level of theory and then not in any detail. The relationship between the child's sociolinguistic coding orientation and the structure of transmission in which he participates will be explicated in the final SRU monograph.

Notes

1 A concrete example will make this clearer. Consider the following three MC children.

	Exophora	Indefinites	Specificity
Child A	0·042 ($\bar{x}$ = 0·111)	0·196 ($\bar{x}$ = 0·153)	0·036 ($\bar{x}$ = 0·054)
Child B	0·134	0·056	0·036
Child C	0·064	0·172	0·084

Child C conforms clearly to the pattern of context-independence and Child B to the pattern of context-dependence (relative to this sub-sample). Child A is also scored context-independent and the text he creates is very general in nature. The expected negative association between exophora and indefinites is conformed to by all three children. The expected negative association between exophora and specificity is conformed to by children B and C only. Child A, although he creates a context-independent *text*, offers a similar proportional use of one sub-index (specificity) as the child who creates a context-dependent text. Thus two children may differ clearly in their orientation to context-independent speech but score similarly on one of the sub-indices. In terms of the overall predictions, all three children conform to one of the theoretical categories. But in correlating the specificity index with either of the other two indices, only two children will contribute to the expected associations, the other will actually work against them. These problems will be more prominent in the social-class sub-groups where the range of scores with which we are dealing is reduced and the distributions tend to be very skewed.

2 Note that this does not mean that those children who give general descriptions never make highly specific realisations. Relative to their own social group they may do so less than others, but relative to the total sample such children may well score above average on specificity. The same argument holds for the suggestion that those children who give detailed descriptions never make reference to generality.

3 It should be noted that three of these children are girls who offered narrative only. For statistical reasons they have been excluded from the remainder of the analysis.

4 To give an indication of the size of these social-class differences we reproduce below the correlations between social class and the textual index and social class and contingencies, backings and affect for the original sample (Turner, in press):

	Total sample		
	(n = 155)	MC (n = 80)	WC (n = 75)
Text	−0·280***	−0·214**	−0·287***
Contingencies, etc.	−0·230***	−0·154*	−0·240***

5 As pointed out on in n.2 the results do not mean that these MC children never make highly specific realisations. Relative to their own social-class group they make fewer detailed statements than others, but relative to the sample as a whole the extent of their use of the specific option is average (see total matrix).

6 A forthcoming SRU publication shows that children orientated to elaborated coding tend to participate in different systems of cultural transmission than children orientated to restricted coding, and that these differences occur along the hypothesised social-class lines.

Appendix 1 Statistical tables of results not included in text

Table A.1 Interrelationships of descriptive indices for WC boys (*tau coefficients*)

	Exophora	Indefinites	Specificity	Text
Exophora		−0·088	−0.097	0·523***
Indefinites			0·262**	−0·543***
Specificity				−0·270***
Text				

Table A.2 Interrelationships of descriptive indices for WC girls (*tau coefficients*)

	Exophora	Indefinites	Specificity	Text
Exophora		−0·121	−0·130	0·528***
Indefinites			0·050	−0·547***
Specificity				−0·317***
Text				

Table A.3 Interrelationships of descriptive indices for MC boys (*tau coefficients*)

	Exophora	Indefinites	Specificity	Text
Exophora		−0·045	−0·006	0·428***
Indefinites			−0·065	−0·552***
Specificity				−0·027
Text				

Table A.4   Interrelationships of descriptive indices for MC girls (tau coefficients)

	Exophora	Indefinites	Specificity	Text
Exophora		−0·064	−0·078	0·475***
Indefinites			−0·200	−0·425***
Specificity				−0·012
Text				

Table A.5   Tau coefficients between the narrative index and the descriptive indices in the Trotin task for the MC sample

	Total MC sample	Boys	Girls
Exophora	−0·103	−0·202*	−0·034
Indefinites	−0·015	−0·026	0·012
Specificity	0·165*	0·187*	0·152
Text	−0·100	−0·176*	−0·019

Table A.6   Interrelationships of instructional indices for WC boys (tau coefficients)

	Mode A	Mode B	Mode C	Text
Mode breakdown	−0·100	0·288**	−0·210*	0·175*
Mode maintenance	0·327***	−0·144	−0·226*	−0·263**

Table A.7   Interrelationships of instructional indices for WC girls (tau coefficients)

	Mode A	Mode B	Mode C	Text
Mode breakdown	−0·024	0·355***	−0·265**	0·129
Mode maintenance	0·179*	0·069	−0·199	−0·100

Table A.8   Interrelationships of instructional indices for MC boys (tau coefficients)

	Mode A	Mode B	Mode C	Text
Mode breakdown	−0·262**	0·231**	0·142	0·252**
Mode maintenance	0·306**	−0·146	−0·161	−0·295**

Table A.9   Interrelationships of instructional indices for MC girls (tau coefficients)

	Mode A	Mode B	Mode C	Text
Mode breakdown	−0·303**	0·407***	0·041	0·327**
Mode maintenance	0·380***	−0·289**	−0·227*	−0·379***

Table A.10   The relationship of narrative in instruction to other instructional indices for MC boys and MC girls (tau coefficients)

	MC boys	MC girls
Mode A	−0·343***	−0·177(*)
Mode B	0·228*	0·462***
Mode C	−0·058	−0·156
Text	0·407***	0·221*

Table A.11   Tau coefficients between the orientation indices for instruction and the context-independent/dependent indices for description for MC boys

	Exophora	Indefinites	Specificity	Text
Mode A	−0·012	−0·027	−0·179*	−0·102
Mode B	−0·071	−0·084	0·184*	0·083
Mode C	0·138	0·129	0·012	0·025
Text	−0·032	−0·014	0·204*	0·107

Table A.12   Tau coefficients between the orientation indices for instruction and the context-independent/dependent indices for description for MC girls

	Exophora	Indefinites	Specificity	Text
Mode A	−0·054	0·051	−0·175	−0·059
Mode B	−0·039	−0·107	0·097	0·177(*)
Mode C	0·095	0·025	0·133	−0·071
Text	0·040	−0·057	0·175	0·076

Table A.13   Tau coefficients between the mode-maintenance categories in instruction and the context-independent/dependent indices in description for MC boys

	Exophora	Indefinites	Specificity	Text
Mode breakdown	0·277*	−0·220*	−0·114	0·338***
Mode maintenance	0·084	−0·027	−0·146	0·072

Table A.14   Tau coefficients between the mode-maintenance categories in instruction and the context-independent/dependent indices in description for MC girls

	Exophora	Indefinites	Specificity	Text
Mode breakdown	0·134	−0·083	0·017	0·219*
Mode maintenance	−0·181	−0·170	0·064	−0·161

Table A.15   Tau coefficients between the indices of control and the context-independent/dependent indices for description for the MC boys' sub-sample

	Exophora	Indefinites	Specificity	Text
Punishment	−0·021	−0·033	0·111	0·052
Contingencies, etc.	−0·269**	0·130	0·104	−0·328***
Directive: imperative	−0·042	−0·029	0·054	−0·074
Directive: modified	0·036	−0·051	−0·012	0·137(*)
Text	−0·056	0·033	0·005	0·003

Table A.16   Tau coefficients between the indices of control and the context-independent/dependent indices for description for the MC girls' sub-sample

	Exophora	Indefinites	Specificity	Text
Punishment	−0·110	0·049	−0·105	−0·150(*)
Contingencies, etc.	0·097	0·098	0·341***	−0·077
Directive: imperative	−0·211*	0·194*	−0·167(*)	−0·239*
Directive: modified	−0·289**	−0·103	0·149(*)	0·016
Text	0·014	−0·002	0·289**	−0·002

Table A.17   Tau coefficients between the indices of control and the narrative index in the descriptive context for the MC sub-sample and the MC boys' and girls' sub-samples

	MC	MCB	MCG
Punishment	0·094	0·111	0·081
Contingencies, etc.	0·300**	0·299**	0·313**
Directive: imperative	−0·066	−0·060	−0·072
Directive: modified	0·299***	0·303**	0·298**
Text	0·300**	0·313**	0·291**

Table A.18   Tau coefficients between the indices of control and the orientation indices for instruction for the MC boys' sub-sample

	Mode A	Mode B	Mode C	Text
Punishment	0·033	−0·011	−0·134(*)	0·007
Contingencies, etc.	0·116	−0·048	−0·057	−0·112
Directive: imperative	0·061	−0·136(*)	0·075	−0·091
Directive: modified	−0·036	0·057	−0·042	0·054
Text	0·026	0·096	−0·120	0·006

Table A.19   Tau coefficients between the indices of control and the orientation indices for instruction for the MC girls' sub-sample

	Mode A	Mode B	Mode C	Text
Punishment	0·032	0·217*	−0·212*	−0·003
Contingencies, etc.	−0·093	0·018	0·098	0·085
Directive: imperative	0·153(*)	0·162(*)	−0·313**	−0·116
Directive: modified	0·157(*)	−0·103	−0·107	−0·155(*)
Text	−0·043	−0·122	0·149(*)	0·023

Table A.20   Tau coefficients between the indices of control and the narrative index in the instructional context for the MC sub-sample and the MC boys' and girls' sub-samples

	MC	MCB	MCG
Punishment	0·303***	0·381***	0·189*
Contingencies, etc.	0·076	0·027	0·123
Directive: imperative	−0·151*	−0·131	−0·192*
Directive: modified	−0·008	0·038	−0·057
Text	0·069	0·105	0·026

Table A.21   Tau coefficients between the indices of control and the indices of mode breakdown and maintenance for the total sample

	Mode breakdown	Mode maintenance
Punishment	0·102*	−0·147**
Contingencies, etc.	−0·056	−0·070(*)
Directive: imperative	0·013	−0·040
Directive: modified	0·009	0·132**
Text	−0·051	0·064

Table A.22   Tau coefficients between the indices of control and the indices of mode breakdown and maintenance for the WC sub-sample

	Mode breakdown	Mode maintenance
Punishment	0·021	−0·013
Contingencies, etc.	0·012	−0·129*
Directive: imperative	0·070	−0·143*
Directive: modified	−0·019	0·146*
Text	−0·066	0·092

Table A.23   Tau coefficients between the indices of control and the indices of mode breakdown and maintenance for the MC sub-sample

	Mode breakdown	Mode maintenance
Punishment	0·085	−0·148*
Contingencies, etc.	0·012	−0·147*
Directive: imperative	−0·178**	0·119(*)
Directive: modified	0·084	0·104(*)
Text	0·094	−0·043

Table A.24   Tau coefficients between the indices of control and the indices of mode breakdown and maintenance for the WC boys' sub-sample

	Mode breakdown	Mode maintenance
Punishment	−0·050	−0·120
Contingencies, etc.	−0·106	−0·108
Directive: imperative	0·116	−0·041
Directive: modified	−0·128	0·230*
Text	−0·173(*)	0·037

*Table A.25 Tau coefficients between the indices of control and the
indices of mode breakdown and maintenance for the WC girls' sub-sample*

	Mode breakdown	Mode maintenance
Punishment	0·098	0·062
Contingencies, etc.	0·093	−0·144(*)
Directive: imperative	0·051	−0·247**
Directive: modified	0·025	0·105
Text	0·010	0·137(*)

*Table A.26 Tau coefficients between the indices of control and the
indices of mode breakdown and maintenance for the MC boys' sub-sample*

	Mode breakdown	Mode maintenance
Punishment	0·070	−0·209*
Contingencies, etc.	−0·167(*)	−0·207*
Directive: imperative	−0·072	0·083
Directive: modified	0·240**	0·088
Text	0·109	−0·081

*Table A.27 Tau coefficients between the indices of control and the
indices of mode breakdown and maintenance for the MC girls' sub-sample*

	Mode breakdown	Mode maintenance
Punishment	0·114	−0·055
Contingencies, etc.	0·173(*)	−0·036
Directive: imperative	−0·238*	0·233*
Directive: modified	−0·040	0·088
Text	0·075	−0·013

Appendix 2 Schedules used in Chapter 4

Reprinted below are the schedules used to compile the two indices used in Chapter 4, Section VIII. The general index of communication comprises the first four schedules. The fifth schedule represents the positional/personal index.

Children often chatter quite a lot. Please say what you usually do if   starts chattering

	Tell him to stop	Tell him to wait	Answer him quickly	Chat with him
1. When you are working around the house.				
2. When you are walking along the street.				
3. When you are trying to relax.				
4. When you are talking to your husband.				
5. When you are in a shop.				
6. When you are in a bus or tube.				
7. At meal-times.				

If you were explaining the meaning of the following words to your child, which *two* of the four statements would you choose? Please put a figure 1 by the statement you would be most likely to choose and a figure 2 by the statement you think is second best.

'cool'

Mark 2

(1) It's when something is no longer hot to touch. ☐

(2) It's the opposite of warm. ☐

(3) It's what you feel when the sun goes in. ☐

(4) It's a little bit warmer than 'cold'. ☐

'mix'

Mark 2

(1) To put things together. ☐

(2) When I make a stew the food is all mixed up. ☐

(3) It's what you do when you put different paints together to make different colours. ☐

(4) It's the opposite of separate. ☐

'dangerous'

Mark 2

(1) It's when you might get hurt. ☐

(2) A road where there are lots of accidents. ☐

(3) It's dangerous to play with fire. ☐

(4) It's the opposite of safe. ☐

'flexible'

Mark 2

(1) Rubber is flexible. ☐

(2) It's the opposite of rigid or stiff. ☐

(3) Your shoes are flexible. ☐

(4) Something that will bend without breaking. ☐

Children sometimes ask unusual questions. If   asked you the following questions, what would you do?

A. Suppose   asked you what would happen if children never grew up. Would you:

	I would *not* do this	I might do this	I *would* do this
(a) Explain why the question does not make sense.			
(b) Ask him what *he* thinks would happen.			
(c) Tell him not to be silly.			
(d) Explain what it would be like if children never grew up.			

B. Suppose   asked you what would happen if it was always dark. Would
you:

	I would *not* do this	I might do this	I *would* do this
(a) Ask him what *he* thinks would happen.			
(b) Explain what it would be like if it was always dark.			
(c) Tell him not to be silly.			
(d) Explain why the question does not make sense.			

Here are some more questions that   might ask. For each question, please
say what you would be most likely to do *first*.
e.g.

1. *Why we have rules*

Tick just one

(a) Make up something until he is older. ☐

(b) Tell him to ask Daddy. ☐

(c) Try and change the subject. ☐

(d) Take the opportunity to discuss the matter with him. ☐

(e) Tell him he's not old enough to understand. ☐

(f) Give him a brief answer and see if he's satisfied. ☐

2. *Why there are wars*

Tick just one

(a) Make up something until he is older. ☐

(b) Tell him to ask Daddy. ☐

(c) Try and change the subject. ☐

(d) Take the opportunity to discuss the matter with him. ☐

(e) Tell him he's not old enough to understand. ☐

(f) Give him a brief answer and see if he's satisfied. ☐

3. *Why boys are different from girls*

Tick just one

(a) Make up something until he is older. ☐

(b) Tell him to ask Daddy. ☐

(c) Try and change the subject ☐

(d) Take the opportunity to discuss the matter with him. ☐

(e) Tell him he's not old enough to understand. ☐

(f) Give him a brief answer and see if he's satisfied. ☐

4. *Why some people are mentally disturbed*

Tick just on

(a) Make up something until he is older. ☐
(b) Tell him to ask Daddy. ☐
(c) Try and change the subject. ☐
(d) Take the opportunity to discuss the matter with him. ☐
(e) Tell him he's not old enough to understand. ☐
(f) Give him a brief answer and see if he's satisfied. ☐

5. *Why some people are rich and others poor*

Tick just one

(a) Make up something until he is older. ☐
(b) Tell him to ask Daddy. ☐
(c) Try and change the subject. ☐
(d) Take the opportunity to discuss the matter with him. ☐
(e) Tell him he's not old enough to understand. ☐
(f) Give him a brief answer and see if he's satisfied. ☐

6. *Why some people are physically disabled*

Tick just one

(a) Make up something until he is older. ☐
(b) Tell him to ask Daddy. ☐
(c) Try and change the subject. ☐
(d) Take the opportunity to discuss the matter with him. ☐
(e) Tell him he's not old enough to understand. ☐
(f) Give him a brief answer and see if he's satisfied. ☐

7. *Daddy's part in making babies*

Tick just one

(a) Make up something until he is older. ☐
(b) Tell him to ask Daddy. ☐
(c) Try and change the subject. ☐
(d) Take the opportunity to discuss the matter with him. ☐
(e) Tell him he's not old enough to understand. ☐
(f) Give him a brief answer and see if he's satisfied. ☐

8. *Why people die*

Tick just one

(a) Make up something until he is older. ☐
(b) Tell him to ask Daddy. ☐
(c) Try and change the subject. ☐
(d) Take the opportunity to discuss the matter with him. ☐
(e) Tell him he's not old enough to understand. ☐
(f) Give him a brief answer and see if he's satisfied. ☐

Parents have to make a lot of arrangements and decisions in bringing up their family; I expect you have done so, and have views about them. We would like to know *your views*, so could you select from *each pair* of statements the *one* which is nearest to your own view.

e.g.   XA   Parents should encourage the whole family to talk together
      at meal-times. ☐

or

    XB   Parents should encourage children to be quiet until they
      have finished eating. ☐

1A   Parents should encourage boys and girls to use different kinds of toys. ☐

or

1B   Parents should encourage boys and girls to use the same kinds of toys. ☐

2A   Parents should make rules that can sometimes be set aside. ☐

or

2B   Parents should only make rules that can always be kept. ☐

3A   Parents should not worry about the occasional argument that the
    children hear. ☐

or

3B   Parents should never argue in front of the children. ☐

4A   Parents should not be afraid to use physical punishment on their
    children. ☐

or

4B   Parents should use physical punishment only as a last resort. ☐

5A   Parents should wait for children to come to them for advice. ☐

or

5B   Parents should give advice to children when they think it is
    necessary. ☐

6A   Parents should not worry about making mistakes sometimes. ☐

or

6B   Parents should always set the child a good example. ☐

7A   Parents should make it clear that they know more than children –
    so they should have the last word. ☐

or

7B   Parents should make it clear that parents and children can
    sometimes see things differently – so both can be right. ☐

8A   Parents should insist on tidiness in children. ☐

or

8B   Parents should not worry too much if children are untidy. ☐

9A   Parents should not make too many sacrifices for their children. ☐

or

9B   Parents should be prepared to make many sacrifices for their
    children. ☐

10A Parents should always appear to be united when dealing with their children. ☐

or

10B Parents should not worry about disagreeing when dealing with their children. ☐

11A Parents should expect children to accept adults' opinions. ☐

or

11B Parents should expect children to question adults' opinions. ☐

12A Parents should generally leave children to sort out their own troubles. ☐

or

12B Parents should generally help children to share their troubles with the family. ☐

13A Parents should try to avoid showing their temper. ☐

or

13B Parents should not worry about losing their temper. ☐

14A Parents should help children put right anything they do wrong outside the home. ☐

or

14B Parents should make children put right anything they do wrong outside the home. ☐

15A Parents should try to see every young child as a different person. ☐

or

15B Parents should try to understand that young children are really very similar. ☐

16A Parents should encourage their children to see them as individuals. ☐

or

16B Parents should encourage their children to respect them because they are their mother and father. ☐

17A Parents should always try to be firm. ☐

or

17B Parents should not worry if they give in sometimes. ☐

18A Parents should get to know the parents of their children's friends. ☐

or

18B Parents should not worry if they don't know the parents of their children's friends. ☐

19A Parents should, occasionally, put their own interests before those of the children. ☐

or

19B Parents should always put the children's interests first. ☐

20A Parents should apply different standards to boys and girls. ☐

or

20B Parents should apply similar standards to boys and girls. ☐

21A   Parents should teach children what duties they have towards the family.   ☐

or

21B   Parents should let children decide what their duties are towards the family.   ☐

22A   Parents should show affection towards their children freely.   ☐

or

22B   Parents should not show affection towards their children too freely.   ☐

23A   Parents should expect children to obey rules without question.   ☐

or

23B   Parents should always explain to children why rules have to be made.   ☐

24A   Parents should have interests separate from the family.   ☐

or

24B   Parents should share all their interests with the family.   ☐

Appendix 3 The expression of uncertainty and descriptive, instructional and regulative speech

Geoffrey Turner

In this appendix we summarise the findings of a correlational analysis carried out as a minor and subsidiary part of the main correlational analysis of the seven-year-old children's use of language in context (Adlam and Turner in the present volume).[1] The aim of the analysis was to examine the relationships between the children's use of expressions of uncertainty in contexts previously examined (Turner, 1973b)[2] and their use of descriptive, instructional and regulative speech. Do the children who make their uncertainty explicit, or certain types of it, tend to be explicit in their descriptive, instructional and regulative speech in the ways described in this volume? Does the children's use of uncertainty expressions point to consistency in their coding behaviour?

For purposes of this analysis the children's scores for uncertainty expressions were expressed as relative frequencies (as proportions of the total number of words). Furthermore, the various categories and sub-categories of uncertainty expressions recognised in Turner and Pickvance (1973) and Turner (1973b) were grouped in terms of two higher order categories, in line with the treatment of the variables in the descriptive, instructional and regulative contexts. The two higher order summarising categories are now given, the complete coding frame being given and discussed at the end of the appendix:

(1) ego-oriented expressions, i.e. egocentric sequence, suppositions based upon perception, other suppositions, assessments of possibility/probability, alternatives, approximations, indirect questions, and questions offering alternatives;

(2) socio-oriented expressions, i.e. sociocentric sequences and direct questions.

The ego-oriented expressions are the ones that we should expect to be related to explicit speech in other contexts, and the socio-oriented to more implicit speech, to relatively context-dependent and particularistic meanings.

The findings are presented in the following order:
(1) groups means for the measures of uncertainty;
(2) inter-correlations of the measures of uncertainty; and correlations between uncertainty expressions in different tasks;

(3) correlations between the measures of uncertainty in the Picture Story and Trotin tasks and the measures of descriptive, instructional and regulative speech.

(1) Group means for the measures of uncertainty

Table A.1   Group means for the measures of uncertainty in the Picture Story and Trotin tasks

	Ego-oriented	Socio-oriented
Total sample	·0058	·0010
MC	·0069	·0008
WC	·0048	·0012
MC B	·0069	·0009
MC G	·0069	·0007
WC B	·0073	·0018
WC G	·0028	·0007
WC B LP	·0130	·0000
WC B non-LP	·0058	·0023
WC G LP	·0030	·0004
WC G non-LP	·0027	·0008

Table A.1 reveals a pattern of class difference, with the middle-class children showing a higher frequency score for ego-oriented expressions and the working-class children showing a higher score for socio-oriented expressions. There is little or no sex variation in the middle-class group for the two major measures; but in the working-class group there is a strong pattern of sex difference, with the boys' scores being twice as high as those of the girls. It is noticeable that the working-class boys obtained a frequency score for ego-oriented expressions which is very similar to that obtained by the middle-class children (·0073 as compared with ·0069). However, it is clear that this result largely reflects the performance of the working-class boys who had taken part in the language programme; these children obtained an exceptionally high score for ego-oriented expressions (·0130). It is of some interest that there is no evidence of a language programme effect among the girls.

(2) Inter-correlations for the measures of uncertainty

Table A.2   Inter-correlation for the measures of uncertainty in the Picture Story and Trotin tasks

	Total sample Socio-o	MC Socio-o	WC Socio-o
Ego-o	·223***	·223**	·277***

Table A.2 shows that the two major measures of uncertainty are positively correlated, and the correlation is significant for the total sample and for each of the sub-samples.

Correlations between uncertainty expressions in different tasks

Table A.3   Correlations between the measures of uncertainty in the Picture Story and Trotin tasks and the measures of uncertainty in social control task

	Total sample		MC		WC	
	Ego-o	*Socio-o*	*Ego-o*	*Socio-o*	*Ego-o*	*Socio-o*
Social control Mainly ego-o	·402***	·226***	·401***	·275***	·401***	·190**

Table A.3 shows that the pattern of relationships in the use of uncertainty expressions across tasks is highly compatible with the pattern of relationships previously observed *within* one set of tasks (Table A.2). In other words, there is a broad pattern of consistency in the children's use of uncertainty expressions across tasks. The children who used expressions of uncertainty in the 'social control' regulative task tended to use both types of uncertainty expressions in the Picture Story and Trotin tasks. But since the uncertainty expressions used in the regulative task were mainly ego-oriented,[3] the correlations with ego-oriented expressions in the *second* set of tasks are very high.

(3) Correlations between the measures of uncertainty in the Picture Story and Trotin tasks and the measures of descriptive, instructional and regulative speech

Table A.4 reveals a definite pattern of relationships for the total sample and each of the sub-samples. It is very clear that the socio-oriented expressions of uncertainty are related to the measures of implicitness and context-dependent, particularistic meanings, whilst the ego-oriented expressions are related to explicitness and specificity, though less strongly. We shall briefly enumerate the *main* findings for the total sample and each of the sub-samples.

For the total sample, the ego-oriented expressions correlate positively with specificity in the descriptive context, and negatively with narrative in the instructional context, but the strongest correlations are the positive ones with contingencies, etc., and the textual index in the regulative context. By contrast, the socio-oriented expressions correlate positively with exophora, narrative and the textual index in the descriptive context; they correlate positively with Mode B but negatively with Mode A, and positively with mode breakdown, narrative and the textual index in the instructional context; finally, they correlate negatively with modified directives in the regulative context.

Table A.4   Correlations between the measures of uncertainty in the Picture Story and Trotin tasks and the measures of descriptive, instructional and regulative speech for total sample, and middle-class and working-class sub-samples

		Total sample		MC		WC	
		Ego-o	Socio-o	Ego-o	Socio-o	Ego-o	Socio-o
Descriptive	Exophora	·025	·188***	·106(*)	·268***	·040	·101(*)
	Indefinites	·024	−·024	−·023	·054	−·006	−·036
	Specificity	·103*	·062	·148*	·110(*)	·016	·072
	Narrative	−·046	·138**	−·037	·027	·007	·198**
	Text	−·013	·113*	·089	·125*	·022	·071
	Mode A	·017	−·124**	−·085	−·085	·043	−·133*
	Mode B	−·060	·162***	·058	·061	−·071	·203**
	Mode C	−·050	−·042	·061	·090	·022	−·159**
Instructional	Mode break.	−·081	·145**	·089	·163*	−·149*	·122*
	Mode maint.	·018	−·032	−·057	−·088	·046	·054
	Narrative	−·102*	·091*	·011	−·075	−·130*	·138*
	Text	−·036	·144**	·079	·071	−·053	·195**
	Punishment	·057	·078(*)	·113(*)	·107(*)	·109(*)	·031
	Contingencies	·187***	−·004	·152*	−·036	·141*	·097
Regulative	Directive: Imp.	−·059	−·057	−·015	−·061	−·054	·143*
	Directive: Mod.	−·019	−·103*	−·053	−·068	−·043	−·124*
	Text	·131**	−·058	·111(*)	·019	·082	−·108(*)

In the middle-class sub-sample, much of the same pattern is evident. Again, the ego-oriented expressions correlate with specificity in the descriptive context and with contingencies, etc., and the textual index in the regulative context. And concerning the socio-oriented expressions, there is a relatively strong correlation with exophora, and the correlation with the textual index reaches significance. What is chiefly missing is the strong pattern of relationships with instructional indices; there is just one significant correlation here, with mode breakdown. However, we know from the main analysis (Adlam and Turner, Chapter 4 in the present volume) that the middle-class children show very little variation in their responses to this context and so the possibility of a statistical relationship with any other variable is greatly reduced.

In the working-class sub-sample, by contrast, there is a very strong pattern of relationships with the instructional indices. In the case of the ego-oriented expressions, there are no significant relationships with the descriptive indices, but there are significant negative correlations with mode breakdown and narrative in the instructional context. There is also a significant positive correlation with contingencies, etc. in the regulative context. Turning to the socio-oriented expressions, there is a tendency for these to be associated with exophora (whereas there was a strong correlation in the case of the middle-class children) and there is a significant positive correlation with narrative in the descriptive context. In the case of the instructional indices, six out of the seven correlations are significant. There is a positive correlation with Mode B and negative correlations with Modes A and C. There are also positive correlations with mode breakdown, narrative and the instructional text index. Finally, in the case of the regulative indices, there is a positive correlation with imperative directives and a negative one with modified directives, and there is an almost significant negative correlation with the regulative text index.

Table A.5 gives the correlations for the working-class boys and girls separately. We know from Table A.1 that there are big differences between the boys and girls in the frequency with which they use uncertainty expression, and we know, too, that the boys who had taken part in the language programme obtained exceptionally high scores for the ego-oriented expressions. Table A.5 shows that, despite the observed variation, there is a degree of compatibility between the results for the boys and those for the girls, though there are some important points of difference. Concerning the ego-oriented expressions, in both sex groups the correlations with the descriptive variables are low, there being just a tendency (an unexpected one) for these expressions to be associated with the textual score for context-dependence in the case of the girls. Of the previously observed relationships between the ego-oriented expressions and the instructional variables and the regulative variables in the working-class sub-sample, it can now be seen that the boys are chiefly responsible for the former and the girls for the latter. The boys have relatively high negative correlations with mode breakdown and narrative in the instructional context, and the girls have positive correlations with contingencies, etc., and the textual index in the regulative context; they also have a negative correlation with

Table A.5 Correlations between the measures of uncertainty in the Picture Story and Trotin tasks and the measures of descriptive, instructional and regulative speech for working-class boys and girls

		WCB Ego-o	WCB Socio-o	WCG Ego-o	WCG Socio-o
Descriptive	Exophora	·082	·324**	·041	·127
	Indefinites	·053	·070	−·072	−·141(*)
	Specificity	−·033	·084	·073	·076
	Narrative	−·015	·267**	·072	·183*
	Text	·029	·146(*)	·139(*)	·041
	Mode A	·054	−·047	−·018	−·262**
	Mode B	−·031	·232*	−·144(*)	·211*
	Mode C	−·047	−·264**	·143(*)	−·072
Instructional	Mode break.	−·287**	·271**	·009	·048
	Mode maint.	·036	·069	−·004	·061
	Narrative	−·257**	·231*	·024	·123
	Text	−·042	·146(*)	−·037	·286**
	Punishment	·103	·022	·036	−·003
	Contingencies	·003	−·036	·380***	·240**
Regulative	Directive: Imp.	−·059	·325**	−·162*	−·082
	Directive: Mod.	−·092	−·088	−·054	−·076
	Text	·099	−·273**	·189*	·119

imperative directives. Turning to the socio-oriented expressions, the boys have positive correlations with exophora and narrative, and there is a tendency for these expressions to be associated with the textual index of context-dependence. The girls do not have a significant correlation with exophora, and, indeed, the sign is reversed. They do, however, have a positive correlation with narrative, but it is of some interest that this correlation is lower than that in the case of the boys. Concerning the instructional context, here there is a very similar pattern in both sex groups, with the socio-oriented expressions correlating positively with Mode B, and negatively with Mode A (chiefly in the case of the girls) and Mode C (chiefly boys). In both groups, too, there is an association of the socio-oriented expressions with the textual index of context-dependence in the instructional context. Where the two groups differ is in this respect: the boys have significant correlations with mode breakdown and narrative whereas the girls do not. Finally, concerning the regulative context, here the boys have two clear results which fit the expected pattern—a positive correlation with imperative directives and a negative correlation with the textual index; whereas the girls have one which does not conform—a positive correlation with contingencies.

Comment

The correlational analysis has demonstrated very clearly a pattern of relationships between the children's use of uncertainty expressions and the type of speech they offer in the descriptive, instructional and regulative contexts. The two main measures of uncertainty, ego-oriented expressions and socio-oriented expressions, although positively correlated, enter into distinct sets of relationships with the other variables. To a large degree, the socio-oriented expressions are associated with implicitness and context-dependent, particularistic meanings, whilst the ego-oriented expressions are associated with explicitness and specificity. And it is important to stress that this result does not merely reflect class differences; it also holds *within* the class groups. It is also important to note that these relationships are not confined to one context; in most cases they operate across two or more contexts. There is, then, some evidence of consistency in coding behaviour.

It is thought that the weak relationships between the ego-oriented expressions and the descriptive variables in the case of the working-class children reflect the influence of the language programme. We know that the boys who had taken part in the programme obtained exceptionally high scores for such expressions, but there is little evidence to suggest that they have also changed in other areas, such as their reference usage. The one-sided influence of the language programme would undoubtedly reduce the size of the correlations.

Our previous interpretation (see Turner, 1973b) that the working-class girls who move to narrative make low use of expressions of uncertainty, receives some support, but not as much support as one might have supposed. There was in fact a significant positive correlation between their use of socio-oriented expressions and narrative in the descriptive context (·183*). It is the case, however, that this correlation is lower than that obtained by the boys (·267**). And it is also true that the correlation between the girls' use of socio-oriented expressions and narrative in the instructional context is not significant (·123), whereas this correlation is significant in the case of the boys (·231*). Once again, the working-class girls have revealed themselves to be less predictable than children from the other groups.

Coding frame

The coding frame gives the complete set of categories on which the two higher order summarising categories used in the correlational analysis were based. The coding frame was first used in its present form in a study of age differences in the expression of uncertainty, comparing the children's usage at five years and seven years (Turner, 1973b). It incorporates an earlier coding frame used when the children were five years old (Turner and Pickvance, 1973); but it also includes three categories, 'alternatives (disjunctives)', 'suppositions' and 'approximations', considered when the children were five years old but rejected at that time because of their extreme rarity.

The coding frame is essentially based on Bernstein's (1962) 'egocentric sequence' and 'sociocentric sequence' categories and Loban's (1966) 'tentative statement' category. It differs, however, from Bernstein's and Loban's work in two respects. One, a number of finer distinctions are made within the categories. Two, wherever possible, the categories are related to their linguistic realisations, using a mode of description based on 'systemic grammar' (see e.g. Halliday, 1970a).

Below we set out the coding frame largely as it appeared in the report of the earlier study (Turner and Pickvance, 1973). Some of the less essential information has been omitted; a number of new comments and references to recent work have been added. Except in the case of the three additional categories, the examples are the original ones, taken from the children's speech when they were five years old.

A. Egocentric sequence

Bernstein (1971, p. 113) associated use of the egocentric sequence with elaborated code and use of sociocentric sequences with restricted code:

> The preface 'I think' is probably as much an indication of semantic uncertainty as the S.C. [sympathetic circularity, later sociocentric] sequences are in a restricted code. The former sequence does not usually require affirmation . . . It invites a further 'I think' on the part of the listener. The sequence signals difference and relates the sequence to the person. It symbolizes the area of discretion which the form of the social relationship permits . . . this sequence, just like the

S.C. sequences, may indicate the strain in the social interaction but in this case the strain is taken wholly by the *individual*.

In the present analysis two types of egocentric sequence were distinguished, the criterion being phonological—whether the tonic fell on *think* or on *I* (for 'tonic', see Halliday, 1966): (1) Tentative, the tonic on *think* (e.g. I *think* it's a man selling bottles); (2) Self-differentiating, the tonic on *I* (e.g. *I* think some of the men'll have to sit in there). Both types select 'mental process: cognitive' (with *think*); Speaker I = Processer (see Halliday, 1970a).

B. **Sociocentric sequences**

These sequences were originally called sympathetic circularity sequences by Bernstein (1961): he gave as a characteristic of a public language (later restricted code) the following:

> A large number of statements/phrases which signal a requirement for the previous speech sequences to be reinforced: 'Wouldn't it?' 'You see?' 'You know?' etc. This process is termed 'sympathetic circularity'.

Bernstein (1971, pp. 111, 114) wrote:

> It is as if the speaker is saying 'Check—are we together on this?' On the whole the speaker expects affirmation. . . . Inasmuch as the S.C. sequences, which are generated basically by uncertainty, invite implicit affirmation of the previous sequence then they tend to close communication in a particular area rather than facilitate its development and elaboration.

The sociocentric sequences were subdivided into two types: (1) 'You know/see' (e.g. Well he's fishing, you see); (2) Tag questions (e.g. He falls in the water, doesn't he?). Type (1) selects 'mental process: cognitive' (with *know*) or 'mental process: cognitive or perceptual (ambiguous)' (with *see*); Hearer *you* = Processer. Tag questions were differentiated into two further types, drawing on Sinclair (1965). (a) Constant polarity tags (e.g. It's a dog, is it?); (b) Reversed polarity tags (e.g. They can't climb up a roof without a ladder, can they?; It's William, isn't it?). In the case of the reversed polarity tags, if the verbal group in the first clause is positive, the verbal group in the tag clause is negative, and vice versa, but in the case of constant polarity tags the polarity of the verbal groups is the same in both clauses. Sinclair (1972, pp. 75–9) calls type (a) copy tags and type (b) checking tags; the latter term requires no explanation but the former does:

> the copy tag copies something that has just been said—it adds nothing except the reaction of the person who speaks it. It is often used to acknowledge statements that cause surprise, and it requests confirmation of the previous statement.

It is possible to make a further distinction within type (b) according to whether the tag is said with a rising tone or a falling tone; we did not make this distinction.[4]

C. Questions

Two main types of question were recognised: (1) Direct (e.g. What's that?); (2) Indirect (e.g. I wonder what that is). Indirect questions contain the preface, 'I wonder', 'I can't think', 'I don't know', etc., the actual query being given in a reported clause. The preface selects 'mental process: cognitive', either 'positive' (with *wonder*) or 'negative' (with *think, know, remember*); Speaker I = Processer. Both types of questions were subdivided into three further types: (a) Polar or Yes/No (e.g. Aren't those naughty cats?; I wonder if I can see a letter); (b) Wh- (e.g. What's that thing?; I wonder what they are); (c) Alternative or disjunctive questions (e.g. Is it a man or a boy?; I don't know if they're going that way or that way). Type (c) is a new category. Alternative or disjunctive questions are noted here but they are considered along with statements offering alternatives under category H. The differences between the three sub-types of question are handled in the mood system.

D. Refusals

These are explicit refusals to answer the interviewer's questions; for example, in response to the interviewer's 'What's the man saying?' a child may give 'I don't know', 'I can't think', 'I can't say', 'I don't know what', 'I don't know what the man's saying', etc. A refusal may be distinguished from an indirect question on two main grounds: one, a refusal always refers to a question put by the interviewer whereas an indirect question never does—the query is the child's own; and two, because the refusal refers to a preceding question, it may be elliptical in form presupposing the preceding question either partially or totally (e.g. I don't know what, I don't know); an indirect question, as defined here, may not presuppose a question put by the interviewer (for 'ellipsis' and 'presupposition', see Halliday and Hasan, 1976).

E. Assessments of possibility and probability

These assessments may be made by two means: (1) Modal adjuncts (e.g. They're eating carrots perhaps or cake; Maybe she's saying . . .); (2) Modal auxiliaries (e.g. Might be a tunnel actually might; Could be a funny aeroplane). There are other ways of making such assessments (e.g. I'm doubtful whether . . .; It is possible that . . .; There is a possibility that . . .) but these were not used by the children. Halliday (1970b) gives a complete systemic description of 'modality' covering probability, possibility, relative certainty and absolute certainty.[5]

F. Supposition based on perception

These are statements with *look/seem* and *as if/as though/like* (e.g. They look as if they're bridesmaids; It looks like it's going to be flooded; It looks like a stream). The (main) clause selects 'mental process: perceptual' (with *look* or *seem*); the Processer may be made explicit (e.g. It looks to me . . .).

G. Other suppositions

Like the tentative egocentric sequence 'I think', these are expressions which focus on the speaker's cognitive state, making explicit his tentative attitude to what he says. Examples are: I suppose she's going in; The air ship's going to land on the tree I suppose. I expect they will [break the window]. They select 'mental process cognitive' (with a verb from Roget §514 (supposition), especially *suppose, expect*).

H. Alternatives (Disjunctives)

The speaker may indicate alternatives by means of *or*. We distinguished: (1) Questions containing alternatives (e.g. Is it a man or a boy?; I don't know if they're going that way or that way); (2) Statements offering alternatives (e.g. There's a cat or a dog; He's bringing his net or shovel; It's just going night-time now or morning; All the cooks have done that or the two old ladies). In the speech we are dealing with *or* is 'disjunctive' (not 'conjunctive'), the alternatives offered being mutually exclusive.

I. Approximations

Approximations may be expressed by several linguistic means. We list the main constructions: those with *sort of/kind of* (e.g. Sort of a tea party; Sort of helicopter balloon; She kind of sells things); *or something (like that)* (e.g. He pulls him off the tree or something; They're having their tea or something; These boys find this old bungalow or something like that); *thing* (e.g. There's that balloon thing again; He's pushing that pole piece of wood thing); *like* (e.g. There's a cart with like a rug in it); and *a bit/more* with *like* (e.g. he looks different from a newspaper man but looks a bit like it; Looks more like a stepmother).

The coding frame is ordered as it was in the original study, except that three additional categories are placed at the end of it. This coding frame was appropriate for identifying which expressions of uncertainty the children used and for making age comparisons. But for other purposes it is appropriate to group the categories in terms of higher order categories. One possible way of arranging the categories is exemplified below (Figure A.1), where the categories are represented in the form of a semantic network (see Halliday, 1973). For purposes of the correlational analysis two higher order summarising categories were recognised:

(1) ego-oriented expressions, i.e. all tentative statements *plus* two types of questions, namely indirect questions and questions offering alternatives, which can be regarded as particularly explicit categories of speech;
(2) socio-oriented expressions, i.e. sociocentric sequences and direct questions.

The socio-oriented expressions are essentially devices which seek feedback from the listener. At first sight, it may appear rather odd to group these together. Are not the sociocentric sequences, particularly the tag questions, typically confirmation-seeking whilst the direct questions are often information-seeking? It was found, however, that the use of these questions seemed to have a similar motivation (Turner and Pickvance, 1973). A considerable number of children who asked direct wh-questions were able to suggest an answer to their queries, either spontaneously or when prompted by the interviewer, a finding which suggests that they were perhaps using these questions to try and check their interpretations against the interviewer's.

Notes

1 To have included the results of the analysis in the main report would have complicated excessively an already complicated and lengthy paper.
2 This study, which was concerned mainly with age differences in the expression of uncertainty, used scores from two tasks *combined*, the Picture Story and Trotin tasks. Also available were scores for uncertainty in the 'social control' task.
3 The children used a much narrower range of uncertainty expressions in the 'social control' task, so it was not profitable to subdivide them according to the ego-oriented/socio-oriented distinction; as stated, the expressions used were predominantly of the ego-oriented type.
4 Sinclair (1972, p. 76) illustrates the distinction as follows:

	The speaker thinks	Events suggest	Expected response
Madge is coming round tonight, isn't she?	Yes	—	Yes
Madge is coming round tonight, isn't she?	Yes	No	Yes
Madge isn't coming round tonight, is she?	No	—	No
Madge isn't coming round tonight, is she?	No	Yes	No

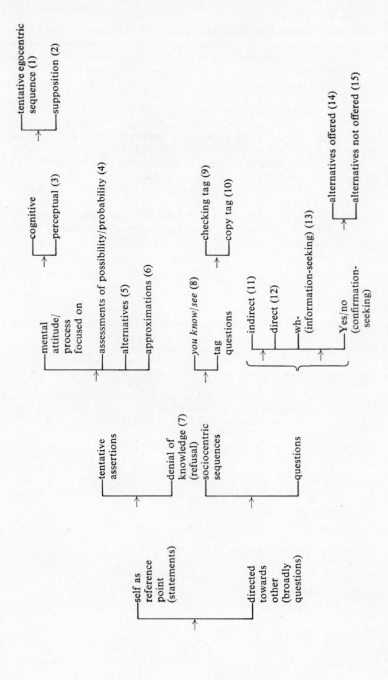

Examples

(1) I *think* it's a wedding.
    cf. *I* think it's a wedding.
(2) I suppose it's a wedding.
    It's a wedding, I expect.
(3) It looks like a wedding to me.
    It looks as if they're having a party.
(4) It could be a wedding.
    It might be a birthday party.
    Perhaps it's a wedding.
    It's probably a wedding.

(5) It's a wedding or a birthday party.
(6) It's a wedding or something.
    It's a sort of party.
(7) I don't know.
    I don't know what's going on.
(8) It's a, you know, wedding.
    Well, it's a wedding, you see.
(9) It's a wedding, isn't it?
    It's not a birthday party, is it?
(10) ——————

(11, 15) I wonder if it is a wedding.
(11, 14) I don't know whether it's a wedding or a birthday party.
(12, 15) Is it a wedding?
(12, 14) Is it a wedding or a birthday party?
(11, 13) I wonder what it is.
(12, 13) What is it?

Figure A.1   A semantic network for expressions of uncertainty in a descriptive context

5 Part of the modality system may be represented thus:

		Neutral	Undertone: tentative, deduced	Overtone: assertive, with reservation (tonic)
Probable		probably will	presumably would (will)	predictably (tone 1) would
	Possible	possibly may, can (could)	perhaps might, could	conceivably (tone 4) may, might, could
Possible/ certain	Virtually certain		assumedly should, ought to	surely (tone 4) should, ought to
	Certain	certainly must (will)	obviously must	surely (tone 1) must

Besides the modal adjuncts and the modal auxiliaries, Halliday lists four other ways of expressing modality, three involving the adjective, one the noun:

(1) as adjective (predicative in impersonal matrix clause *it is . . . that . . .*): *possible, likely, obvious, conceivable*, etc.

(2) as adjective (predicative in interpersonal, speaker-hearer matrix clause *I am . . . that . . ., are you . . . that . . .?*: *sure, certain*, etc.; also *doubtful* (*whether . . .*). (Compare *I think that . . .*, etc.)

(3) as adjective (predicative in clauses as *he is sure to have known*): *sure, certain, likely*

(4) as noun (complement in impersonal matrix clause *there is a . . . that . . .*): *possibility, chance, likelihood, presumption*, etc.

Bibliography

BERNSTEIN, B. (1961), 'Social class and linguistic development: a theory of social learning', in A. H. Halsey, J. Floud and C. A. Anderson (eds), *Education, Economy and Society*, Collier-Macmillan, London, 288–314.

BERNSTEIN, B. (1962), 'Social class, linguistic codes and grammatical elements', in B. Bernstein (1971).

BERNSTEIN, B. (1971), *Class, Codes and Control*: Vol. 1. *Theoretical Studies Towards a Sociology of Language*, Routledge & Kegan Paul, London.

BERNSTEIN, B., ed. (1973a), *Class, Codes and Control*: Vol. 2. *Applied Studies Towards a Sociology of Language*, Routledge & Kegan Paul, London.

BERNSTEIN, B. (1973b), 'A brief account of the theory of codes', Appendix I in *Social Relationships and Language: Some Aspects of the Work of Basil Bernstein*, The Open University, E 262, Block 3.

BERNSTEIN, B. (1975), *Class, Codes and Control*: Vol. 3. *Towards a Theory of Educational Transmissions*, Routledge & Kegan Paul, London.

BERNSTEIN, B. and COOK, J. (1965), 'Social control grid', in J. Cook-Gumperz (1973), ch. 2.

BLOM, J. P. and GUMPERZ, J. (1972), 'Some social determinants of verbal behaviour', in J. J. Gumperz and D. Hymes (eds), *Directions in Sociolinguistics*, Holt, Rinehart & Winston, New York.

BRANDIS, W. and BERNSTEIN, B. (1974), *Selection and Control, Teachers' Ratings of Children in the Infant School*, Routledge & Kegan Paul, London.

BRANDIS, W. and HENDERSON, D. (1970), *Social Class, Language and Communication*, Routledge & Kegan Paul, London.

BROWN, R. and GILMAN, A. (1960), 'The pronouns of power and solidarity', in T. Sebeok (ed.), *Style and Language*, M.I.T. Press, Cambridge, Mass.

CAZDEN, C. (1971), 'The situation: a neglected source of social class difference in language use', in J. B. Pride and J. Holmes (eds), *Sociolinguistics*, Penguin, Harmondsworth.

COOK-GUMPERZ, J. (1973), *Social Control and Socialization*, Routledge & Kegan Paul, London.

ERVIN-TRIPP, S. (1964), 'An analysis of the interaction of language, topic and listener', *American Anthropologist*, 66, no. 6, part 2, 86–102.

FISHMAN, J. A. (1965), 'Who speaks what language to whom and when?', *Linguistique*, no. 2, 67–88.

245

GAHAGAN, D. M. and GAHAGAN, G. A. (1970), *Talk Reform*, Routledge & Kegan Paul, London.

GUMPERZ, J. and HERNANDEZ-CHAVEZ, E. (1972), 'Bilingualism, bidialectalism, and classroom interaction', in C. Cazden, P. John and D. Hymes (eds), *Functions of Language in the Classroom*, Teachers College Press, New York.

HALLIDAY, M. A. K. (1966), 'Intonation systems in English', in A. McIntosh and M. A. K. Halliday, *Patterns of Language: Papers in General, Descriptive and Applied Linguistics*, Longmans, London.

HALLIDAY, M. A. K. (1970a), 'Language structure and language function', in J. Lyons (ed.), *New Horizons in Linguistics*, Penguin, Harmondsworth, 140–65.

HALLIDAY, M. A. K. (1970b), 'Functional diversity in language', *Foundations of Language*, 6, 322–61.

HALLIDAY, M. A. K. (1973), *Explorations in the Functions of Language*, Edward Arnold, London.

HALLIDAY, M. A. K. and HASAN, R. (1976), *Cohesion in English*, Longmans, London.

HASAN, R. (1968), *Grammatical Cohesion in Spoken and Written English*, Part 1, Nuffield Programme in Linguistics and English Teaching, Paper no. 7, Longmans, London.

HASAN, R. (1973), 'Code, register and social dialect', in B. Bernstein, *Class, Codes and Control*, vol. 2.

HAWKINS, P. R. (1969), 'Social class, the nominal group and reference', in B. Bernstein (1973a).

HAWKINS, P. R. (1973), 'The influence of sex, social class and pause-location in the hesitation phenomena of seven-year-old children', in B. Bernstein, *Class, Codes and Control*, vol. 2.

HEIDER, E. R., CAZDEN, C. and BROWN, R. (1968), *Social Class Differences in the Effectiveness and Style of Children's Coding Ability*, Project Literacy Reports, no. 9, Cornell University Press, Ithaca, N.Y.

HYMES, D. (1971), 'Competence and performance in linguistic theory', in R. Huxley and E. Ingram (eds), *Language Acquisition: Models and Methods*, Academic Press, New York.

HYMES, D. (1972), Introduction to C. Cazden, P. John and D. Hymes (eds), *Functions of Language in the Classroom*, Teachers College Press, New York.

KANTOROVICH, I. (1966), *Ty and Vy: A Writer's Notes*, quoted by S. Ervin-Tripp, 'Sociolinguistics', in J. Fishman (ed.), *Advances in the Sociology of Language*, vol. 1, Mouton, The Hague.

LABOV, W. (1964), 'Phonological correlates of social stratification', *American Anthropologist*, 66, no. 2, 164–76.

LABOV, W. (1969), 'The logic of non-standard English', in R. D. Abrahams and R. D. Troike (eds), *Language and Cultural Diversity in American Education*, Prentice-Hall, Englewood Cliffs, N.J., 1972.

LOBAN, W. D. (1966), *Language Ability: Grades Seven, Eight and Nine*, US Government Printing Office, Washington.

POLGAR, S. (1960), Quoted by Hymes, D. (1971), 'Competence and performance in linguistic theory', in R. Huxley and E. Ingram (eds), *Language Acquisition: Models and Methods*, Academic Press, New York.

ROBINSON, W. P. (1973), 'Where do children's answers come from?', in B. Bernstein, *Class, Codes and Control*, vol. 2.

ROBINSON, W. P. and RACKSTRAW, S. (1971), *A Question of Answers*, 2 vols, Routledge & Kegan Paul, London.

SINCLAIR, J. MCH. (1965, 1972), *A Course in Spoken English*, Oxford University Press, London. Pre-publication edition, 1965.

TURNER, G. J. (1973a), 'Social class and children's language of control at age five and age seven', in B. Bernstein, *Class, Codes and Control*, vol. 2.

TURNER, G. J. (1973b), 'Social class, age and the expression of uncertainty', unpublished document, Sociological Research Unit, University of London Institute of Education.

TURNER, G. J. (in press), *The Regulative Context: a Sociolinguistic Enquiry*, Routledge & Kegan Paul, London.

TURNER, G. J. and PICKVANCE, R. E. (1973), 'Social class differences in the expression of uncertainty in five-year-old children', in B. Bernstein (1973a).

WOOTTON, A. J. (1974), 'Talk in the homes of young children', *Sociology*, 8, 278–95.

Index

Routledge Social Science Series

Routledge & Kegan Paul   London and Boston

68–74 Carter Lane   London EC4V 5EL
9 Park Street   Boston   Mass 02108

Contents

*Authors wishing to submit manuscripts for any series in
this catalogue should send them to the Social Science Editor,
Routledge & Kegan Paul Ltd, 68–74 Carter Lane,
London EC4V 5EL*

●*Books so marked are available in paperback*
All books are in Metric Demy 8vo format (216 × 138mm approx.)

International Library of Sociology

General Editor John Rex

GENERAL SOCIOLOGY

Barnsley, J. H. The Social Reality of Ethics. *464 pp.*
Belshaw, Cyril. The Conditions of Social Performance. *An Exploratory Theory. 144 pp.*
Brown, Robert. Explanation in Social Science. *208 pp.*
● Rules and Laws in Sociology. *192 pp.*
Bruford, W. H. Chekhov and His Russia. *A Sociological Study. 244 pp.*
Cain, Maureen E. Society and the Policeman's Role. *326 pp.*
●**Fletcher, Colin.** Beneath the Surface. *An Account of Three Styles of Sociological Research. 221 pp.*
Gibson, Quentin. The Logic of Social Enquiry. *240 pp.*
Glucksmann, M. Structuralist Analysis in Contemporary Social Thought. *212 pp.*
Gurvitch, Georges. Sociology of Law. *Preface by Roscoe Pound. 264 pp.*
Hodge, H. A. Wilhelm Dilthey. *An Introduction. 184 pp.*
Homans, George C. Sentiments and Activities. *336 pp.*
Johnson, Harry M. Sociology: *a Systematic Introduction. Foreword by Robert K. Merton. 710 pp.*
●**Keat, Russell, and Urry, John.** Social Theory as Science. *278 pp.*
Mannheim, Karl. Essays on Sociology and Social Psychology. *Edited by Paul Keckskemeti. With Editorial Note by Adolph Lowe. 344 pp.*
Systematic Sociology: *An Introduction to the Study of Society. Edited by J. S. Erös and Professor W. A. C. Stewart. 220 pp.*
Martindale, Don. The Nature and Types of Sociological Theory. *292 pp.*
●**Maus, Heinz.** A Short History of Sociology. *234 pp.*
Mey, Harald. Field-Theory. *A Study of its Application in the Social Sciences. 352 pp.*
Myrdal, Gunnar. Value in Social Theory: *A Collection of Essays on Methodology. Edited by Paul Streeten. 332 pp.*
Ogburn, William F., and Nimkoff, Meyer F. A Handbook of Sociology. *Preface by Karl Mannheim. 656 pp. 46 figures. 35 tables.*
Parsons, Talcott, and Smelser, Neil J. Economy and Society: *A Study in the Integration of Economic and Social Theory. 362 pp.*
Podgórecki, Adam. Practical Social Sciences. *About 200 pp.*
●**Rex, John.** Key Problems of Sociological Theory. *220 pp.*
Discovering Sociology. *278 pp.*
Sociology and the Demystification of the Modern World. *282 pp.*
●**Rex, John** (Ed.) Approaches to Sociology. *Contributions by Peter Abell, Frank Bechhofer, Basil Bernstein, Ronald Fletcher, David Frisby, Miriam Glucksmann, Peter Lassman, Herminio Martins, John Rex, Roland Robertson, John Westergaard and Jock Young. 302 pp.*
Rigby, A. Alternative Realities. *352 pp.*

Roche, M. Phenomenology, Language and the Social Sciences. *374 pp.*
Sahay, A. Sociological Analysis. *220 pp.*
Strasser, Hermann. The Normative Structure of Sociology. *Conservative and Emancipatory Themes in Social Thought. About 340 pp.*
Urry, John. Reference Groups and the Theory of Revolution. *244 pp.*
Weinberg, E. Development of Sociology in the Soviet Union. *173 pp.*

FOREIGN CLASSICS OF SOCIOLOGY

●**Durkheim, Emile.** Suicide. *A Study in Sociology. Edited and with an Introduction by George Simpson. 404 pp.*
   Professional Ethics and Civic Morals. *Translated by Cornelia Brookfield. 288 pp.*
●**Gerth, H. H.,** and **Mills, C. Wright.** From Max Weber: *Essays in Sociology. 502 pp.*
●**Tönnies, Ferdinand.** Community and Association. (*Gemeinschaft und Gesellschaft.) Translated and Supplemented by Charles P. Loomis. Foreword by Pitirim A. Sorokin. 334 pp.*

SOCIAL STRUCTURE

Andreski, Stanislav. Military Organization and Society. *Foreword by Professor A. R. Radcliffe-Brown. 226 pp. 1 folder.*
Coontz, Sydney H. Population Theories and the Economic Interpretation. *202 pp.*
Coser, Lewis. The Functions of Social Conflict. *204 pp.*
Dickie-Clark, H. F. Marginal Situation: *A Sociological Study of a Coloured Group. 240 pp. 11 tables.*
Glaser, Barney, and **Strauss, Anselm L.** Status Passage. *A Formal Theory. 208 pp.*
Glass, D. V. (Ed.) Social Mobility in Britain. *Contributions by J. Berent, T. Bottomore, R. C. Chambers, J. Floud, D. V. Glass, J. R. Hall, H. T. Himmelweit, R. K. Kelsall, F. M. Martin, C. A. Moser, R. Mukherjee, and W. Ziegel. 420 pp.*
Jones, Garth N. Planned Organizational Change: *An Exploratory Study Using an Empirical Approach. 268 pp.*
Kelsall, R. K. Higher Civil Servants in Britain: *From 1870 to the Present Day. 268 pp. 31 tables.*
König, René. The Community. *232 pp. Illustrated.*
●**Lawton, Denis.** Social Class, Language and Education. *192 pp.*
McLeish, John. The Theory of Social Change: *Four Views Considered. 128 pp.*
Marsh, David C. The Changing Social Structure of England and Wales, 1871-1961. *288 pp.*
●**Mouzelis, Nicos.** Organization and Bureaucracy. *An Analysis of Modern Theories. 240 pp.*
Mulkay, M. J. Functionalism, Exchange and Theoretical Strategy. *272 pp.*
Ossowski, Stanislaw. Class Structure in the Social Consciousness. *210 pp.*
●**Podgórecki, Adam.** Law and Society. *302 pp.*

SOCIOLOGY AND POLITICS

Acton, T. A. Gypsy Politics and Social Change. *316 pp.*

Clegg, Stuart. Power, Rule and Domination. *A Critical and Empirical Understanding of Power in Sociological Theory and Organisational Life. About 300 pp.*

Hechter, Michael. Internal Colonialism. *The Celtic Fringe in British National Development, 1536–1966. 361 pp.*

Hertz, Frederick. Nationality in History and Politics: *A Psychology and Sociology of National Sentiment and Nationalism. 432 pp.*

Kornhauser, William. The Politics of Mass Society. *272 pp. 20 tables.*

●**Kroes, R.** Soldiers and Students. *A Study of Right- and Left-wing Students. 174 pp.*

Laidler, Harry W. History of Socialism. *Social-Economic Movements: An Historical and Comparative Survey of Socialism, Communism, Co-operation, Utopianism; and other Systems of Reform and Reconstruction. 992 pp.*

Lasswell, H. D. Analysis of Political Behaviour. *324 pp.*

Mannheim, Karl. Freedom, Power and Democratic Planning. *Edited by Hans Gerth and Ernest K. Bramstedt. 424 pp.*

Mansur, Fatma. Process of Independence. *Foreword by A. H. Hanson. 208 pp.*

Martin, David A. Pacifism: *an Historical and Sociological Study. 262 pp.*

Myrdal, Gunnar. The Political Element in the Development of Economic Theory. *Translated from the German by Paul Streeten. 282 pp.*

Wootton, Graham. Workers, Unions and the State. *188 pp.*

FOREIGN AFFAIRS: THEIR SOCIAL, POLITICAL AND ECONOMIC FOUNDATIONS

Mayer, J. P. Political Thought in France from the Revolution to the Fifth Republic. *164 pp.*

CRIMINOLOGY

Ancel, Marc. Social Defence: *A Modern Approach to Criminal Problems. Foreword by Leon Radzinowicz. 240 pp.*

Cain, Maureen E. Society and the Policeman's Role. *326 pp.*

Cloward, Richard A., and **Ohlin, Lloyd E.** Delinquency and Opportunity: *A Theory of Delinquent Gangs. 248 pp.*

Downes, David M. The Delinquent Solution. *A Study in Subcultural Theory. 296 pp.*

Dunlop, A. B., and **McCabe, S.** Young Men in Detention Centres. *192 pp.*

Friedlander, Kate. The Psycho-Analytical Approach to Juvenile Delinquency: *Theory, Case Studies, Treatment. 320 pp.*

Glueck, Sheldon, and **Eleanor.** Family Environment and Delinquency. *With the statistical assistance of Rose W. Kneznek. 340 pp.*

Lopez-Rey, Manuel. Crime. *An Analytical Appraisal. 288 pp.*

Mannheim, Hermann. Comparative Criminology: *a Text Book. Two volumes. 442 pp. and 380 pp.*

Morris, Terence. The Criminal Area: *A Study in Social Ecology. Foreword by Hermann Mannheim. 232 pp. 25 tables. 4 maps.*

Rock, Paul. Making People Pay. *338 pp.*

●**Taylor, Ian, Walton, Paul,** and **Young, Jock.** The New Criminology. *For a Social Theory of Deviance. 325 pp.*

●**Taylor, Ian, Walton, Paul,** and **Young, Jock** (Eds). Critical Criminology. *268 pp.*

SOCIAL PSYCHOLOGY

Bagley, Christopher. The Social Psychology of the Epileptic Child. *320 pp.*

Barbu, Zevedei. Problems of Historical Psychology. *248 pp.*

Blackburn, Julian. Psychology and the Social Pattern. *184 pp.*

●**Brittan, Arthur.** Meanings and Situations. *224 pp.*

Carroll, J. Break-Out from the Crystal Palace. *200 pp.*

●**Fleming, C. M.** Adolescence: Its Social Psychology. *With an Introduction to recent findings from the fields of Anthropology, Physiology, Medicine, Psychometrics and Sociometry. 288 pp.*

● The Social Psychology of Education: *An Introduction and Guide to Its Study. 136 pp.*

●**Homans, George C.** The Human Group. *Foreword by Bernard DeVoto. Introduction by Robert K. Merton. 526 pp.*

● Social Behaviour: *its Elementary Forms. 416 pp.*

●**Klein, Josephine.** The Study of Groups. *226 pp. 31 figures. 5 tables.*

Linton, Ralph. The Cultural Background of Personality. *132 pp.*

●**Mayo, Elton.** The Social Problems of an Industrial Civilization. *With an appendix on the Political Problem. 180 pp.*

Ottaway, A. K. C. Learning Through Group Experience. *176 pp.*

Plummer, Ken. Sexual Stigma. *An Interactionist Account. 254 pp.*

Ridder, J. C. de. The Personality of the Urban African in South Africa. *A Thermatic Apperception Test Study. 196 pp. 12 plates.*

●**Rose, Arnold M.** (Ed.) Human Behaviour and Social Processes: *an Interactionist Approach. Contributions by Arnold M. Rose, Ralph H. Turner, Anselm Strauss, Everett C. Hughes, E. Franklin Frazier, Howard S. Becker, et al. 696 pp.*

Smelser, Neil J. Theory of Collective Behaviour. *448 pp.*

Stephenson, Geoffrey M. The Development of Conscience. *128 pp.*

Young, Kimball. Handbook of Social Psychology. *658 pp. 16 figures. 10 tables.*

SOCIOLOGY OF THE FAMILY

Banks, J. A. Prosperity and Parenthood: *A Study of Family Planning among The Victorian Middle Classes. 262 pp.*

Bell, Colin R. Middle Class Families: *Social and Geographical Mobility. 224 pp.*

Burton, Lindy. Vulnerable Children. *272 pp.*

Gavron, Hannah. The Captive Wife: *Conflicts of Household Mothers. 190 pp.*

George, Victor, and **Wilding, Paul.** Motherless Families. *248 pp.*

Klein, Josephine. Samples from English Cultures.
1. Three Preliminary Studies and Aspects of Adult Life in England.
447 pp.
2. Child-Rearing Practices and Index. *247 pp.*

Klein, Viola. Britain's Married Women Workers. *180 pp.*
The Feminine Character. *History of an Ideology. 244 pp.*

McWhinnie, Alexina M. Adopted Children. *How They Grow Up. 304 pp.*

● **Morgan, D. H. J.** Social Theory and the Family. *About 320 pp.*

● **Myrdal, Alva,** and **Klein, Viola.** Women's Two Roles: *Home and Work.*
238 pp. 27 tables.

Parsons, Talcott, and **Bales, Robert F.** Family: Socialization and Interaction Process. *In collaboration with James Olds, Morris Zelditch and
Philip E. Slater. 456 pp. 50 figures and tables.*

SOCIAL SERVICES

Bastide, Roger. The Sociology of Mental Disorder. *Translated from the
French by Jean McNeil. 260 pp.*

Carlebach, Julius. Caring For Children in Trouble. *266 pp.*

George, Victor. Foster Care. *Theory and Practice. 234 pp.*
Social Security: *Beveridge and After. 258 pp.*

George, V., and **Wilding, P.** Motherless Families. *248 pp.*

●**Goetschius, George W.** Working with Community Groups. *256 pp.*

Goetschius, George W., and **Tash, Joan.** Working with Unattached Youth.
416 pp.

Hall, M. P., and **Howes, I. V.** The Church in Social Work. *A Study of
Moral Welfare Work undertaken by the Church of England. 320 pp.*

Heywood, Jean S. Children in Care: *the Development of the Service for the
Deprived Child. 264 pp.*

Hoenig, J., and **Hamilton, Marian W.** The De-Segregation of the Mentally
Ill. *284 pp.*

Jones, Kathleen. Mental Health and Social Policy, 1845-1959. *264 pp.*

King, Roy D., Raynes, Norma V., and **Tizard, Jack.** Patterns of Residential
Care. *356 pp.*

Leigh, John. Young People and Leisure. *256 pp.*

●**Mays, John.** (Ed.) Penelope Hall's Social Services of England and Wales.
About 324 pp.

Morris, Mary. Voluntary Work and the Welfare State. *300 pp.*

Morris, Pauline. Put Away: *A Sociological Study of Institutions for the
Mentally Retarded. 364 pp.*

Nokes, P. L. The Professional Task in Welfare Practice. *152 pp.*

Timms, Noel. Psychiatric Social Work in Great Britain (1939-1962).
280 pp.

● Social Casework: *Principles and Practice. 256 pp.*

Young, A. F. Social Services in British Industry. *272 pp.*

Young, A. F., and **Ashton, E. T.** British Social Work in the Nineteenth
Century. *288 pp.*

SOCIOLOGY OF EDUCATION

Banks, Olive. Parity and Prestige in English Secondary Education: a Study in Educational Sociology. *272 pp.*

Bentwich, Joseph. Education in Israel. *224 pp. 8 pp. plates.*

●**Blyth, W. A. L.** English Primary Education. *A Sociological Description.*
   1. Schools. *232 pp.*
   2. Background. *168 pp.*

Collier, K. G. The Social Purposes of Education: *Personal and Social Values in Education. 268 pp.*

Dale, R. R., and **Griffith, S.** Down Stream: *Failure in the Grammar School. 108 pp.*

Dore, R. P. Education in Tokugawa Japan. *356 pp. 9 pp. plates.*

Evans, K. M. Sociometry and Education. *158 pp.*

●**Ford, Julienne.** Social Class and the Comprehensive School. *192 pp.*

Foster, P. J. Education and Social Change in Ghana. *336 pp. 3 maps.*

Fraser, W. R. Education and Society in Modern France. *150 pp.*

Grace, Gerald R. Role Conflict and the Teacher. *150 pp.*

Hans, Nicholas. New Trends in Education in the Eighteenth Century. *278 pp. 19 tables.*

● Comparative Education: *A Study of Educational Factors and Traditions. 360 pp.*

●**Hargreaves, David.** Interpersonal Relations and Education. *432 pp.*

● Social Relations in a Secondary School. *240 pp.*

Holmes, Brian. Problems in Education. *A Comparative Approach. 336 pp.*

King, Ronald. Values and Involvement in a Grammar School. *164 pp.*

   School Organization and Pupil Involvement. *A Study of Secondary Schools.*

●**Mannheim, Karl,** and **Stewart, W. A. C.** An Introduction to the Sociology of Education. *206 pp.*

Morris, Raymond N. The Sixth Form and College Entrance. *231 pp.*

●**Musgrove, F.** Youth and the Social Order. *176 pp.*

●**Ottaway, A. K. C.** Education and Society: An Introduction to the Sociology of Education. *With an Introduction by W. O. Lester Smith. 212 pp.*

Peers, Robert. Adult Education: *A Comparative Study. 398 pp.*

Pritchard, D. G. Education and the Handicapped: *1760 to 1960. 258 pp.*

Richardson, Helen. Adolescent Girls in Approved Schools. *308 pp.*

Stratta, Erica. The Education of Borstal Boys. *A Study of their Educational Experiences prior to, and during, Borstal Training. 256 pp.*

Taylor, P. H., Reid, W. A., and **Holley, B. J.** The English Sixth Form. *A Case Study in Curriculum Research. 200 pp.*

SOCIOLOGY OF CULTURE

Eppel, E. M., and **M.** Adolescents and Morality: *A Study of some Moral Values and Dilemmas of Working Adolescents in the Context of a changing Climate of Opinion. Foreword by W. J. H. Sprott. 268 pp. 39 tables.*

● **Fromm, Erich.** The Fear of Freedom. *286 pp.*
● The Sane Society. *400 pp.*
Mannheim, Karl. Essays on the Sociology of Culture. *Edited by Ernst Mannheim in co-operation with Paul Kecskemeti. Editorial Note by Adolph Lowe. 280 pp.*
Weber, Alfred. Farewell to European History: *or The Conquest of Nihilism. Translated from the German by R. F. C. Hull. 224 pp.*

SOCIOLOGY OF RELIGION

Argyle, Michael and **Beit-Hallahmi, Benjamin.** The Social Psychology of Religion. *About 256 pp.*
Nelson, G. K. Spiritualism and Society. *313 pp.*
Stark, Werner. The Sociology of Religion. *A Study of Christendom.*
Volume I. *Established Religion. 248 pp.*
Volume II. *Sectarian Religion. 368 pp.*
Volume III. *The Universal Church. 464 pp.*
Volume IV. *Types of Religious Man. 352 pp.*
Volume V. *Types of Religious Culture. 464 pp.*
Turner, B. S. Weber and Islam. *216 pp.*
Watt, W. Montgomery. Islam and the Integration of Society. *320 pp.*

SOCIOLOGY OF ART AND LITERATURE

Jarvie, Ian C. Towards a Sociology of the Cinema. *A Comparative Essay on the Structure and Functioning of a Major Entertainment Industry. 405 pp.*
Rust, Frances S. Dance in Society. *An Analysis of the Relationships between the Social Dance and Society in England from the Middle Ages to the Present Day. 256 pp. 8 pp. of plates.*
Schücking, L. L. The Sociology of Literary Taste. *112 pp.*
Wolff, Janet. Hermeneutic Philosophy and the Sociology of Art. *150 pp.*

SOCIOLOGY OF KNOWLEDGE

Diesing, P. Patterns of Discovery in the Social Sciences. *262 pp.*
● **Douglas, J. D.** (Ed.) Understanding Everyday Life. *370 pp.*
● **Hamilton, P.** Knowledge and Social Structure. *174 pp.*
Jarvie, I. C. Concepts and Society. *232 pp.*
Mannheim, Karl. Essays on the Sociology of Knowledge. *Edited by Paul Kecskemeti. Editorial Note by Adolph Lowe. 353 pp.*
Remmling, Gunter W. The Sociology of Karl Mannheim. *With a Bibliographical Guide to the Sociology of Knowledge, Ideological Analysis, and Social Planning. 255 pp.*

Remmling, Gunter W. (Ed.) Towards the Sociology of Knowledge. *Origin and Development of a Sociological Thought Style. 463 pp.*

Stark, Werner. The Sociology of Knowledge: *An Essay in Aid of a Deeper Understanding of the History of Ideas. 384 pp.*

URBAN SOCIOLOGY

Ashworth, William. The Genesis of Modern British Town Planning: *A Study in Economic and Social History of the Nineteenth and Twentieth Centuries. 288 pp.*

Cullingworth, J. B. Housing Needs and Planning Policy: *A Restatement of the Problems of Housing Need and 'Overspill' in England and Wales. 232 pp. 44 tables. 8 maps.*

Dickinson, Robert E. City and Region: *A Geographical Interpretation 608 pp. 125 figures.*

The West European City: *A Geographical Interpretation. 600 pp. 129 maps. 29 plates.*

● The City Region in Western Europe. *320 pp. Maps.*

Humphreys, Alexander J. New Dubliners: *Urbanization and the Irish Family. Foreword by George C. Homans. 304 pp.*

Jackson, Brian. Working Class Community: *Some General Notions raised by a Series of Studies in Northern England. 192 pp.*

Jennings, Hilda. Societies in the Making: *a Study of Development and Re-development within a County Borough. Foreword by D. A. Clark. 286 pp.*

●**Mann, P. H.** An Approach to Urban Sociology. *240 pp.*

Morris, R. N., and **Mogey, J.** The Sociology of Housing. *Studies at Berinsfield. 232 pp. 4 pp. plates.*

Rosser, C., and **Harris, C.** The Family and Social Change. *A Study of Family and Kinship in a South Wales Town. 352 pp. 8 maps.*

●**Stacey, Margaret, Batsone, Eric, Bell, Colin,** and **Thurcott, Anne.** Power, Persistence and Change. *A Second Study of Banbury. 196 pp.*

RURAL SOCIOLOGY

Chambers, R. J. H. Settlement Schemes in Tropical Africa: *A Selective Study. 268 pp.*

Haswell, M. R. The Economics of Development in Village India. *120 pp.*

Littlejohn, James. Westrigg: *the Sociology of a Cheviot Parish. 172 pp. 5 figures.*

Mayer, Adrian C. Peasants in the Pacific. *A Study of Fiji Indian Rural Society. 248 pp. 20 plates.*

Williams, W. M. The Sociology of an English Village: *Gosforth. 272 pp. 12 figures. 13 tables.*

SOCIOLOGY OF INDUSTRY AND DISTRIBUTION

Anderson, Nels. Work and Leisure. *280 pp.*
●**Blau, Peter M.**, and **Scott, W. Richard.** Formal Organizations: *a Comparative approach. Introduction and Additional Bibliography by J. H. Smith. 326 pp.*
Dunkerley, David. The Foreman. *Aspects of Task and Structure. 192 pp.*
Eldridge, J. E. T. Industrial Disputes. *Essays in the Sociology of Industrial Relations. 288 pp.*
Hetzler, Stanley. Applied Measures for Promoting Technological Growth. *352 pp.*
Technological Growth and Social Change. *Achieving Modernization. 269 pp.*
Hollowell, Peter G. The Lorry Driver. *272 pp.*
Jefferys, Margot, *with the assistance of Winifred Moss.* Mobility in the Labour Market: *Employment Changes in Battersea and Dagenham. Preface by Barbara Wootton. 186 pp. 51 tables.*
Millerson, Geoffrey. The Qualifying Associations: *a Study in Professionalization. 320 pp.*
●**Oxaal, I., Barnett, T.,** and **Booth, D.** (Eds). Beyond the Sociology of Development. *Economy and Society in Latin America and Africa. 295 pp.*
Smelser, Neil J. Social Change in the Industrial Revolution: *An Application of Theory to the Lancashire Cotton Industry, 1770–1840. 468 pp. 12 figures. 14 tables.*
Williams, Gertrude. Recruitment to Skilled Trades. *240 pp.*
Young, A. F. Industrial Injuries Insurance: *an Examination of British Policy. 192 pp.*

DOCUMENTARY

Schlesinger, Rudolf (Ed.) Changing Attitudes in Soviet Russia.
2. The Nationalities Problem and Soviet Administration. *Selected Readings on the Development of Soviet Nationalities Policies. Introduced by the editor. Translated by W. W. Gottlieb. 324 pp.*

ANTHROPOLOGY

Ammar, Hamed. Growing up in an Egyptian Village: *Silwa, Province of Aswan. 336 pp.*
Brandel-Syrier, Mia. Reeftown Elite. *A Study of Social Mobility in a Modern African Community on the Reef. 376 pp.*
Crook, David, and **Isabel.** Revolution in a Chinese Village: *Ten Mile Inn. 230 pp. 8 plates. 1 map.*
Dickie-Clark, H. F. The Marginal Situation. *A Sociological Study of a Coloured Group. 236 pp.*
Dube, S. C. Indian Village. *Foreword by Morris Edward Opler. 276 pp. 4 plates.*

India's Changing Villages: *Human Factors in Community Development.* *260 pp. 8 plates. 1 map.*

Firth, Raymond. Malay Fishermen. *Their Peasant Economy. 420 pp. 17 pp. plates.*

Firth, R., Hubert, J., and Forge, A. Families and their Relatives. *Kinship in a Middle-Class Sector of London: An Anthropological Study. 456 pp.*

Gulliver, P. H. Social Control in an African Society: a Study of the Arusha, Agricultural Masai of Northern Tanganyika. *320 pp. 8 plates. 10 figures.*

Family Herds. *288 pp.*

Ishwaran, K. Shivapur. *A South Indian Village. 216 pp.*

Tradition and Economy in Village India: *An Interactionist Approach. Foreword by Conrad Arensburg. 176 pp.*

Jarvie, Ian C. The Revolution in Anthropology. *268 pp.*

Little, Kenneth L. Mende of Sierra Leone. *308 pp. and folder.*

Negroes in Britain. *With a New Introduction and Contemporary Study by Leonard Bloom. 320 pp.*

Lowie, Robert H. Social Organization. *494 pp.*

Peasants in the Pacific. *A Study of Fiji Indian Rural Society. 248 pp.*

Smith, Raymond T. The Negro Family in British Guiana: *Family Structure and Social Status in the Villages. With a Foreword by Meyer Fortes. 314 pp. 8 plates. 1 figure. 4 maps.*

SOCIOLOGY AND PHILOSOPHY

Barnsley, John H. The Social Reality of Ethics. *A Comparative Analysis of Moral Codes. 448 pp.*

Diesing, Paul. Patterns of Discovery in the Social Sciences. *362 pp.*

●**Douglas, Jack D.** (Ed.) Understanding Everyday Life. *Toward the Reconstruction of Sociological Knowledge. Contributions by Alan F. Blum. Aaron W. Cicourel, Norman K. Denzin, Jack D. Douglas, John Heeren, Peter McHugh, Peter K. Manning, Melvin Power, Matthew Speier, Roy Turner, D. Lawrence Wieder, Thomas P. Wilson and Don H. Zimmerman. 370 pp.*

Jarvie, Ian C. Concepts and Society. *216 pp.*

●**Pelz, Werner.** The Scope of Understanding in Sociology. *Towards a more radical reorientation in the social humanistic sciences. 283 pp.*

Roche, Maurice. Phenomenology, Language and the Social Sciences. *371 pp.*

Sahay, Arun. Sociological Analysis. *212 pp.*

Sklair, Leslie. The Sociology of Progress. *320 pp.*

International Library of Anthropology

General Editor Adam Kuper

Brown, Paula. The Chimbu. *A Study of Change in the New Guinea Highlands. 151 pp.*

Hamnett, Ian. Chieftainship and Legitimacy. *An Anthropological Study of Executive Law in Lesotho. 163 pp.*
Hanson, F. Allan. Meaning in Culture. *127 pp.*
Lloyd, P. C. Power and Independence. *Urban Africans' Perception of Social Inequality. 264 pp.*
Pettigrew, Joyce. Robber Noblemen. *A Study of the Political System of the Sikh Jats. 284 pp.*
Street, Brian V. The Savage in Literature. *Representations of 'Primitive' Society in English Fiction, 1858–1920. 207 pp.*
Van Den Berghe, Pierre L. Power and Privilege at an African University. *278 pp.*

International Library of Social Policy

General Editor Kathleen Jones

Bayley, M. Mental Handicap and Community Care. *426 pp.*
Butler, J. R. Family Doctors and Public Policy. *208 pp.*
Davies, Martin. Prisoners of Society. *Attitudes and Aftercare. 204 pp.*
Holman, Robert. Trading in Children. *A Study of Private Fostering. 355 pp.*
Jones, Kathleen. History of the Mental Health Service. *428 pp.*
Opening the Door. *A Study of New Policies for the Mentally Handicapped. 260 pp.*
Thomas, J. E. The English Prison Officer since 1850: *A Study in Conflict. 258 pp.*
Walton, R. G. Women in Social Work. *303 pp.*
Woodward, J. To Do the Sick No Harm. *A Study of the British Voluntary Hospital System to 1875. 221 pp.*

International Library of Welfare and Philosophy

General Editors Noel Timms and David Watson

● **Plant, Raymond.** Community and Ideology. *104 pp.*

Primary Socialization, Language and Education

General Editor Basil Bernstein

Bernstein, Basil. Class, Codes and Control. *3 volumes.*
  1. *Theoretical Studies Towards a Sociology of Language. 254 pp.*
  2. *Applied Studies Towards a Sociology of Language. 377 pp.*
  3. *Towards a Theory of Educational Transmission. 167 pp.*
Brandis, W., and **Bernstein, B.** Selection and Control. *176 pp.*
Brandis, Walter, and **Henderson, Dorothy.** Social Class, Language and Communication. *288 pp.*

Cook-Gumperz, Jenny. Social Control and Socialization. *A Study of Class Differences in the Language of Maternal Control. 290 pp.*

● **Gahagan, D. M.,** and **G. A.** Talk Reform. *Exploration in Language for Infant School Children. 160 pp.*

Robinson, W. P., and **Rackstraw, Susan D. A.** A Question of Answers. *2 volumes. 192 pp. and 180 pp.*

Turner, Geoffrey J., and **Mohan, Bernard A.** A Linguistic Description and Computer Programme for Children's Speech. *208 pp.*

Reports of the Institute of Community Studies

Cartwright, Ann. Human Relations and Hospital Care. *272 pp.*

● Parents and Family Planning Services. *306 pp.*

Patients and their Doctors. *A Study of General Practice. 304 pp.*

Dench, Geoff. Maltese in London. *A Case-study in the Erosion of Ethnic Consciousness. 302 pp.*

● **Jackson, Brian.** Streaming: *an Education System in Miniature. 168 pp.*

Jackson, Brian, and **Marsden, Dennis.** Education and the Working Class: *Some General Themes raised by a Study of 88 Working-class Children in a Northern Industrial City. 268 pp. 2 folders.*

Marris, Peter. The Experience of Higher Education. *232 pp. 27 tables.* Loss and Change. *192 pp.*

Marris, Peter, and **Rein, Martin.** Dilemmas of Social Reform. *Poverty and Community Action in the United States. 256 pp.*

Marris, Peter, and **Somerset, Anthony.** African Businessmen. *A Study of Entrepreneurship and Development in Kenya. 256 pp.*

Mills, Richard. Young Outsiders: *a Study in Alternative Communities. 216 pp.*

Runciman, W. G. Relative Deprivation and Social Justice. *A Study of Attitudes to Social Inequality in Twentieth-Century England. 352 pp.*

Willmott, Peter. Adolescent Boys in East London. *230 pp.*

Willmott, Peter, and **Young, Michael.** Family and Class in a London Suburb. *202 pp. 47 tables.*

Young, Michael. Innovation and Research in Education. *192 pp.*

● **Young, Michael,** and **McGeeney, Patrick.** Learning Begins at Home. *A Study of a Junior School and its Parents. 128 pp.*

Young, Michael, and **Willmott, Peter.** Family and Kinship in East London. *Foreword by Richard M. Titmuss. 252 pp. 39 tables.* The Symmetrical Family. *410 pp.*

Reports of the Institute for Social Studies in Medical Care

Cartwright, Ann, Hockey, Lisbeth, and **Anderson, John L.** Life Before Death. *310 pp.*

Dunnell, Karen, and **Cartwright, Ann.** Medicine Takers, Prescribers and Hoarders. *190 pp.*

Medicine, Illness and Society

General Editor   W. M. Williams

Robinson, David. The Process of Becoming Ill. *142 pp.*

Stacey, Margaret, *et al.* Hospitals, Children and Their Families. *The Report of a Pilot Study. 202 pp.*

Stimson, G. V., and **Webb, B.** Going to See the Doctor. *The Consultation Process in General Practice. 155 pp.*

Monographs in Social Theory

General Editor   Arthur Brittan

● **Barnes, B.** Scientific Knowledge and Sociological Theory. *192 pp.*

Bauman, Zygmunt. Culture as Praxis. *204 pp.*

● **Dixon, Keith.** Sociological Theory. *Pretence and Possibility. 142 pp.*

Meltzer, B. N., Petras, J. W., and **Reynolds, L. T.** Symbolic Interactionism. *Genesis, Varieties and Criticisms. 144 pp.*

● **Smith, Anthony D.** The Concept of Social Change. *A Critique of the Functionalist Theory of Social Change. 208 pp.*

Routledge Social Science Journals

The British Journal of Sociology. *Managing Editor – Angus Stewart; Associate Editor – Michael Hill. Vol. 1, No. 1 – March 1950 and Quarterly. Roy. 8vo. All back issues available. An international journal publishing original papers in the field of sociology and related areas.*

Community Work. *Edited by David Jones and Marjorie Mayo. 1973. Published annually.*

Economy and Society. *Vol. 1, No. 1. February 1972 and Quarterly. Metric Roy. 8vo. A journal for all social scientists covering sociology, philosophy, anthropology, economics and history. Back numbers available.*

Religion. Journal of Religion and Religions. *Chairman of Editorial Board, Ninian Smart. Vol. 1, No. 1, Spring 1971. A journal with an interdisciplinary approach to the study of the phenomena of religion.*

Year Book of Social Policy in Britain, The. *Edited by Kathleen Jones. 1971. Published annually.*

Printed in Great Britain by Unwin Brothers Limited
The Gresham Press Old Woking Surrey
A member of the Staples Printing Group

June 1975